THE MINISTRY OF HEALING IN THE

CHURCH OF ENGLAND:

AN ECUMENICAL-LITURGICAL STUDY

ALCUIN CLUB COLLECTIONS
No. 56

The Ministry of Healing in the Church of England an Ecumenical-Liturgical Study

Charles W. Gusmer

Professor of Sacramental Theology and Liturgy

Darlington Seminary, New Jersey

THE ALCUIN CLUB

MAYHEW-McCRIMMON
Great Wakering

First published in Great Britain in 1974
on behalf of the Alcuin Club by

MAYHEW-McCRIMMON LTD
10-12 High Street
Great Wakering
Essex SS3 0EQ
Great Britain

ISBN 0-85597-081-2

Printed in Great Britain by
Silver End Press,
Letterpress Division of E. T. Heron & Co. Ltd, Essex and London

To
HILDEGARDE WALLICH GUSMER
who first taught me how to worship.

CONTENTS

FOREWORD

The healing ministry of the Church has been a topic of much concern in recent years. Theologians use terms such as healing and wholeness interchangeably with salvation and redemption. The World Council of Churches has sponsored seminars and papers on this subject. Pentecostal communities, even within the Roman Catholic Communion, have revived an interest in charismatic healing : and the Roman Church itself has recently revised its rites for the sick and dying, most notably the anointing of the sick.

This work began as a doctoral dissertation, which was accepted by the Theological Faculty of Trier, Germany, and was subsequently rewritten for publication. It is an ecumenical study, in the manner of a *Konfessionskunde*, of the ministry of healing in the Church of England. It is also a liturgical study of this movement, with special emphasis given to the rites of the laying on of hands and the unction of the sick. The progression of chapters deserves some explanation. The first two chapters deal with Anglican healing in general, in order to place the sacramental and liturgical aspects of this ministry in proper perspective. Chapter I accordingly describes the development of the healing ministry beginning at the turn of this century. Chapter II attempts to portray a self-understanding of the healing movement, i.e. how the advocates of this ministry understand the theology and meaning of healing. In this regard it should be noted that the definitive monograph — if such is possible — on anointing of the sick has yet to be written. The poverty of serious scholarship in this area has, for example, been a source of embarrassment to theologians of the Roman Communion where this rite has been practised. This observation has particular bearing on the sub-chapter entitled "Orientation on the early Church", where we must for the most part be content to relate the research of preponents of the Anglican healing movement — some obscure, some dated, but nevertheless pioneers in their day — with the judicious use of footnotes to show where modern scholarship, meagre as it is, may have corrected or surpassed them.

Then comes the heart of this study — the liturgical and sacramental features of the healing ministry. Chapter III deals with the Prayer Book and healing : the Order for the Visitation of the Sick,

5

6

the Anglican tradition of unction, and the curious rite of touching for the King's Evil. Chapter IV describes the unction of the sick and laying on of hands as practised in the Church of England today : the liturgical services — official and "unofficial" — and a sacramental synthesis of their meaning.

The conclusion is an evaluation of the Anglican healing ministry, especially in its liturgical aspects, and a relation of this to the reform of the Roman rites for the sick.

Many people have made this work possible. I would like to thank first of all the Immaculate Conception Seminary, Darlington, which afforded me the time to complete this study. I am especially indebted to my friends in the Trier Liturgical Institute : Prof. Dr. Balthasar Fischer for his incisive and kindly direction; and Father Lucas Brinkhoff, O.F.M., the librarian. I am also very grateful to my friends in England, where much of the research for this study was done : the Rev. Geoffrey Harding and his associates in the Churches' Council for Health and Healing; the library staffs at Sion College and the British Museum; and the Alcuin Club, which accepted this work for publication.

May this volume be a modest contribution to liturgical science, which at the same time will instil in the reader a greater compassion towards the sick and suffering.

ABBREVIATIONS

AAS   *Acta Apostolicæ Sedis.* Rome, 1909 ff.

AC   Alcuin Club Collections. London.

BCP   *The Book of Common Prayer and Administration of the Sacraments and Other Rites and Ceremonies of the Church according to the Use of the Church of England.*

CC   *Corpus christianorum.* Series latina. Turnhout and Paris, 1953 ff.

CH   *Die ältesten Quellen des orientalischen Kirchenrechts. Die Canones Hippolyti,* ed. H. Achelis. Texte und Untersuchungen zur Geschichte der altchristlichen Literatur 6/4. Leipzig, 1891.

CSEL   *Corpus scriptorum ecclesiasticorum latinorum.* Vienna, 1866 ff.

CT   *Concilium Tridentinum. Diariorum, Actorum, Epistularum, Tractatum nova Collectio,* ed. Societas Goerresiana promovendis inter Catholicos Germaniae Litterarum Studiis. Freiburg, 1901 ff.

DS   *Enchiridion Symbolorum, definitionum et declarationum de rebus fidei et morum,* edd. H. Denzinger and A. Schönmetzer. Freiburg, 1967.

EP   *Enchiridion Patristicum,* ed. M. J. Rouët de Journel. Freiburg, 1959.

FlP   *Florilegium patristicum,* edd. B. Geyer and J. Zellinger. Bonn, 1904 ff.

Funk   *Didascalia et Constitutiones apostolorum,* ed. F. X. Funk. Paderborn, 1905. Reprinted Turin, 1964.

8

GCS   *Die griechischen christlichen Schriftsteller der ersten drei Jahrhunderte.* Leipzig, 1897 ff.

Goodspeed *Die ältesten Apologeten,* ed. Edgar J. Goodspeed. Göttingen, 1914.

HBS   *Henry Bradshaw Society.* London, 1891 ff.

PG   *Patrologia Græca,* ed. J. P. Migne. Paris, 1857-66.

PL   *Patrologia Latina,* ed. J. P. Migne. Paris, 1878-90.

SCh   *Sources chrétiennes,* edd. H. de Lubac and J. Daniélou. Paris, 1941 ff.

CHAPTER I

The Growth and Development of the Ministry of Healing in the Church of England

At the turn of the century, John Wordsworth, Bishop of Salisbury, wrote a small exposition of the teaching of the Church of England for the benefit of the Eastern Orthodox Christians. Seeking to find an Anglican counterpart to the Eastern rite of Euchelaion or "prayer oil", the Bishop could state only that "it [i.e. the Church of England] provides a special office for the Visitation of the Sick, with prayers for the sick man's recovery, and it enjoins upon its bishops in particular to 'heal the sick'."[1] He could make no mention of unction of the sick, for this rite, although included in the first Prayer Book of 1549, had been eliminated in subsequent revisions.

Were a similar monograph to be written today, the author could cite Canon 37, "Of the Ministry to the Sick", from Section B, "Divine Service and the Administration of the Sacraments", of the recently revised *Canons of the Church of England*. After exhorting the minister to visit the sick parishioner and making provision for the Communion of the Sick, the Canon continues in paragraph 3 :

> If any such person so desires, the priest may lay hands upon him and may anoint him with oil on the forehead with the sign of the Cross using the form of service sanctioned by lawful authority and using pure olive oil consecrated by the bishop of the diocese or otherwise by the priest himself in accordance with such form of service.[2]

Or again, the author could now refer to the *Revised Catechism* issued in 1962. In addition to the Gospel sacraments of baptism and holy communion, the Church provides for other "sacramental ministries of grace" : confirmation, ordination, holy matrimony, the ministry of absolution and the ministry of healing. The ministry of healing is described in these words :

9

The sacramental ministry of healing is the ministry by which God's grace is given for the healing of spirit, mind and body, in response to faith and prayer, by the laying on of hands, or by anointing with oil.[3]

The revised Canons and Catechism are but two witnesses to the emergence of the ministry of healing in the Church of England in the twentieth century. This development has been influenced by a number of factors : the important work of the guilds and fellow-ships of healing; the discussion of the ministry of healing at the Lambeth Conferences of 1908, 1920, 1930 and 1958; the promulgation of official rites of healing by the Canterbury (1935) and York (1936) Convocations; the Churches' Council for Health and Healing and the ensuing co-operation with the medical profession; and the Report of the Archbishops' Commission appointed in 1953 to study the ministry of healing.

1 Guilds and Fellowships of Healing

A compelling factor in promoting the healing ministry has been the existence of various guilds and fellowships of healing, notably the Guild of Health, the Guild of St. Raphael, the Divine Healing Mission and the Dorothy Kerin Trust.[4]

The Guild of Health was founded in 1904. The original committee consisted of three members, with the distinguished liturgist Percy Dearmer (d. 1936) acting as chairman. Dearmer had for some time previously been engaged in a study of faith or spiritual healing, which led to the publication of a work of his own on the subject.[5] Conrad Noel, one of the original members of the Guild of Health, described its origins :

> The idea was that Christian Science and other health movements outside the Church had been driven into heresy by the Church herself having forgotten to preach spiritual healing and having lost the power to practise it. Hence this revival in the Church of England. I think the Guild of Health was the parent society from which various other mental-healing societies sprang.[6]

The Guild of Health began within the Church of England, but in 1915 its membership was widened to include all Christian denominations. In 1934 it published the book *Spiritual Healing,* the outcome of a round-table conference between clergy, doctors, nurses and others.[7] Since 1952 the Edward Wilson House in London has served as the centre for the Guild's activities, which include some three hundred local groups meeting regularly to pray, to study, to promote Christian fellowship and to plan various projects such as hospital visiting, caring for shut-ins and rehabilitating the mentally ill. The Guild also sponsors an annual conference and has published since 1905 a magazine entitled *For Health and Healing*. In July, 1968, however, as an indication of the closer co-operation among the healing associations, the Guild of Health and the Divine Healing Mission decided to merge their respective publications into a joint bi-monthly journal, *The Way of Life*.

The general aim of this Guild is "to restore the healing ministry of Christ in and through His Church". Accepting the challenge of Christ's commission to preach and to teach, to heal and to cast out evil, the Guild believes that health, translated as wholeness or completeness, is essential to the building of the Kingdom of God and is the task of all the Churches. For this reason the Church and Medicine should be brought into closer fellowship, for both have a place in the redemptive plan of God. Medical science has demonstrated the interaction of the mind and body of man, considered as a unity both in health and in sickness. As the Bible teaches, this unity is fulfilled in community. The Constitution of the Guild summarizes its objectives as follows :

1. To bring together Christian people, particularly doctors, psychiatrists, and ministers of religion to work in fellowship for fuller health, both for the individual and the community.
2. To enable all members to study the interaction between physical, mental and spiritual factors in well-being.
3. To sustain and strengthen by prayer the sick, those who minister to them, and all those who exercise the divine gift of healing.
4. To help men and women to realize in themselves, as members of the Christian family, the abundant life offered in Christ.[8]

The Guild of St. Raphael was founded in 1915 with the aim of restoring the ministry of healing as part of the normal functions of the Church. It is exclusively Anglican, consisting of communicant members at home and abroad, with a threefold purpose :

1. To unite in a fellowship of prayer within the Catholic Church, those who hold the faith that our Lord wills to work in and through His Church for the health of her members in spirit, mind and body.
2. To promote the belief that God wills the conquest of disease, as well as sin, through the power of the living Christ.
3. To guide the sick, and those who care for them, to Christ as the source of healing.[9]

The Guild's method are to teach the sick the need for repentance and faith, to encourage the use of the sacrament of holy unction and the rite of laying on of hands for healing, and to further individual and corporate intercessory prayer. These methods were given prominence by Archbishop Lang in an address on the occasion of the twenty-first anniversary of the founding of the Guild. This address, *Divine Healing. Its place in the normal Ministry of the Church of England,* is sometimes considered as a charter of the Guild, for it singles out four features of the ministry of healing : the ministry of prayer and intercession, the ministry of absolution, the ministry of unction and the laying on of hands, and the sacrament of the Lord's Body and Blood.[10]

In pursuance of these methods, admittedly liturgical and sacramental in emphasis, the Guild has published a great deal of literature, including *S. Raphael's Prayer Book for the Use of the Sick; The Priest's Vademecum,* a popular source of instruction and prayer for visiting the sick; and several pamphlets promoting the use of unction.[11] The Guild also issues a quarterly periodical entitled *Chrism.*

The Divine Healing Mission originated as the Society of Emmanuel, founded by James Moore Hickson in 1905. Hickson is the most notable example of a charismatic lay healer in the Church of England in this century. He first discovered his gift of healing when at the age of fourteen he felt moved to lay hands on a cousin suffering from neuralgia and gave her immediate relief. In 1908 he published a pamphlet, *The Healing of Christ in His Church,* which so impressed Archbishop Davidson that a copy was sent to all bishops then assembled for the Lambeth Conference. In 1921 Hickson embarked on a world tour which took him to America, South Africa, Palestine, India, China, Japan, Australia and New Zealand. The success which greeted the healing missions he conducted during this tour is described in his book *Heal the Sick.*[12]

In 1910 under Hickson's leadership the Society of Emmanuel attempted to establish a small hospital where spiritual healing could be practised in co-operation with medical treatment, but the plan never came to fruition. Today, however, the Divine Healing Mission has its headquarters at the Crowhurst Home of Healing in Sussex, which was founded in 1928 to provide a therapeutic programme centred on the Church's ministry of healing. The programme develops over a week from Tuesday to Tuesday, the highlight of the week being a Service of Healing with the imposition of hands every Monday evening. *The Healer* has been the bi-monthly publication of the Divine Healing Mission since 1910 until the recent merger with *For Health and Healing* to become *The Way of Life*.

The Dorothy Kerin Trust bears the name of another outstanding lay healer of the Church of England.[13] On the verge of death resulting from tubercular meningitis, on February 18, 1912 Dorothy Kerin was miraculously cured during a vision of an angel. After some years of spiritual preparation, she felt called to be a channel to convey to others our Lord's gift of wholeness of body, mind and spirit and proceeded to open a small nursing home in Ealing. Always working closely with the Church, she was commissioned by Archbishop Lang to exercise her charismatic gift through the laying on of hands. Her healing missions took her throughout Britain, to Europe and to America.

After the war she transferred her home to Burrswood, then a derelict mansion near Tunbridge Wells in Kent. Upon her death in January 1963, the Dorothy Kerin Trust was established to continue her work. Burrswood today consists of the Dorothy Kerin Home of Healing, the Haven and the Church of Christ the Healer. The Home of Healing is a registered nursing home, staffed by qualified nurses and a resident physician, where religion and medicine are intimately associated. The Haven is a home for guests seeking rest and spiritual retreat. The Church of Christ the Healer was built for daily worship and for the services of healing conducted three times a week by a resident chaplain according to a rite composed by Miss Kerin. There is also a Burrswood International Fellowship, under the patronage of the Archbishop of Canterbury, comprising members who support the activities of the Dorothy Kerin Trust with their prayers and gifts. *The Burrswood Herald* is the quarterly periodical of the Fellowship.

2. *The Lambeth Conferences*

For the 1908 Lambeth Conference a committee was appointed "to consider the report upon the subject of the ministries of healing".[14] It admitted that the growing interest in spiritual and mental healing could be the result of the Church's neglect to proclaim the full meaning of the Incarnation. In the ministrations of the Church to the sick, a disproportionate stress may sometimes have been laid upon preparation for death. Sickness has too often been regarded as a cross to be borne with passive resignation, whereas the proper approach would be to regard it as "a weakness to be overcome by the power of the Spirit". The Committee stated that "sickness and disease are in one aspect a breach in the harmony of the divine purpose, not only analogous to, but sometimes at least caused by, want of moral harmony with the divine will". The restoration of harmony in mind and will can often bring about the restoration of the harmony of the body. The Report expressed gratitude to Almighty God for the wonderful works of healing wrought by the medical and nursing professions, and emphasized the role of medicine in the divine redemptive plan as "the ordinary means appointed by Almighty God for the care and healing of the human body".

As regards practical recommendations in the ordinary pastoral ministrations of the clergy to the sick, the Committee urged that "more hopeful and less ambiguous petitions for the restoration of health, always subject to the Will of God", be added to the Office for the Visitation of the Sick in the Prayer Book. These petitions should be used in close conjunction with prayer for pardon and peace and might suitably be accompanied by the "apostolic act of the laying-on of hands". But the basic attitude of the 1908 Lambeth Committee Report was one of watchfulness and reserve. The Report cautioned against the danger of the faithful being "thoughtlessly drawn into alliance, in the desire for health, with any who, under whatever attractive name, are in antagonism with the Christian faith upon such subjects as the Incarnation, the Resurrection, the reality of Sin, and the use of the Holy Sacraments". The obvious reference was to Christian Science.[15] Too little was known about the phenomenon of spiritual healing to make a mature judgement at this time. While not wishing to discourage "those who may be pioneers in a new branch of service", the Committee could not bring itself to recommend any authoritative recognition to individuals claiming special gifts of healing.

The Committee's opinion on unction of the sick was incon-
clusive. On the one hand it was unclear if the references Mark
6:13 and James 5:14 were to be interpreted as intended for
general and lasting use among later generations of Christians,
since there was no other record of anointing with oil by Christ
or by his disciples after Pentecost. The application of oil was a
common medicinal remedy at the time of St. James and therefore
an appropriate symbol of healing. Furthermore, the Committee
discerned no clear use of unction of the sick in the Christian
Church until the fourth century; the subsequent history of unction
was likewise obscure. On the other hand, while not recommending
the restoration of unction of the sick, the Committee did not wish
to prohibit its use, "if it be earnestly desired by the sick person".
In all such cases recourse should be made to the bishop of the
diocese.

Four of the resolutions of the 1908 Lambeth Conference concerned the ministry of healing. The resolutions for the most part
incorporated the findings of the Committee Report. Resolution 33
called for a renewal of the Church's spiritual life. The clergy were
exhorted to proclaim to their people Christ, the Incarnate Son of
God and his abiding presence in the Church and in Christian
souls by the Holy Spirit,

> that all may realise and lay hold of the power of the indwelling
> Spirit to sanctify both soul and body, and thus, through a har-
> mony of man's will with God's Will, to gain a fuller control over
> temptation, pain, and disease, whether for themselves or others,
> with a firmer serenity and a more confident hope.[16]

With a view towards resisting dangerous tendencies of the times,
Resolution 34 advised the clergy to teach the sick the privilege of
those who are called "to enter especially into the fellowship of
Christ's sufferings and to follow the example of His patience".
Resolution 35 adopted the Committee's suggestions for an enrichment of the pastoral visitation of the sick by "some additional
prayers for the restoration of health more hopeful and direct than
those contained in the present Office for the Visitation of the
Sick". No mention, however, was made of the laying on of hands
suggested in the Committee Report. And finally, Resolution 36
reiterated the Committee's position concerning unction of the sick,
which was neither recommended as a rite of the Church, nor expressly prohibited. An interesting warning was sounded: "Care

must be taken that no return be made to the later custom of anointing as a preparation for death".

At the Lambeth Conference of 1920 a Committee Report on Spiritualism, Christian Science and Theosophy provided the context for a discussion of healing.[17] All three movements were roundly disavowed. The topic of healing came to light especially in the treatment of Christian Science.

Commenting on recent developments since the previous Report on the Ministries of Healing at the 1908 Conference, the Committee deplored the wide distinction which had often been made between "spiritual" and "physical" means of healing. While there was some foundation for the three departments of healing considered as physical science, psychology and religion insofar as this corresponded to the threefold division of human nature into body, mind and spirit; nevertheless "no one of these aspects of healing can possibly be excluded from the scope of the term spiritual".

The rise of Christian Science was a reaction to the negligence of the Church to preach sufficiently God's concern for the body as well as for the soul. The Report rejected various tenets of Christian Science: the inherent pantheism, the implicit revived dualism of matter and spirit, the distinction between "Christ the ideal Truth and Jesus the human prophet of Galilee", and the impoverishment of the Atonement resulting upon the denial of the reality of sin.

The practical recommendations included a call for a fuller presentation of the Church's doctrine on true spirituality and for teaching on the efficacy of individual and corporate prayer and the effects of Holy Communion. Most important of all, for the first time a Committee of the Lambeth Conference urged the "recognition of the Ministry and gifts of healing in the Church, and that these should be exercised under due license and authority". In the judgement of the Committee these recommendations involved four further suggestions: instruction of both clergy and laity so that the corporate faith of the Church might be stimulated and the power to heal released; training of candidates for holy orders, especially in psychology; either the revision of the Office for the Visitation of the Sick, or else provision for "an alternative office containing recommendations and regulations for the laying-on of hands with prayer for recovery with or without unction"; and the licensing of the healers who were both orthodox in belief and willing to co-operate with the medical profession and the parochial clergy. The Report concluded its treatment of healing with a statement on the positive value of pain and suffering as "a means of true spiritual growth and of intimate fellowship with our Saviour".

The 1920 Lambeth Conference adopted five resolutions on Christian Science and healing.[18] Resolution 59 rejected the errors of Christian Science as outlined in the Committee Report. Resolution 60 reminded the Church that intimate communion with God realized in union with Christ through the Holy Spirit "influences the whole personality of man, physical and spiritual, enabling him to share his Lord's triumph over sin, disease and death". Resolution 61 proposed an intensive study and practice of prayer and meditation, so that "the corporate faith of the Church may be renewed, and the fruit of the Spirit may be more manifest in the daily lives of professing Christians, and the power of Christ to heal may be released". Resolution 62 expressed appreciation for those engaged in scientific research and in the medical profession. Because of its subsequent importance, Resolution 63 deserves quotation in full :

> For the general guidance of the Church the Conference requests the Archbishop of Canterbury to appoint a Committee to consider and report as early as possible upon the use with prayer of the laying on of hands, of the unction of the sick and other spiritual means of healing, the findings of such a Committee to be reported forthwith to the authorities of the national, provincial, and regional Churches of the Anglican Communion.

As may be readily observed, the Conference declined to incorporate into its resolutions the suggestion of the Committee that the ministry of healing be officially recognized; neither was there any encouragement given to the laying on of hands or to unction. This recognition had to await a fuller investigation into the ministry of healing, which the Committee envisaged by Resolution 63 would present to the 1930 Lambeth Conference.

This Committee published its report, *The Ministry of Healing,* in 1924. The two problems considered were "A comparison between the different methods of healing and the consideration of their relation to Christian thought", and "The question whether a Ministry of Healing should now be recognised and sanctioned".[19]

The Committee discerned three methods of bodily healing :

1. Material — surgery, drugs, diet, etc.

2. Psychical — suggestion and different forms of mental analysis.
3. Devotional and sacramental.

"Spiritual healing" may be called "that which makes use of all or any of these factors in reliance upon God", although in popular language the term is frequently and inaccurately restricted to the third method of bodily healing. The appeal of this third approach, devotional and sacramental healing, is "direct to God as the immediate source of life and health without the use of any material means".[20] The revival within the Church of systems of healing based on the redemptive work of Christ all spring from belief in a fundamental principle "that the power to exercise spiritual healing is taught by Christ to be the natural heritage of Christian people who are living in fellowship with God, and is part of the ministry of Christ through His Body the Church".

In the strongest terms of any official document on the ministry of healing, the Report regarded disease as an evil to be repelled:

Theologically stated, this means that health, or an orderly condition of body, mind and spirit, is God's primary Will for all his children; and that disease, as a specific violation or falling short of this orderly condition, is not only to be combated, but to be combated in God's Name and as a way of carrying out His Will.[21]

Disease, whatever its immediate source, and however it may be overruled for good, is in itself evil. Like other forms of evil, disease is permitted by God, either as a result of man's misuse of freedom, or as a stimulus to human sympathy or scientific research, or as a means of spiritual discipline.

The aim of spiritual healing is the restoration of the whole man, especially by strengthening the spiritual life as the centre of personality. "By awakening a sense of the Power and the Love of God, by emphasizing the true relationship of the patient to God, and by helping him to realize the healing presence of Christ", spiritual healing will often include physical healing, although this should not be an exclusive preoccupation. The results achieved by spiritual healing may thus be considered twofold: complete or partial bodily recovery, and even more important, spiritual strengthening. When the "stake" was not removed, St. Paul learned that God's grace was sufficient. Summing up its description of spiritual healing, the Report gave due recognition to the role of medical means in the resulting recovery. The primary concern of spiritual healing was the healing of the spirit; the healing of the body was secondary.

On the question whether a ministry of healing should now be officially recognized, the Report laid down the following general principles :

1. The Church's paramount task in regard to disease is to inculcate in all its members "a right attitude of confidence, love and understanding towards God"; to bring those caring for the soul and those caring for the body into closer co-operation and to insist on the importance of hygiene and plain living.
2. The Church "must sanction methods of religious treatment of disease", while giving full credit to scientific discoveries about the interrelation of spirit, mind and body.
3. If no higher goal than the recovery of bodily health is sought, the Church should not apply its means of restoration. To do so would be to compromise the rites and sacraments of the Church. "No sick person must look to the clergyman to do what it is the physician's or surgeon's duty to do."
4. Whatever ministration employed by the Church, the primary purpose is to deepen "the sense of fellowship with God secured for us in Jesus Christ". If this is achieved, the work of the Church has been effective.[22]

More specifically, the Committee made some concrete suggestions about the form the healing ministry should take. The stress given to the preparation preceding the sacramental rites is particularly significant :

a. Prayer and sacrament should be used conjointly. Before the administration of any sacramental rites, "earnest and united prayer should be offered on behalf of the sick person in church as well as by the patient himself and his friends at home".
b. Religious methods, while applicable to all cases of sickness, were especially appropriate "where moral or intellectual difficulties and perplexities have contributed to the disorder". Here again, a preliminary treatment which attempts to deal with the deep-rooted sources of evil and offers the patient

an opportunity for confession and absolution was considered essential.

c. Then follows treatment more immediately aimed at the complete restoration of the patient through the use of sacramental rites.

This may take the form of Unction (i.e. anointing with oil by a priest), or of the Laying on of Hands (either by a priest or a lay person), or of both. These rites have scriptural authority and are sacramental in the sense that a blessing is sought and received through the performance of outward and visible actions. The motive with which they are used is the dedication of the bodily life of the patient to God's Will; and the blessing received will be either restoration of health, or grace to bear sickness patiently.[23]

d. The religious ministration is fittingly concluded with the patient's reception of Holy Communion.

This Report exhibited a very positive approach towards the ministry of healing. It urged the endorsement of the ministry of healing and referred to unction and the laying on of hands as having "scriptural authority" and being "sacramental". The 1930 Lambeth Conference accepted its findings and in Resolution 73 commended it to the Church.[24] Thus the prevailing attitude of the Lambeth Conferences had noticeably shifted from the initial scepticism of 1908 to reserved encouragement in 1920, and to official endorsement in 1930. They had gradually come to realize that the ministry of healing was not the monopoly of Christian Science or other sects, but rather a fundamental element of orthodox Christianity. This ministry was to be practised in close co-operation with the medical profession through prayer and the sacramental rites of unction and the laying on of hands.

The subject of healing was also briefly discussed at the 1958 Lambeth Conference. In a Committee Report on the Book of Common Prayer, with the recommendation that this ministry find a clearer expression in any future revision of the Prayer Book.[25]

3. Official Services of Healing

To what extent have unction of the sick and the laying on of hands found official sanction in the Church of England? The 1927/28 Proposed Prayer Book contained an improved Order for the Visitation of the Sick, which provided for the laying on of hands.[26] When this Book failed to receive Parliamentary approval, the advocates of the healing ministry introduced a motion in the Lower House of the Convocation of Canterbury in January 1931 petitioning the Archbishop to appoint a committee to draw up and submit for approval services for unction and the imposition of hands, and for the imposition of hands without unction. Both Houses agreed to this proposal; and on June 6, 1935 they approved services for the "Administration of Holy Unction and the Laying-on of Hands" issued "for provisional use in the Province subject to due diocesan sanction".[27] The Convocation of York followed a similar course in the following year.[28] A detailed examination of these services, as well as of the various unofficial services of the guilds and fellowships of healing, will be given later.

4. The Churches' Council for Health and Healing

In 1944 Archbishop Temple invited the Development Committee of the Guild of Health to found a new organization whose aims were to act as a co-ordinating centre for all Christian healing movements in Britain, to promote the co-operation between doctors and clergy, and to bring the work of healing into closer relation with the regular work of the Churches.[29] In 1946 this committee became the Churches' Council of Healing. Although the Archbishop of Canterbury serves as president, the Free Churches are likewise represented in this ecumenical enterprise.[30] The constituent members of the Churches' Council for Health and Healing agree on the following principles:

1. All healing proceeds from the activity of the eternal creative power of God ever seeking to restore harmony to His world. God's will for man is perfect health, but sickness and disease are facts which must be faced. Part of the victory of the Cross is the truth that suffering can be completely transformed by being offered to God and being taken up into the fellowship of Christ's redemptive sacrifice.
2. God's infinite power can work within His responsive creation to remake the whole human personality. Divine Healing means essentially the healing of the whole man by the power of God, through a clearer understanding of His love and purpose and in obedience to His laws.
3. Doctors, clergy and ministers are instruments of God's healing power in the faithful exercise of their skill and patience;

and all members of the churches can be used by God for healing, through their ministries of prayer and intercession, meditation and direction; and through the sacraments and other means of grace.[31]

The Churches' Council for Health and Healing has probably achieved the most success in its endeavour to achieve closer co-operation with the medical profession. In 1947 the British Medical Association issued a statement welcoming the existence of the Churches' Council of Healing and encouraging further clergy-doctor co-operation, especially through joint discussions. The statement frankly acknowledged the need for a closer relationship :

Medicine and the Church working together should encourage a dynamic philosophy of health which would enable every citizen to find a way of life based on moral principles and on a sound knowledge of the factors which promote health and well being. Health is more than a physical problem, and the patient's attitude both to illness and to other problems is an important factor to his recovery and adjustment to life.[32]

In 1956 the British Medical Association issued a more detailed study, *Divine Healing and Co-operation between Doctors and Clergy,* the result of an ad hoc committee appointed by the BMA to answer certain questions posed by the Archbishops' Commission on the Ministry of Healing. The memorandum, written from a strictly medical point of view, found no evidence of any type of illness *"cured by 'spiritual healing' alone which could not have been cured by medical treatment which necessarily includes consideration of environmental factors".*[33] But the BMA committee admitted the psychological value of sound religious ministrations and further encouraged co-operation between clergy and doctors.

In April 1962 Archbishop Ramsey invited a group of doctors and clergymen to establish a small working party to explore some of the practical problems involved in the co-operation between the medical profession and the clergy. Their report considered the training of ordinands and medical undergraduates, post-ordination and post-medical training, and the continued association between the two professions in clergy-doctor discussion groups.[34] The report's recommendation of the formation of an organization devoted to "the study and advancement of matters of mutual interest to clergy and doctors" has since been adopted through the creation in 1964 of the Institute of Religion and Medicine with headquarters in London. The Institute attempts to provide "a purposeful meeting ground for doctors, ministers of religion, social workers, nurses and members of other professions concerned with the care of the sick and the health of the community".[35]

6. *Report of the Archbishops' Commission*

The most authoritative document to date is the Report of the Archbishops' Commission, *The Church's Ministry of Healing*. A discussion of the concepts employed in the Report will serve to clarify further what is meant by the healing ministry.

On January 18, 1952 two motions were carried in the Lower House of the Convocation of Canterbury. The first motion commended "to the sympathetic attention of the Church, and particularly of parish priests, the modern revival of spiritual healing". A second consequential motion requested the Archbishop of Canterbury to appoint a committee "to examine the problems and opportunities" raised by spiritual healing and to report.[36] In October 1953 the Archbishops of Canterbury and York appointed a commission with the following terms of reference :

To consider the theological, medical, psychological and pastoral aspects of "Divine Healing" with a view to providing within two or three years a report designed to guide the Church to clearer understanding of the subject; and in particular to help the clergy in the exercise of the ministry of healing and to encourage increasing understanding and co-operation between them and the medical profession.[37]

The Commission, composed of both clergy and representatives of the medical and nursing professions, collected written and oral evidence from a wide variety of sources and published its Report in 1958.

It reached some valuable conclusions regarding such commonly-used terms as health, disease and healing.[38] Health is ordinarily used to denote the normal functioning of the bodily organism. The word "health", however, is etymologically allied to the word "whole".[39] Since the interrelation of physical and mental factors in the health of the whole person is now an accepted fact, it would be better to speak of health as "a condition of the full functioning of the whole organism".

Disease was defined as "a condition in which the functions of the individual are deranged by internal or external forces inimical to their harmonius activity". Although few major diseases can be directly attributed to the misdemeanours of the patient or his ancestors, society is responsible for considerable suffering stemming from war, inadequate diet, poor housing, etc. There are "no such things as diseased entities but only diseased persons". The cause of disease is always at least twofold: in the nature of the individual and in the nature of his environment at a given point in time. In practice it is impossible to separate disease into physical or psychological states, although some diseases respond more readily to physical and others to psychological methods.

Healing generally means "the restoration to normality of deranged physical functions". But in the wider perspective required by a Christian view of man, healing means "the enabling of a man to function as a whole in accordance with God's will for him". In the absence of any universally recognized absolute standard for measuring physical, mental or spiritual fitness, the word healing can be used only relatively of man in this life, for God alone knows the capacities of each individual. "It is the high calling of all who are engaged in the work of healing at every level to help in various degrees and by various means those whom God created in his image to come to completeness."

"Divine Healing" was the original term of reference given to the Archbishops' Commission. "Spiritual healing", and to a lesser extent "faith healing", are also phrases used by various authors.[40] But the Commission chose to speak of "the Church's ministry of healing", because the terms faith healing, spiritual healing and divine healing were often used by people "thinking of the cure of bodily ailments by means other than medical science". The Commission insisted that the Church's ministry to the sick is concerned with "the redemption of the whole man", the cure of bodily ailments being but one element in this ministry.

The terms faith healing, spiritual healing and divine healing were also found inadequate for other reasons. Faith healing is imprecise because it can imply as a prerequisite of healing a belief in the healer's powers, or belief that the sufferer will actually recover, or belief that God wills the recovery from a specific ailment. Spiritual healing, while conveying the important truth that the restoration to health is the work of the Holy Spirit, has in actual practice too often been misappropriated by the advocates of Spiritualism. A more serious objection is that the application of "spiritual" to certain methods of healing would imply that other methods of healing were necessarily not spiritual, an implication which cannot be substantiated. Divine healing is also subject to misgivings. In the first place the term could lead to a misrepresentation of divine providence by intimating that God only cares for the sick by means of extraordinary cures, whereas "in one sense all healing is divine". Secondly, divine healing could tend to imply that "those who have received some special gift of healing and who work outside the Church's life and fellowship, have not received their gift from God".

Rejecting faith healing, spiritual healing and divine healing as inadequate designations, the Commission thus referred to the Church's ministrations to the sick as "the Church's ministry of healing". This name assumes that the Church really has such a ministry, yet is not subject to the ambiguity which results from the qualification of "healing" by any of the aforementioned adjectives. In an effort to avoid any narrow cultist misunderstanding, the Report of the Archbishops' Commission wisely placed the Church's ministry of healing in the broadest possible context by describing it in these words :

This ministry is an integral part of the Church's total work by which men and women are to become true sons and daughters of God's kingdom. In it are to be employed all means God has put at our disposal; the administration of the Word and Sacraments; the exercise of pastoral care; and the employment of all the many gifts of special kinds which God has given to individuals. Among the latter the skill and knowledge of those who have given themselves to the discipline of medical and nursing training are by no means the least.[41]

CHAPTER II

The Anglican Understanding of Healing

The development of the ministry of healing in the Church of England during the twentieth century has often been regarded as a revival of a Christian ministry which had been long neglected. This chapter will attempt to show how the ministry of healing is understood. It begins with a survey of the Anglican literature on healing which deals with the New Testament evidence and the practice of the early Church. The viewpoint of the authors — some obscure, some dated — is nonetheless remarkably in accord with the most recent yet scanty studies on the early history of anointing and its decline from a rite for the sick into a sacrament for the dying — a change in liturgical practice which took place during the Carolingian renaissance of the eighth and ninth centuries, and which was further solidified in the teaching of the scholastic doctors of the twelfth and thirteenth centuries. A final section of the chapter will summarize the theology of the Anglican healing ministry by elucidating some common misconceptions. No claim can be made to an exhaustive treatment of the theology of healing in all its ramifications. The aim here is rather to present a solid background of the thought and spirituality of the ministry in order to make the present-day rites more comprehensible.

A. THE NEW TESTAMENT

Upholding a principle which is consonant with Anglican tradition, the Archbishops' Report of 1958 declared that the example and precepts of Christ must be normative for the exercise of the Church's ministry of healing.[1] The New Testament evidence may be conveniently grouped under three headings.

1. General principles of the New Testament which apply to healing;
2. The significance of Jesus' ministry to the sick : the healing miracles;
3. Christ's commission to the Church.

26

1. General Principles

A study of the Gospels reveals the following broad principles about Christ's practice of healing.[2]

a) The importance of the human body.

This truth is implied in the doctrine of the Incarnation. Already in 1908 the Lambeth Conference Report stressed that the teaching of the Incarnation requires that "the whole of creation is included in the work of Redemption, and that the body, no less than the spirit, of man received the eternal benediction of the Lord when He took our nature upon Him."[3] Phyllis Garlick adds a further reflection :

> The Incarnation is indeed the living demonstration of the truth that there *is* a gospel for the body; that far from being evil because it is material, the body is holy since it is designed to be the temple of the Holy Spirit (1 Cor 6 :19).[4]

The nobility of the human body is perhaps best summed up in three dictums : God was Creator of the flesh; God was incarnate in the flesh; God promised the resurrection of the flesh.[5]

b) The supremacy of the eternal.

Lest a misguided zeal lead to a quest for physical healing at any cost, the Archbishops' Report, quoting Mt. 18 :8, cautioned that "no temporal deprivation is too dire to accept or incur in order to possess and secure the one gift of eternal life".[6] There is a real danger of confusing ends and means by using religion as a therapeutic means for recovering health, rather than "seeking to bring the whole personality into conscious touch with the love and power of God".[7] In other words, eternal salvation in Jesus Christ is the goal to be sought before everything else, including physical health.

c) The unity of man.

A study of Jesus' treatment of human suffering and sin admits an intimate interdependence of body and soul, whereby one inevitably has repercussions on the other. In his healing actions Jesus granted forgiveness; when restoring the sick he bestowed salvation. Sickness and sin were different expressions of the one supreme evil whose overthrow was signalled by the presence of the Kingdom of God.[8]

R. A. Lambourne in *Community, Church and Healing* forcefully demonstrates the reciprocal aspects of human wholeness in an analysis of the Greek verbs used in describing the healing miracles : *therapeuein* (heal), *iaomai* (heal), *sōzein* (make whole), *katharizein* (cleanse), *apokathistēmi* (restore whole).[9] He concludes : "The mutual illumination of 'healing' and 'redemption', 'wholeness' and 'salvation' rests on historic fact, the fact that there was in Palestine under Christ, and there is in the world under Christ today, a real relation between health and redemption."[10] Lambourne cautions, however, against interpreting this close connection between faith and physical healing, or faith and the burden of sin, as a "total connection" or "mathematical ratio".[11]

2. *The Significance of Jesus' Ministry to the Sick*

What was Christ's attitude towards the sick and suffering, as shown by the healing miracles? In the Anglican healing literature the complex subject of the healing miracles is often summarily described as proof that disease is an evil to be combatted as a way of carrying out the will of God.[12] Jesus' attitude towards sickness —bodily, spiritual and mental—was one of "uncompromising hostility".[13] Sickness, like sin, belonged to the kingdom of Satan which Christ came to destroy. One author even goes so far as to regard all illness as "a form of possession by the powers of evil".[14]

The exegesis and theology underlying such assumptions is usually weak and ill-conceived. Percy Dearmer in *Body and Soul* has a chapter "Therapeutics of the Gospels" which presents a table of the healing miracles catalogued according to place and method.[15] Leslie Weatherhead, whose *Psychology, Religion and Healing* is one of the most widely accepted monographs on the healing ministry, classifies Jesus' healing miracles into the following psychological categories : "Cures which involve the Mechanism of Suggestion", "Cures which involve a more Complicated Technique", and "Cures which involve the Influence of a Psychic 'Atmosphere' or the 'Faith' of People other than the Patient".[16] Lambourne rightly observes that much of the theology of the healing movement has been "sparse and often unsound".[17]

It is Lambourne himself who has provided the most serious

biblical theology of the healing miracles. He emphasizes the sign value of the miracles : the healing works of Jesus are signs of his Messiahship and of the coming of a new age; they are effective signs which bring about the condition they signify; the miracles are also public effective signs which call for a decision on the part of those who witnessed them.[18]

The healing works of Jesus are signs of his Messiahship and of the coming of a new age. Those who witnessed the healing works of Christ were not called simply to observe edifying wonders, but were confronted with the claim that Jesus was the Messiah and that the Kingdom of God had come among them. The question for Jesus' witnesses was not whether a miracle had actually taken place, but rather what the miracle signified. To the Pharisees accusing him of casting out devils through Beelzebub, Jesus responds : "But if it is through the Spirit of God that I cast devils out, then know that the Kingdom of God has overtaken you" (Lk. 11 :14-22; see also Mt. 12 :22-28). The point of controversy between the Pharisees and Jesus was that Jesus by his wonders was fulfilling the "day" fore-shadowed by the prophetic and apocalyptic literature of the Old Testament, such as in the Isaianic signs : the lame walk, the lepers are cleansed, the deaf hear, the dead are raised, and the poor have the Gospel preached to them (Mt. 11 :2-5; Is. 35 :5-6). The miracles of Christ are mighty signs which point to the present rule of God. "By these acted parables, Jesus at one and the same time *proclaims* the coming of the kingdom, *portrays* what the kingdom is like, and actually *initiates* and spreads the kingdom."[19]

The healing works of Jesus are also effective signs. They are signs not only in the sense of indications or signposts, but are integral to the realities they demonstrate. The miracles not only point to the Messiah and the Kingdom of God, they are part of it. They are effective signs, bringing about the very kingdom they signify. The concept of a sign which accomplishes the condition it describes is called "prophetic symbolism" in the Old Testament, while New Testament scholars prefer to speak of an "acted parable."

Thus the gift of healing given by the Father to the Son was used by him to announce the Rule of God, to describe it, and to usher it in. Thereby he marked healing work done by all men in all ages not only, nor perhaps mainly, as imitation of his compassion but as proclamation and description of the good news of the Gospel, the announcing and bringing in of forgiveness and salvation.[20]

Finally, the healing works of Jesus are public effective signs. They are not private affairs between man and God, an individual test, but are *"public* acts, *corporate* matters, *public* effective signs".[21] The sickness-healing situation was a crisis situation for the entire community in which it occurred. There were no passive spectators. Either the witnesses had their eyes opened and were brought to belief, or else culpably closed their eyes and even deliberately distorted what they saw. In the mission of Christ, therefore, preaching and healing go together. Such also is the injunction handed on to the followers of Jesus :

> It is not just a coincidence, nor a pair of listed duties, that Jesus, when commissioning his disciples, commands them both to heal the sick and preach the kingdom (Mk. 6 :7-13; Mt. 10 :1-15; Lk. 9 :1-6, 10 :1-20). To heal the sick and to preach the kingdom are neither complementary, nor supplementary, but both are manifestations of the same word of God.[22]

Awe and wonder is not the response Jesus seeks to elicit by his acts of healing, rather he is asking that men and women will recognize in the healing miracle a theophany, God's presence. The proper response is that God's people should repent and enter into the promises of the covenant.

Lambourne also discerns a representative "cast" in the New Testament healings : the healer, the sick man and the witnesses of healing are all representative of the community.[23] The term "representative" is used not in the modern everyday usage of one who does something "for" or "instead of" those he represents, but rather in the Hebraic sense of the group speaking "in" the representative : the biblical concept of corporate personality. Of special interest here is how Lambourne interprets the sick man as representative of the community, for this will disclose the particular significance of the healing miracles. While Jesus had perfect compassion on all sick men and women, the Gospels — taking his humanity and limitations seriously — only occasionally suggest compassion as a criterion for selecting those who would cure.[24] In choosing to preach the Gospel through his healing work, Jesus made his selection of patients so that in them the work of God should be made manifest (Jn. 9 :1ff : the man born blind). Those who were healed are representative of the sickness of man. A wealth of Old Testament imagery lies behind the Isaianic categories of sickness (Is. 35 :5-6, 61 :1-2). The deaf, the blind, the dumb and the halt are representative of mankind in its "fallen-sickness-sin aspect" : mankind which "cannot hear the word of the Lord, nor see his glory, nor speak good of his name, nor walk in his ways".[25]

The selection of mighty works which illustrate the mission of Christ is particularly impressive in John's Gospel, so that through Jesus' healing "you may believe that Jesus is the Christ, the Son of God, and that believing this you may have life through his name" (Jn. 20 : 31). Yet even in the Synoptic Gospels the witnesses of the healing miracles are called to regard the sick man as their representative. In Mark's Gospel the healing activity of Jesus progresses from the first healing in the synagogue (1 : 21) — representative of worshipping Israel — through Simon Peter's Jewish home (1 : 30) and the Jewish city (1 : 33), to the Jewish outcast (1 : 40). The Syro-phoenician's daughter, whose cure is recorded in a later Markan chapter, represents the Gentile world. Lambourne comments : "Jesus, having first stretched forth his hand to cleanse worshipping Israel, and followed this by taking away the uncleanness of leprous, outcast Israel, finally takes the burden of the Gentiles".[26] The representative nature of the sick man in the Gospels receives its strongest, although indirect, support from the prevailing Jewish mentality that the relationship between sin and disease was extremely close. Nor was there any doubt about the corporate nature of sin.[27] The sick man thus represents the community of man in its "fallen-sickness-sin situation".

Amid a surprising dearth of serious scholarship in the Anglican healing literature on the significance of Christ's healing ministry to the sick, Lambourne's contribution excels. Summarizing his reflections as outlined above : the healing works of Jesus are public effective signs of Messiahship and the coming of a new age, in which the sick person is representative of the fallen-sickness-sin situation of the community. The Archbishops' Report arrived at a similar conclusion concerning Jesus' healing purpose and the centrality of the healing miracles to his mission :

> It would seem, then, that our Lord's works of healing were integral to his whole purpose, the salvation and redemption of the whole man. They were one of the glad signs of the Kingdom of God which helped to make the Gospel "good news". Physical sickness was a symptom of the grip of evil over the world of men and in Christ was found available the only authority and power that could achieve a complete restoration.[28]

3. Christ's Commission to the Church (Jas. 5:14-16)

The Anglican interpretation of the New Testament data does not regard the ministry of healing as terminating with the resurrection and ascension of the Lord. It sees this ministry as continuing throughout all ages by reason of a special commission entrusted to the Church. In sending forth the disciples on their mission, Jesus bade them to preach the kingdom and to heal the sick (Mk. 6:7ff; Lk. 10:1ff). The nineteen works of healing recorded in the Acts of the Apostles illustrate how the Apostolic Church fulfilled the injunction of the Lord to heal in his name.[29] The ministry of healing was "a recognized ministry within the Body of Christ"; the gifts of healing were comparable to other charisma from the same Holy Spirit (1 Cor. 12:9, 28-30).[30] James 5.14 discloses that the general commission to heal was exercised by the elders of the Church and not by talented individuals. In short, the Spirit was at work in the Church imparting the wholeness and life of the risen Lord.

The interpretation given by the Anglican healing literature to James 5:14-16 is of particular importance for this liturgical study.[31]

> Is any among you sick? Let him call for the elders of the Church; and let them pray over him, anointing him with oil in the name of the Lord: and the prayer of faith shall save him that is sick, and the Lord shall raise him up; and if he have committed sins, it shall be forgiven him. Confess therefore your sins one to another, and pray one for another that ye may be healed. The supplication of a righteous man availeth much in its working.[32]

The Committee Report of the 1908 Lambeth Conference recognized that the biblical authority (Mk. 6:13; Jas. 5:14) for anointing of the sick was of great significance for those Christians who pattern their lives on the word of Holy Scripture. St. James, however, "emphatically connects the 'saving' of the sick with the 'Prayer of Faith', of which the anointing was an accompaniment".[33] As the Committee could find no record of anointing by Christ or by his disciples after Pentecost, apart from the James passage, the Report cautiously stated that it was unclear if James recommended this rite to later generations of Christians. Unction with oil was a common medicinal practice at that time; oil provided a suitable symbol of healing.

An appendix to the 1924 Lambeth Report on the ministry of healing, written by Canon A. J. Mason, examined the historical evidence for the ministry of healing in greater detail. The method of treatment suggested by James was not unknown to his audience. He is not "prescribing it for the first time, nor 'promulgating' it, as a thing previously instituted but hitherto kept secret", although James does seem to have wished it was better known.[34] The Apostle claims no special sanction for the anointing he prescribes, such as Paul's commendation of the eucharist (1 Cor. 11 :23). Anointing the sick with oil had already been practised by the Twelve before the Ascension (Mk. 6 :13). It is unknown whether the disciples were following an express command of Jesus, or using an old traditional Jewish means of soothing ailments, such as indicated by the prophets (Is. 1 :6; Jer. 8 :22, 46 :11, 51 :8).

Was the unction suggested by James considered by him to be remedial or religious? Such a question would be reading into the text different categories from those of James. The science of medicine was little developed in his day; there was a tendency to regard all sickness as sent by God or by evil spirits. Just as it was common to look for sin as the cause of sickness and misfortune, so likewise healing was never solely physical in the "dim, half-explored region that St. James moves".[35] The subsequent healing is not merely the result of a medicinal application with oil, for it is the elders of the Church, and not a physician, who are summoned.

Was the healing expected by James sacramental? Canon Mason defined a sacrament as "a rite in which God pledges himself to give the benefit desired, unless the recipient nullifies the action by wrong dispositions".[36] To say that such a definition was the meaning of James would imply that every anointed Christian would never have died. The promise of healing attached to the James's prescription is not unconditional; it is equally removed from magical practice. The whole benefit is traceable to prayer : "the prayer of faith shall save the sick". This prayer of faith is offered by the elders of the Church, the official leaders of the local community, and not by Christians endowed with particular charisma of healing. The effects ascribed to this visitation of the sick are not confined to physical healing, but extend to spiritual benefits as well. Later theological analysis can point to two sacraments in question : "a sacrament of unction for bodily infirmity, and a sacrament of penance for the remission of sins".[37] But James does not make this distinction. Everything is attributed to one undivided action : "the 'fervent prayer' of the elders of the Church, which obtains healing of the sick, and, in case the sick has committed grave sins, forgiveness also".[38]

A considerable vagueness enshrouds A. J. Mason's reflections on the James passage. Perhaps he was influenced by the remarkable monograph *Anointing of the Sick in Scripture and Tradition* (1904) by Rev. F. W. Puller of the Society of St. John the Evangelist.[39] Though not undisposed towards the revival of unction in the Church of England, Puller was adamant in insisting that the unction referred to in James was identical with the unction conferred by the disciples in Mark 6 : 13. It is not a sacrament conveying sanctifying grace *ex opere operato,* but rather a sacramental providing of supernatural means for the recovery of health.

Puller comes to this conclusion by making a sharp distinction between James 5 : 14-15a and 5 : 15b-16. James 5 : 14-15a pertains to all sick people, who are urged to call the elders of the Church to pray over them and to anoint them with oil. The Greek verb in v.15, while elsewhere in the New Testament sometimes denoting salvation through Jesus, is here used in reference to bodily healing. Likewise the Greek   , often misunderstood by Roman Catholic writers to imply that Christ will "comfort" the soul of the sick person, actually means "to raise up" and bespeaks a physical cure.[40] Puller translates James 5 : 14-15a as follows :

> Is any one among you sick? Let him call for the Presbyters of the Church; and let them pray over him, anointing him with oil in the Name of the Lord; and the prayer of faith *shall restore to health* him that is ailing, and the Lord *will cause him to recover.*[41]

Puller sees the second division of the passage (Jas. 5 : 15b-16) as relating to a further category of sick persons : those in serious sins which have yet to be remitted. Here it is not a question of one of the effects of unction, but of the power of the keys, the sacrament of penance. The particle *oun* closely connects the confession of sins mentioned in v.16 with the remission (*aphethēsetai*) of sins confessed in v.15 James thus instructs those sick persons who find themselves in serious sin to confess their sins and to receive absolution from the elders.

Charles Harris, who writes from the same Catholic persuasion and whose article in *Liturgy and Worship* marks him as a leading champion of the revival of anointing, agrees with Puller's findings in declaring that the "late medieval theory that Unction was primarily ordained for remission of sins — particularly those of the senses" finds no solid support in the famous James passage.[42] This theory is largely traceable to an unfortunate rendering in the Vulgate : "et si in peccatis sit, dimittentur ei". But the Greek (*kai hamartias ē pepoiēkōs aphethēsetai autō*) shows that "sins" cannot possibly be the subject of the passive impersonal *aphethēsetai*. The natural translation would be : "and if he is in a state of having committed sins, forgiveness (*or more technically* 'absolution') shall be imparted to him".[43] The reference is therefore to the sacramental absolution conferred by the elders to whom the sick man has confessed his sins.[44]

Harris agrees with Puller in the prima facie physical sense given to *sōsei* and *egerei* : but unlike him, does not make a strict distinction between James 5 :14-15a and 5 :15b-16, and prefers a wider interpretation of the entire passage. Harris regards James 5 :14-16 as pertaining to the healing of the whole personality for the following reasons : the comprehensive sense of *iathēte* of v.16, which has reference to the healing of both body and soul; James's insistence on faith; the close relation of physical and spiritual healing in primitive times; the use in early orders of unction of terms such as "heal", "save", "safety", "salvation" in a composite physical and spiritual sense; and especially the all-embracing sweep of the ministry of healing entrusted by Christ to the Apostles. This is where Puller and Harris differ, for the latter regards unction of the sick as a sacrament, and supported by liturgical evidence, even accepts the remission of sins as among the "secondary and indirect effects" of the sacrament.[45] For Harris the passage on anointing of the sick in James 5 :14-16 speaks of unction as a sacrament of healing of the whole person, a view which has been gaining acceptance in Anglican theology and will be discussed more fully later.

B. ORIENTATION ON THE EARLY CHURCH

1. *Healing in the Ante-Nicene Church*

Virtually every book promoting the healing ministry in England cites the evidence of healing in the primitive Church.[46] The most complete study of patristic passages is found in Evelyn Frost's *Christian Healing*.[47] Dr. Frost's thesis is that the Ante-Nicene

Church was completely transformed by the power of the Risen Lord, the Second Man who brought life to regenerate a fallen mankind. The power of the Easter victory of Christ is not confined to the sanctification of the soul, but extends also to the preservation of the whole human person — spirit, soul and body — especially in the sacraments of Baptism and the Eucharist. The Fathers of the pre-Nicene Church, largely in their apologetical writings, point to the victory of Christ manifesting itself in powers shown in direct relation to persecution, powers over what was earlier attributed to demons, and in powers over physical death and disease. Instances of healing occur in patristic passages dealing with powers against demons and powers against physical disease. The early Church was firmly convinced that Christians were engaged in a struggle against not merely human enemies, but against the Powers and Principalities (Eph. 6:12).[48] As healing from sickness was often the result of exorcism, one may consider how the healing writers interpret both of these patristic witnesses to the victory of Christ.[49]

In the oldest extant fragment of a Christian Apology, Quadratus (c.125) tells of the witnesses of the healing works of Christ, especially those still living who themselves had been cured or raised from the dead.[50] Justin Martyr (d.c.165) refers to the great success of Christian exorcists who exorcize in the name of Jesus Christ, thus healing countless demoniacs.[51] In the Dialogue with Trypho, Justin speaks of the gift of healing as one of the charismata still received in the Church.[52]

For Theophilus of Antioch divine healing from sickness was a proof of the power of the resurrection at work upon man's physical nature.[53] In his Epistle to the Greeks, Tatian (c.160) chides Christians who seek out material remedies such as herbs and roots, rather than relying on the power of the Logos.[54]

Irenaeus of Lyons (d.c.202), in refuting the claims of Gnostic heretics, points to the superior works of healing performed by Christians. These works of healing include giving sight to the blind and hearing to the deaf; casting out demons; curing the weak, lame, paralytic and all kinds of infirmity; and even raising the dead.[55] In a world which saw a close relationship between sickness and sin, Christ was the medicus who came to cure the sick.[56]

The writings of Tertullian (d.c.220) are another fruitful source of information about healing by exorcism and the methods employed.[57] The demons are completely under the control of Christ and his followers.[58] Tertullian relates how the Christian Proculus healed the ailing pagan emperor Severus by anointing with oil.[59]

Exorcism and healing play an important role in Origen's (d.c.254) polemic with the pagan Celsus. The power of the name of Jesus is so great that, even when pronounced by wicked men, demons are put to flight.[60] Instances of healing were traces of the Holy Spirit.[61] Many Greek and barbarian converts have received gifts of healing.[62] Some of the cures are even more remarkable than those witnessed by the Jews at the time of Christ.[63]

However, the Spirit-filled life of the Church, and consequently instances of healing, were beginning to wane. Cyprian (d.258) observes that the sins of Christians had weakened the power of the Church.[64] Lactantius (d.c.320) remarks that demons flee as long as there is peace in the Church.[65] A noticeable change had set in. Dr. Frost writes :

> From the time of Cyprian onwards the Church is involved in controversy; the problems of discipline and order and of theological definition land the Church in a battlefield; the first freshness of the Spirit-filled life of the previous centuries has passed away, no longer has the Church all things in common, no longer is it of one heart and mind, no longer is there the same degree of power in prayer, no longer is there a rich harvest of testimony to healing, although never has the power of healing the sick by prayer and sacrament been completely lost.[66]

A loss of spiritual vitality, of unity and of the fullness of Christ's revelation weakened the Church's witness to the world and signalled its retreat "from the earlier vital experience of the presence and power of the Holy Spirit".[67] Equally disastrous was the rise of conventional Christianity occasioned by the conversion of the Emperor Constantine which ultimately led to the acceptance of Christianity as the state religion :

> With the conversion of Constantine Christianity passed from the tropical zone of the Spirit's life and activity to the temperate zone where the exotic exuberance of the fruitage of the earlier years was no longer produced by the Church for the inestimable benefit of the world.[68]

By the time of Augustine (d.430) healing miracles, while still occurring, were considered very unusual and were becoming more and more infrequent.[69]

It is well-nigh impossible to evaluate objectively the case for healing in the primitive Church made out by the healing propagandists. Surely they are not the first to note the prolific evidence of healing in the early Church.[70] Whilst Frost's findings have found general acceptance in the Anglican healing movement, it should be pointed out that Puller and Dearmer cite instances of charismatic healing which take us into the twentieth century. Puller lists some twenty-two cures resulting from anointing as late as St. Cuthbert (d.687).[71] Dearmer has compiled instances of healing from the lives of such saints and worthies as Martin Luther (d.1546), Philip Neri (d.1595), George Fox (d.1691), John Wesley (d.1791), Prince Alexander of Hohenlohe (d.1849), Father Matthew (d.1856), Dorothea Trüdel (d.1862), Pastor Blumhardt (d.1880), and Father John of Cronstadt (d.1908).[72] Other authors record the Church's compassionate care for the sick and suffering throughout the centuries. Although admittedly a ministry less spectacular than charismatic healing, this Christian concern for the sick led to the founding of hospitals as early as 369 in Asia Minor by St. Basil, 375 in Edessa by St. Ephraim, and in Rome in the year 400.[73]

2. The Pastoral Ministry to the Sick

Even more striking than the patristic evidence for miraculous healings is the rich harvest the healing literature has reaped from the liturgical sources of the first Christian millennium on the pastoral ministry to the sick. Harris' article on the visitation of the sick, although now somewhat dated, is still one of the most comprehensive studies of the early Church's ministry to the sick.[74]

According to Harris, from the earliest times the pastoral care of the sick was entrusted primarily to the bishop and his college of presbyters. The Canons of Hippolytus disclose that the charism of healing was a qualification recommending a candidate for ordination.[75] The same Canons contain a prayer for the ordination of a bishop or presbyter in which the petition is made that the ordinand be granted special exorcistic and healing powers : " 'Grant to him, O Lord, a mild spirit, and power to remit sins, and grant to him power to loose all bonds of the iniquity of demons (i.e. by exorcism), and to heal all diseases, and to beat down Satan under his feet quickly' ".[76] A similar petition, wth reference to exorcism, occurs in the ordination prayer of a deacon : " 'Grant (to this deacon) power to vanquish every power of the Deceitful One by the sign of thy Cross wherewith he himself is signed' ".[77] At the rite of priestly ordination as found in the Apostolic Constitutions, the bishop prays that the candidate be " 'filled with the gifts of healing' ".[78]

Every Sunday at the eucharistic liturgy the bishop would pray for and bless the sick, as well as exorcize the "energumenoi" (the mentally afflicted who were considered in some way possessed). Two such prayers are contained in the fourth-century *Sacramentary of Serapion* : "A Prayer for the Sick", and "The Imposition of Hands upon the Sick".[79] One of the *Canons of Hippolytus* stresses that the recovery of the sick depends largely upon their frequent attendance at church and participation in prayer, when at all possible.[80] Harris remarks that in primitive times the Christian churches were considered "temples of healing" which rivalled and surpassed the pagan temples of Aesculapius.[81]

Sick Christians who were too ill to be brought to church were visited by the bishop and clergy. The ancient services found in Martene's *De Antiquis Ecclesiæ Ritibus* highlight the therapeutic value of the daily choral offices rendered by clerics at the sick person's bedside. In a rubric at the close of the Visitation Office in Menard's *"Gregorian" Sacramentary,* the priests and ministers are called upon to celebrate the daily chanted recitation of Vespers and Matins, together with the hymn *Christe cœlestis medicina Patris* ("O Christ, Heavenly Medicine of the Father") in the presence of the sick person.[82]

A special efficacy was accorded to the visitation of the sick by the bishop himself. A *Canon of Hippolytus* compares the visit by the prince of priests with the shadow of Peter which healed the sick.[83] Citing examples from the lives of Saints Ambrose and Martin, Harris sees the role of the bishop as the principal exorcist of the diocese.[84] Moreover, from an analysis of prayers for the sick, Harris identifies much of the ministry to the sick as exorcistic or semi-exorcistic in character.[85] For instance, the phrase "rebuke the disease" in Serapion's prayer for the sick implies that even in ordinary cases of sickness diabolical influences were at work which required rebuking.[86] Harris adds :

There was a marked disinclination in the primitive and medieval period to attribute sickness directly to God, though this was occasionally done. The tendency was to regard God as the *healer* of disease, not as its author. The sick person, after confession of sins, and full reconciliation to God, was expected to recover rapidly, aided by the daily ministrations of the Bishop and his presbyters.[87]

The ninth-century *Pontifical of Milan,* the *Missal of Leofric* in Anglo-Saxon England and much of the ancient material in the modern *Rituale Romanum* include many exorcistic prayers for use in the pastoral ministry to the sick.[88]

Not only did the bishop bless and exorcize the sick Christian, but also his medicine and food, particularly bread and water. These blessed substances, when used with faith, were considered "therapeutic agencies, auxiliary to the major ministrations of unction and the imposition of hands".[89] The sprinkling with blessed water was a sign of purification and healing of body and soul. The bread for the sick was usually blessed in commemoration of the miraculous five loaves in the wilderness. The *Sacramentary of Serapion* and the *Apostolic Constitutions* reveal that the bread and water were frequently blessed together with, and under the same formula, as the oil.[90] Harris, however, is quick to add that "a far greater and more definitely sacramental efficacy was attributed to anointing than to the administration of blessed bread and water".[91]

The laity also had an important role in the early Church's ministry to the sick. Perhaps somewhat overstating his Catholic position, Harris asserts that the lay ministry, while officially recognized, was always of "an auxiliary and subordinate, never of a primary and independent character".[92] In both East and West the laity offered oil at the Sunday Eucharist, where it was blessed by the bishop and afterwards used for domestic application. Pope Innocent I in his letter to Decentius (416) states that the faithful have the right not only to be anointed by the clergy, but also to use the oil for further anointings by themselves at home.[93] The Venerable Bede (*d.*735), referring to Innocent's letter, attests to a similar practice in England.[94] Harris observes that "though unction and imposition of hands by lay persons were widely in use in early and mediæval times for the cure of minor ailments, recourse was always had to the more potent ministrations of the bishop and his presbyters, where the disease was serious".[95]

3. *Unction and the Laying on of Hands*

The 1924 Lambeth Report regarded unction and the associated rite of laying on of hands as possessing "scriptural authority" and being "sacramental in the sense that a blessing is sought and received through the performance of outward and visible actions".[96] In all cases where these sacramental rites are worthily celebrated, a spiritual blessing is imparted and sometimes also the complete or partial recovery of health.[97]

a) Unction in the Western Church

The authors agree that the earliest liturgical source for the consecration of oil for the sick is found in the early third-century *Apostolic Tradition* of Hippolytus as represented in the Latin Verona Fragment and the Ethiopic version, the so-called "Egyptian Church Order".[98] Harris translates the Latin version as follows :

> If anyone offers oil (let the bishop bless it) after the manner of the oblation of bread and wine; and let him not speak according to these exact words, but let him give thanks with similar meaning (*or* efficacy), saying, "Sanctifying this oil, O God, mayest thou give health to those who use and receive it. With this unction thou didst anoint kings, priests and prophets. So (now) may it afford strengthening to all who taste it, and health to those who use it".[99]

Harris sees herein a spiritual unction analogous to that bestowed upon the baptized at confirmation and to that poured forth upon the prophets, priests and kings of the Old Testament. Hippolytus attributed a healing power to the oil because he regarded it as a *"spiritual unction* conveying grace to the soul".[100] The "strengthening" and "health" mentioned in the Verona Fragment apply as much to the soul as to the body. Together with other promoters of the ministry of healing—usually of Catholic principles, Harris holds that unction is "a sacrament, conveying sanctifying grace to the soul of the worthy recipient".[101] He vigorously rejects the theory advanced by Puller and Dearmer that unction is merely a supernatural means for the healing of physical and mental disease. Harris likewise disavows a possible interpretation of some psychologists who would see in unction simply another method of therapeutic suggestion.

Harris finds this theology of unction as a sacrament, "a ministry of the Spirit", especially verified in the ancient form in the *Pontificale Romanum* (1595) for consecrating oil of the sick on Maundy Thursday, a prayer which is in part derivative from Hippolytus and dates from the fifth century. The opening exorcism (*Exorcizo te, immundissime spiritus,* etc.), although absent in the ancient sacramentaries, is attested in many older liturgical sources and may be considered to antedate the ninth century. Then follows the actual prayer of consecration, as witnessed in the Gelasian and Gregorian Sacramentaries.[102]

> Send down from heaven, we beseech thee, Lord, thy Holy Spirit, the Paraclete, upon this richness of oil, which thou has deigned to bring forth from the green tree for the refreshment of mind and body. May thy holy blessing be to all who are anointed with this celestial medicine, a protection of mind and body, for the expulsion of all pains, all infirmities, and every sickness of mind and body, wherewith thou didst anoint priests, kings, prophets and martyrs. May it be for us thy perfect chrism, Lord, blessed by you, abiding in our inward parts : In the name of the Lord Jesus Christ.[103]

Harris summarizes the teaching of the Roman Pontifical :

1. The unction is "a spiritual unction" and a "perfect chrism" parallel to the unction at confirmation. Not only is the oil called *chrisma*, but the words "wherewith thou didst anoint priests, kings, prophets and martyrs" also occur in the form for consecrating the chrism for confirmation.

2. The anointing with oil is intended to renew "the indwelling of the Holy Spirit, for the strengthening, healing and consecrating of the sick man's personality" ("celestial medicine", "a protection of mind and body").[104]

3. This indwelling of the Spirit is meant to be permanent : a "perfect chrism . . . abiding in our inward parts".

4. The use of this consecrated oil is effectual for bodily disease as well as for mental and spiritual afflictions : "for the expulsion of all pains, all infirmities, and every sickness of mind and body". In this brief formula, three times reference is made to the mind (*mens*).

5. The oil is to be used for sick persons generally, and not necessarily those in danger of death. This is clear not only from the title, *oleum infirmorum*, but also from the description of the oil as a remedy for every kind of pain and infirmity, and especially for mental and spiritual disorders.

In his appendix to the 1924 Lambeth Report, Canon A. J. Mason correctly observes that the earliest sacramentaries and ritual books contain only formulas for blessing, but not for applying the consecrated oil.[105] He suggests that the prayer at the actual anointing with oil was originally left to the inspiration of the moment. Harris, while admitting that the office for unction found in Menard's edition of the *"Gregorian" Sacramentary* and reproduced in Migne is not the actual Gregorian order for the rite, nonetheless regards the Codex Ratoldi (Paris, Nat. lat. 12052) from which it is derived as the nearest extant approximation to the Gregorian office and thus the "most ancient full Service for the Administration of Unction now in existence".[106]

The "Gregorian" service foresees the presence of a number of priests and ministers, a choir, and perhaps even a congregation of concerned fellow Christians. The rite begins with the exorcism and blessing of holy water in the presence of the sick man. The sprinkling of the sick with holy water, "a semi-sacramental ministration of a remedial character auxiliary to Unction", is found in virtually all the ancient and medieval rituals.[107] After a series of prayers for recovery, a remarkable rubric appears which clearly indicates that in earlier times the sick person was usually not *in extremis* :

> And thus let the sick man bend his knee or knees, and stand at the right hand of the priest, and thus let this Antiphon be chanted : *The Lord said to his disciples, Cast out devils in my name and lay your hands upon the sick, and they shall recover.*

Harris suspects that the imposition of hands by the presbyters followed the Antiphon, although any rubric to this effect has been omitted in Menard's edition. The sick person would presumably remain kneeling for the imposition of hands as well as for the ensuing unction.

After the recitation of another antiphon, an interesting rubric on the manner of unction comes to light :

> And thus let him thoroughly anoint the sick man with consecrated oil, on the neck and throat, and between the shoulders, and on the breast; also let him be more thoroughly and liberally anointed where the pain is more threatening. And let the sick man pray while he is being anointed, and let one of the priests recite this prayer: "I anoint thee with Holy Oil in the name of the Father, and of the Son, and of the Holy Ghost, that no unclean spirit may lie hid in thee, or in thy members, or in thy marrow(s), or in any joint of thy limbs, but that the power

of Christ most high and of the Holy Ghost may dwell in thee, —etc".[109]

This prayer is the second of three prayers for anointing provided in the "Gregorian" office. It deals almost exclusively with physical ailments. The first prayer, *Inungo te de oleo sancto,* occurring somewhat earlier in the service, refers to anointing as a spiritual unction. The third prayer, *Domine Deus, Salvator noster,* makes reference to moral and spiritual disorders amid a rather extensive listing of physical maladies. This final prayer concludes : "May this holy anointing with oil be the expulsion of the present disease and languor, and the wished-for remission of all sins".[110]

Following the communion of the sick under both species, there follows another remarkable directive :

And let (the priests) do this to him *for seven days,* if necessary, not only with regard to communion, but also with regard to any other administration; and the Lord shall raise him up, and if he is in sins, they shall be forgiven him.[111]

Evidently at this time the repetition of unction during the same illness was not only not prohibited, but even expressly encouraged. The final rubric stipulates that choral services are to be rendered twice daily at the sick man's bedside. An appended note, of later provenance, follows :

Many priests also anoint the sick on the five senses of the body ... This they do, that if any stain has inhered in the five senses of the mind and body, it may be healed by this medicine of God.[112]

b) Unction in the Eastern Church

Harris perceives the theology of anointing of the sick as a spiritual unction, a sacrament conveying grace to the sick man's personality, equally substantiated in the liturgical tradition of the Eastern Church.

The earliest extant liturgical document of the East which treats of unction is the so-called *Sacramentary of Serapion* of Thmuis in Egypt (c.350). The Sacramentary includes two forms for the blessing of oil of the sick, together with bread and wine. The first form is entitled "A Prayer concerning the Offerings of Oil and

Water" which are presented by the faithful at the eucharist. The prayer expressly mentions bodily and mental healing, and concludes : "that the partaking of these creatures may be a *healing medicine (pharmakon therapeutikon)*, and *a medicine of complete soundness (pharmakon holoklērias)*.[113]

The term "complete soundness" (*holoklēria*) recurs in the second form given in Serapion's Sacramentary : "A Prayer for Oil of the Sick, or for Bread, or for Water". The principal section of this prayer is as follows :

. . . Send forth (a) healing power of the Only-begotten from heaven upon this oil, that it may become to those who are anointed, or partake of these creatures, unto the driving away of every sickness and every weakness, unto a medicine of preservation against every demon; unto the expulsion of every unclean spirit; unto the separation of every evil spirit; unto the chasing away of every fever and shivering fit and every infirmity; *unto good grace and remission of sins; unto a medicine of life and salvation (pharmakon zōēs kai sōtērias); unto health and complete wholeness of soul, body, spirit (holoklēriam psukēs sōmatos pneumatos)*; unto complete strengthening (*hrōsin teleian*) . . .[114]

F. W. Puller, who refuses to recognize in unction any claim to being a sacrament of the Church which imparts grace, has considerable difficulty integrating this second prayer of Serapion into his hypothesis, and thereby rejects the phrase "unto good grace and remission of sins" as a later interpolation.[115] F. E. Brightman, who edited the *Sacramentary of Serapion* in 1900, does not concur with Puller's interpretation; neither do Harris nor A. J. Mason.[116] Harris points to other early formulas for anointing, in the *Book of Dimna* (possibly seventh century) and the *Stowe Missal* (eighth or ninth century), which likewise refer to the spiritual effects of unction.[117]

The Eastern tradition of unction is authoritatively expressed in the service for anointing in the Greek *Euchologion* (seventh century). The service is a public ceremony, when possible performed by seven priests, at least one deacon, together with a choir and a representative congregation. The oil is consecrated by the ministering priests in the presence of the sick man. All persons seriously ill may be anointed; the danger of death is not a prerequisite. The rite may also be repeated in the course of the same illness. Harris notes that the *Euchologion* service stresses physical and mental healing, but even more the spiritual benefits, especially the remission of sins.[118]

The *Euchologion* is in agreement with the earlier Western tradition that anointing of the sick is a spiritual unction. The priests pray "that this oil may be blessed by thy power and mercy, and by the descent of the Holy Ghost upon it".[119] And again : "Send down thy Holy Spirit and hallow this oil, and make it to be unto this thy servant *N.*, who is anointed therewith, unto perfect remission of his sins, and unto inheritance of the kingdom of heaven".[120] The anointing service or Euchelaion ("oil of prayer"), as contained in the *Euchologion,* has also served as a model for the Armenian, Syriac and Coptic offices, although these have today largely fallen into desuetude.[121]

c. Laying on of Hands

While unction is usually treated more extensively in the Anglican healing literature, the imposition of hands upon the sick is a rite which the authors see closely interwoven with the history of unction.[122] Jesus laid hands upon the sick; it may have been his usual manner of healing. The author of the epilogue to Mark's Gospel regarded the imposition of hands as a means of healing definitely recommended by Christ : "They will lay their hands upon the sick, who will recover" (Mk. 16 : 18).

The expression "imposition of hands" in earlier times often implied the joint use of unction. Origen, even when quoting James' Epistle, interpolates the words : "Let them lay hands on him".[123] In the Ambrosian liturgy of Milan, unction was frequently called *impositio manuum.*[124] A. J. Mason, drawing a parallel between confirmation and the sacramental rites of healing, suggests that unction and the imposition of hands were two "symbolic actions" which were "identical and interchangeable".[125] Apart from its use associated with anointing, the laying on of hands seems to have been the usual method of healing by those endowed with a charismatic gift from the early times of the Church until even today among such lay healers as James Moore Hickson and Dorothy Kerin.[126]

d. Subsequent History of Unction

The Anglican orientation on the doctrine and practice of the early Church has led the way in demonstrating that unction and the related rite of the laying on of hands were sacramental rites of healing employed by the primitive Church in its pastoral ministry to the sick. In both the Western and Eastern Church these rites were administered to sick, by no means dying, persons with the hopeful assumption that healing would often result.[127] How do the authors view the subsequent development of the anointing of the sick?

It is generally agreed that a change in the conception of unction came about in the Western Church in the eighth and ninth centuries, perhaps somewhat earlier in the East.[128] In the West unction became the sacrament of the dying: extreme unction. In the Eastern Orthodox Church the Euchelaion became a means of grace frequently resorted to as part of the normal preparation for communion. A. J. Mason intimates that men began to look for spiritual rather than bodily benefits, as experience had taught them that bodily healing was rarely granted as a result of anointing.[129]

F. W. Puller rejects this hypothesis and attributes the change in unction to a misinterpretation of James 5 : 14-16.[130] James actually refers to two classes of sick people : all sick Christians, and then a minority of these sick Christians who are in a state of deadly sin. To this latter category of sick people the presbyters were enjoined to administer the sacrament of penance. But with the growth of the Celtic practice of private penance in the sixth and seventh centuries, frequent confession became a means of grace accessible to all Christians. This change in the Church's penitential discipline had far-reaching ramifications : the conditional clause of James referring to sick Christians in serious sin came to be considered as applicable to all sick Christians. The remission of sins was then understood to be a spiritual effect no longer exclusive to the sacrament of penance, but to unction as well. Thus unction became a sacrament.[131]

As might be expected, Harris also expresses his opinion on this point. Harris discounts the "Ordo Ministrandi Sacramentum Extremae Unctionis" of the *Rituale Romanum* (1614) as a valid witness to primitive doctrine and practice.[132] While many of the earlier prayers for recovery have been retained, the service for unction in the Ritual is at present restricted to those in danger of death from sickness or old age. What had previously been a sacrament of healing has now become extreme unction, the sacrament of the dying. Another reprehensible feature of the Ritual service is the excessive emphasis upon the remission of sins; e.g. the form for anointing : "By this holy unction, and his most merciful pity, the Lord pardon thee all sins committed through *sight,* etc.".[133] Harris regards the *Second Capitulaire* of Theodulf of Orleans and the Council of Mainz (847) as decisive turning points from the primitive to the medieval conception of unction. The *Capitulaire* shows that the accepted view of unction was beginning to be as follows :

1. that the primary—or one of the primary—effects of unction is *remission of sins;*
2. that unction, when applied to the organs of the bodily senses (eyes, ears, nostrils, etc.) remits *the sins committed through those senses;* and
3. that, though unction is not without efficacy for the healing of bodily and mental infirmities, yet its more important effect is *preparation for death.*[134]

A lesser known advocate of the healing ministry, J. R. Pridie, observes that the gradual "narrowing process" in the practice of unction at work in the Carolingian reform councils reached its climax at the Council of Florence (1439), which definitely restricted anointing to dying persons.[135] In the following century the Council of Trent tried to retrieve this position : the term "extreme unction" was explained as the last of all unctions. But Trent goes on to speak of unction as the sacrament of the dying (*sacramentum exeuntium*), thus stereotyping a medieval view which has dominated Western thought ever since.[136] Pridie personally considers that the reason for the change in the use of unction is to be found in a much deeper change of thinking within the Church which began already in the fourth century. In language reminiscent of Dr. Frost, Pridie remarks : "It is the change from her ideal of herself as the Body of Christ enshrining His life, His power (*dunamis*), to the ideal of herself as His Body expressing His authority (*exousia*)". The repercussions of this changing image of the Church were felt in the sacrament of unction. Originally anointing of the sick was "a sacrament of power for help to live"; it was later used as "a sacrament of authority to assure the passing soul that all was well as he went forward into the unknown.[137]

C. COMMON MISCONCEPTIONS ABOUT THE CHURCH'S MINISTRY OF HEALING

It is important to recognize how the healing movement interprets the evidence of the New Testament and the early Church. Numerous other questions about the theology and practice of healing today still remain to be answered. What is the relationship between faith and healing? What is the will of God regarding health and sickness? What is the role of the Church's ministry of healing in the world of modern medicine? Who is called to practice the ministry of healing? What place does this ministry occupy in the life and mission of the Church? What should be expected from the healing ministrations? The Archbishops' Report anticipates questions such as these within the framework of nine possible misconceptions which may arise about the Church's ministry of healing, so as both to correct a false impression about healing by those outside this ministry and to check the possible excesses of those within the ministry. This schema of the Archbishops' Report also provides a useful framework with which to sum up and conclude this chapter.[138]

1. That healing inevitably follows faith

Several of the authors speak of the necessity of inducing the patient into "the faith state" preliminary to any healing ministrations.[139] By this technical term is not meant a mere psychological expectation of recovery or "suggestion", but rather a state of "*spiritual communion* with God and trust in Him".[140] The faith state means directing the patient's thoughts toward God, implying repentance on the part of the sick person and the submission of his will entirely to God, whether for recovery of for continued illness. The Archbishops' Report would agree that faith, understood here as trust and confidence in God as shown to us in Jesus Christ, renders a person more receptive to any healing influence. But the Report, together with other authors, branded as "cruel" and "false" any approach which makes physical healing as an inevitable answer to faith into a principle applicable to all healing.[141] Such a doctrine is cruel, because when the expected healing does not ensue, the result may be a spirit of despair and revolt against God; it is false because it contradicts common experience and the teaching of the New Testament. The Commission concluded that it was impossible from any given instance of illness to dogmatize about the causal relationship between faith and recovery.

The Archbishops' Report probably had the writings of such propagandists as E. Howard Cobb in mind. On several occasions

Cobb intimates that divine healing is the inevitable result of faith. If healing has not been forthcoming, our faith in God is at fault.[142] A more subtle expression of the same fallacy is found in the thesis of Evelyn Frost, who contends that the renewal of Christian healing is attendant upon the renewal of the Church as a community of faith and love.[143]

Amid the discussion of faith and healing, Leslie Weatherhead —a Methodist whose writings have exerted a strong influence on the Anglican healing ministry—attempts to define Christian faith. It is not faith in getting better, a mental gymnastic which may not have anything to do with religion. Neither is the concept of Christian faith exhausted when understood as belief in credal statements. *"Christian faith is the response of the whole man, thinking, feeling and willing, to the impact of God in Christ, by which man comes into a conscious, personal relationship with God."*[144]

2. That suffering is always contrary to God's will

This misconception about the Church's ministry of healing is directed primarily against certain extremist elements in the ministry who would argue in this fashion : Christ healed all the sick people who came to him; if Jesus healed sick people then, he must heal them now; otherwise he is not "the same yesterday, today, and forever".[145] This problem is central to the entire ministry of healing : what is the will of God concerning health and sickness? Whether or not there is a healing ministry at all depends upon the answer to this question, which is posed against a medieval mentality as reflected in the Order for the Visitation of the Sick in the Prayer Book : sickness is sent by God, a cross to be patiently endured. The general answer of the healing movement to this crucial problem of the will of God is that sickness and disease are not sent by God, but are an evil sometimes merely permitted by him. As this problem is so crucial, it is important to consider more specifically how the various writers approach the question.

The 1930 Lambeth Conference Committee Report drew an interesting analogy between temptation and sickness. Temptation is an evil from which we are told to pray for deliverance. Nevertheless, all mankind, including Christ himself, was subject to temptation. In fact, it sometimes appears to be God's will that we continue to suffer from temptation and even to count such suffering a joy. So likewise disease is a liability for humanity and an evil against which the Lord has enjoined us to struggle. Yet complete harmony with the will of God sometimes dictates "a suffering that exalts and purifies", rather than the recovery of physical health.[146]

Some authors make a distinction between the primary and secondary will of God.[147] The primary will of God is perfect health or wholeness. But by the misuse of his freedom man has frustrated the Creator's design, thus necessitating God's secondary or contingent will which sometimes permits sickness and disease. Sickness and disease remain, as always, an evil, something which ought not to be. Yet it is an evil which, for instance, as a means of spiritual discipline, may be overruled for good.

Other authors prefer to distinguish between pain and disease.[148] Pain is something positive; it may be a sign pointing to some unsuspected danger or lack of harmony within the human organism; it may also have an educative value by signalling that the forces of life are adapting themselves in a struggle against a disruptive power. Disease, on the contrary, is entirely negative, leading to deterioration and destruction. In the words of Phyllis Garlick: "Disease is something altogether alien, a destroying, death-dealing evil to be combated by all the powers and resources God have given us".[149]

Another line of thought would distinguish between kinds or sources of suffering. Jim Wilson of the Guild of Health discerns two types of suffering: a suffering such as disease which stems from sin and evil; and a suffering which comes from opposing evil and its manifestations. The Christian is called to resist the first kind of suffering and to embrace the second.[150] In her study of the Ante-Nicene period Evelyn Frost makes a much more elaborate distinction between three sources of suffering: an evil source resulting from the Fall or subsequent sins of man; a natural source which is a law of the natural order; and a directly divine source of suffering for which God is immediately responsible. The evil source of suffering arises in relation to disease, in the working out of the sequel to sin in history, and in sufferings caused by the conflict with sin and evil. Pain arising from any of these three sources of suffering may be used by God as a means for good: for the manifestation of the glory of God, for stimulation of growth, and for educative purposes as a means of healing from sin. The responsibility of the individual Christian is not to acquiesce in suffering, but to press on towards the final goal, which is the healing for which the suffering is permitted. Christianity is not "a way of escape *from* suffering but rather a way of healing *through* suffering".[151] In relation to sickness, for the early Church it was "in conquest of disease, not in submission under it, that the Christian victory was won".[152]

R. A. Lambourne underlines the fact that the ministry of healing involves suffering. Christ is the Son of Man who must suffer as a consequence of joining himself to a mankind he set out to heal. So the Church, which is the Body of Christ, must likewise share in this victorious suffering of Christ which reveals his glory. Lambourne is also rightly suspicious of views which admit that Christian healing implies suffering, but which would suppose that "the man made whole by faith" has transferred his suffering to higher plane. Such an attitude would be tantamount to claiming that the Incarnation did not involve genuine suffering in the flesh. Lambourne illustrates this fallacy in vivid terms:

> It may well be that the salvation by faith into the people of God may mean the healing of a man's duodenal ulcer which was caused by worries which are now felt to be only trivialities; but on the other hand the fit and healthy young man without a worry in the world may be by faith "made whole" into a change of job which will put him at risk to all sorts of new physical, mental, and moral dangers.[153]

The Archbishops' Commission is especially impatient with subtle distinctions which presume that pain, sickness and disease, wherever they occur, are contrary to the will of God. Christian theology has always allotted a place to suffering in the redemptive plan of God:

> It is central to Christian doctrine that the sufferings of Christ were borne in accordance with the will of the Father for the sake of man's salvation. Christians, with St. Paul (Col. 1:24; Phil. 3:10) discern in suffering a means of union with Christ in his redemptive work.[154]

What positive value do the other authors ascribe to suffering in the Christian life? Weatherhead, who generally discounts suffering as a means to sanctification, does however admit that God's will in special circumstances may be to choose suffering as a way of unselfish service.[155] Many authors would probably agree with Purcell Fox, who affirms the value of offering to God not the diseased body, but the suffering incident upon sickness.[156] Garlick sees the redemptive suffering of the cross of Christ not as a solution to the problem of suffering, but a transcendence of it, because

God in Christ has shared the sufferings of mankind.[157] Pridie regards the vicarious suffering of Christ as continued in his Body the Church.[158] The most contemporary approach is that of Michael Wilson, who on this point takes up a theme of Pierre Teilhard de Chardin.[159] Wilson argues for the necessity of a positive ministry to those who have resisted disease to the limit of their endurance and remain uncured. Healing is only one of God's answers. When we have done all we could to resist and have sought God's help in every way possible, we should trustfully allow God to draw us closer to himself.

The soundest approach to the whole problem of the will of God concerning health and sickness has been expressed by Bishop John A. T. Robinson, who places healing within the scriptural context of the Kingdom of God in its eschatological dimension. Bishop Robinson agrees with the proponents of the healing ministry that health is the will of God and that disease is "the work of the devil". He also agrees that the command to heal is integral to the Gospel message. Health and healing are signs of the Kingdom. But the perfect reign of God which will put an end to pain, disease and death belongs to an age which has not yet dawned. We are now living between the time of the Resurrection and the Day of the Lord. And because the Kingdom of God has not yet been fully revealed, we should be very cautious about what we promise to people who are ill. The most manifest sign of the final redemption of all flesh is the "Spirit's power to heal", but it is an anticipation vouchsafed mysteriously and graciously to some, withheld equally mysteriously and graciously from others; and it should not be offered as more.[160] Perfect wholeness of body, mind and spirit does not belong to men of this aeon.

3. That sickness is always caused by sin

Although some authors speak of man's original misuse of his freedom—the Fall of man—as causative of suffering and sickness in the world, this misconception has special reference to the personal sin of the sick person.[161] Obvious examples where sickness and disease would be attributable to sin are dissipation and drunkenness. But it would be incorrect to say that sickness is always a punishment for the sin of the sick person or of his parents, for a conception of an avenging God lurks behind this false theory of sickness. But the Archbishops' Report confesses that much of the sickness and suffering in the world is due to sin on someone's part : "selfishness, carelessness and neglect on the part of the community as a whole, or of individual members of it".[162]

4. That modern medicine has superseded the Church's ministry of healing

The relationship between the Church and medicine is an extremely delicate topic burdened with a history of unpleasant memories. The present cleavage is well known, a phenomenon which hangs together with the overall process of secularism.[163] But as one author remarks, an approach to patients which sees priests as responsible for the souls of men and doctors for their bodies ignores the basic unity of the human person.[164]

The Archbishops' Report seeks a rapprochement between the Church and medicine, without compromising the mission entrusted to the Church by its founder.[165] On the one hand the Commission, recalling a theme expressed at every Lambeth Conference where healing was discussed, praises the progress achieved by medical science. The physician and surgeon are "instruments of God", who are included in our Lord's injunction to the entire Church to heal the sick.

On the other hand, the Commission noted that the Church's role in the healing ministry encompasses more than the important work of Christian doctors and nurses. Although healing wonders may no longer be as profuse as in Apostolic times, "the Church as the Body of Christ and the extension of the Incarnation has a mission to the whole man to teach, to preach and to heal (Mt. 4:23; 9:35)". Nor can any limit be affixed to the intervention of the power of God in answer to the prayer of faith (Jas. 5:15). The misconception that Christ's commission to heal is now the exclusive prerogative of the medical profession disregards the truth that man's destiny includes more than his psycho-physical existence. The need for "inward peace, forgiveness, faith in God and acceptance of Christ" always remains. The Church ministers to these needs of the whole man—body, mind and spirit—through prayer, the sacraments and pastoral care. The Commission hopes that medical science is likewise becoming aware of the essential unity of man's nature by realizing that many of the causes of physical and mental disorders are found "in the deep and intimate relationship of the physical, mental, moral and spiritual in man". The time is ripe for a renewed partnership between medicine and the Church.

5. That only the specially gifted can practice the Church's ministry of healing

The Archbishops' Commission strove to offset the impression that the ministry of healing is restricted to a few specially qualified priests or laymen. While the Report acknowledges the existence of special gifts of healing, "the sacramental ministry for the strengthening of body and soul", which includes the ministry of healing, is bestowed upon every priest at ordination.[166] The ministry of healing is not merely the vocation of a small minority with successful experience in this field, but belongs to the overall pastoral ministry of the clergy. Neither is the ministry of healing a clerical prerogative, but a corporate responsibility for the whole Church. A happy development in the healing ministry has been the growing awareness that the entire local community is called to minister to the needs of the sick through prayer or intercession groups, by visiting the sick, and by displaying understanding and acceptance of the sick person.[167] The thesis of Lambourne's study is that the local Church must "remember and recapitulate the public healing work of Christ by acts of mercy and healing done to the sick and suffering in its neighbourhood, and thereby make Christ 'really present' in the community".[168]

6. That the Church's ministry of healing is separate from its other work

Closely allied with the preceding misconception is another misconstruction which would assign the ministry of healing an isolated existence within the Church. If the ministry of healing is not the province of an elite minority, neither is it separate from the whole of the Church's mission. This danger of eccentricity seems to have been recognized by the Lambeth Conference of 1930, where the subject of spiritual healing was discussed together with other topics in a committee report entitled "The Ministry of the Church".[169] The commission of Christ to his Church was a single commission : to preach the Kingdom of God and to heal the sick. The work of the Church in the world is precisely to preach the Kingdom and to bring "the healing power of Christ to the disorders and evils of our common life".[170] By placing the ministry of healing in this broader context, it is evident that poor social conditions, inadequate housing and diet, poverty and ignorance account for much of the evil in the world. Disease and disorder are often the result of the vices of our society. As Michael Wilson puts it: "Sickness is only one symptom of man's estrangement from God, neighbour and environment".[171] In other words, the Church's ministry of healing belongs to the total mission of the Church in the world.

7. *That physical healing is all that matters*

The Lambeth Report of 1924 also warned against this false notion in the practice of spiritual healing. Correctly stated, the healing of the spirit should be the primary concern; the healing of the body is secondary. If recovery of bodily health is the sole objective, the Church has no right to apply its ministrations.[172] Other writers concur with this assessment. In his critique of Christian Science, Weatherhead remarks:

> A religion which makes the individual's health its main preoccupation cannot bear comparison with real Christianity, in which man is a means and God the end; in which, indeed, nothing matters so long as God is glorified.[173]

Other authors equally insist that the glory of God in whatever results is the proper goal of the Church's ministry of healing.[174] Fox also speaks of the sanctification of man.[175] Weatherhead sees the patient's unity with God as having priority over the restoration to health.[176] The occasion for Christian patience and love which the sick man's condition solicits is also mentioned.[177]

The Archbishops' Report stated that God wills even greater things than the relief of pain and the cure of disease.[178] Spiritual preparation, repentance, absolution and the entire pastoral work of the Church are essential components in the Church's ministry to the sick. This ministry should be continuous in the life of the parish and available to the varying needs of the faithful. The ministry of healing is not a deus ex machina called forth as a last resort or as a short cut to physical health when all other methods fail. The Church is concerned with "the redemption of the whole man, the cure of bodily ailments being but one element in its ministry to him".[179]

8. *That the Communion of the Sick and Unction are part of the "last rites" only*

The closing words of the 1908 Lambeth Committee Report on healing counselled against the revival of unction as a preparation for death.[180] Perhaps the Committee feared the introduction of the current Roman Catholic practice, especially on the part of the Anglo-Catholic wing within the Church of England. This fear has proved unfounded. None of the healing authors refer to the laying on of hands or the anointing of the sick as the "last rites". None envisage these rites as a preparation for death, although Harris encourages the administration of unction to the dying, "but always with some degree of hope, however faint, that recovery may take place.[181] Harris also discusses the Communion of the Sick in its occasional application as Viaticum for the dying.[182] Nevertheless, the Archbishops' Commission felt obliged to expose the superstitious reluctance of some sick people who are disturbed to receive a pastoral visit, to have their names placed on the parish intercession list, or to receive the Communion of the Sick. The Report endeavoured to obviate this persistent anxiety.[183]

9. That a medically unexplained healing is more wonderful than one brought about by medical means

Leslie Weatherhead suggests that if Christ had come upon a man with an obstruction in his throat, he would have sent the afflicted person to a physician or else have removed the obstruction himself. The laying on of hands would not have been the appropriate remedy.[184] Nothing could be more disruptive of the growing co-operation between the Church and medicine than a misconception of the ministry of healing which looks for the marvellous in a medically inexplicable healing at the expense of proper medical treatment. A constant theme of the 1924 Lambeth Report was the importance of medical science in the diagnosis and treatment of illness in which methods of spiritual healing are employed.[185] The Church is not competing with medicine; both are engaged in restoring the wholeness of man in body, mind and spirit.[186]

A correct understanding of this matter is so important that the Archbishops' Report analysed the roots of the above misinterpretation:

a. the wonder commonly felt at the unusual and
b. the popular idea that what can be scientifically explained has little or nothing to do with God.[187]

a) The unusual generally evokes a sense of wonder which directs one's thoughts to God. But Christ, especially in his parables, shows no contempt for the normal processes of nature. Rather it is the one God at work "in analogous ways in the spheres of nature and grace".

Related to this subject are evidences of healing, to which the Report devoted a special chapter.[188] Should the Church claim instances of supernatural healing? The Commission was wisely cautious, balancing the presence of God revealed both in the natural order of creation and in the supernatural order of redemption. A claim that healing has resulted from non-medical methods may imply four assertions :

(1) The sick man has actually been healed;
(2) the healing depended upon a definite non-medical intervention;
(3) the healing is extraordinary and medically unaccountable;
(4) the cause of the healing is supernatural.

The Commission concluded that, while medical science may help disprove unwarranted claims of extraordinary healings, the Church cannot expect science to prove the activity of the supernatural. But this does not exclude reasons for believing that the cure may be of a supernatural order. Even in this case, however, the important thing is to see the healing in the context of reconciliation with God, a sign to the believer of the Kingdom of God.

The function of "signs following" (Mark 16 :20) is to "confirm the word" and the signs consist not in physical or mental healings in isolation, but in the whole complex of effects, including conversion and sanctification, which follows the impact of the Kingdom.[189]

Nonetheless, the basic witness of the "healing action of Christ in His Body" is not to be sought in occasional wonders, but in the many instances where the eyes of faith detect the presence of God "acting through the ministry of grace as well as through medical means".

b) The other source of this misconception is the popular idea that healings are less marvellous and less religious when medically explicable. The Report declared that cures which medicine can explain also point to the Creator, whose power alone ultimately heals. But the belief that all healing truly comes from God should not obscure the necessary distinction between "the works of God in creation" and "the works of God in Christ". The same creative power of God in nature is operative in Jesus Christ, but is used for the specific purpose of "the restoring and perfecting of creation", the inauguration of the Kingdom of God. Once again reflecting a balanced judgment, the Commission urged that "the wonder of God's love in redemption" should not detract from "the wonder of God's love in creation".[190]

Having considered the Church's ministry of healing within the framework of nine common misconceptions, as suggested by the Archbishops' Report, one can now briefly summarize these findings of the Anglican healing literature in positive terms. The ministry of healing is an integral part of the Church's mission in the world, in obedience to the command of Christ to preach the Kingdom and to heal the sick. All members of the Church are called to participate in this ministry : priests in their pastoral care which includes the celebration of the sacraments, Christians with special skills such as doctors and nurses, and the other members of the local community by their prayers and concern. The aim of the ministry of healing is to restore wholeness of body, mind and spirit, as far as is possible in this age which awaits the fuller revelation of the Kingdom of God.

CHAPTER III

The Prayer Book and Healing

Whatever official ministrations the Church of England has provided for its sick members in the past are found in the Book of Common Prayer. This chapter will consider the Visitation Office of the Prayer Book, the Anglican tradition regarding the unction of the sick, and the curious practice of Touching for the King's Evil.

A. VISITATION OFFICE

The Order for the Visitation of the Sick is a formal rite, whose strictly liturgical character marks it as a ministration to be applied to those who are in full communion with the Church and conversant with her services.[1] The Visitation Office has largely fallen into disuse today; it may indeed be doubtful if it was ever widely employed.[2] A fixed structure renders the service inadequate for the varied pastoral situations which present themselves. This innate deficiency appears to have been recognized by Canon 67 of 1604, which liberates a "preacher" from the obligation of using the office and directs him to minister to the sick person "as he shall think most needful and convenient".[3] *The Manual for the Sick* by Lancelot Andrewes (*d*.1626), a posthumous publication of private devotions of the Caroline bishop, is one example of this alternative.[4] As F. E. Brightman suggests, the Visitation Office is perhaps most useful as "a series of suggestions for the visitor to follow and apply as best he can in accordance with his own judgement, experience, and opportunity".[5]

What is the theology of sickness expressed in the Visitation Office? It is certainly not that of healing. The melancholic atmosphere which pervades the order is immediately evident. One commentator on the Prayer Book sees the service as originally drafted as an Anglican substitute for extreme unction and thus reserved for those *in extremis*.[6] The unrelenting gloom of the Visitation Office has been vehemently assailed by the healing literature, especially the exhortations conveying the impression of a God who rains down sickness upon his disobedient and sinful servants.[7]

J. R. Pridie attributes this attitude to a "forensic" notion which dominated sixteenth century thought : where wrong had been committed, a penalty must be exacted. One must submit to the penalty imposed, and the very fact that the penalty was imposed was a verification that it was deserved. In civil life this "forensic" approach respected the Divine Right of Kings. In theological thought it was reflected in the prevailing Post-Reformation stress on the doctrine of the Atonement. Man's relationship with God has been sundered by his failure and sin; a theory of satisfaction was necessary to restore normal relations.[8]

The protest of the healing movement has not been in vain. The inadequacy of the Visitation Office has provoked numerous recommendations from the Lambeth Conferences that the service be revised in such a manner so as to express a more hopeful and positive approach to the Church's ministry to the sick.[9]

1. 1549 Prayer Book: Sources and Structure

At the time of the Reformation there existed in England several local variations or "uses" of the Roman rite. The Use of Salisbury or Sarum was the most influential of the local adaptations and was widely followed in other dioceses during the later middle ages.[10] The Sarum Use furnished valuable material which the compilers of the new Prayer Book could draw upon. The Order for the Visitation and Communion of the Sick was modelled upon the office for the visitation of the sick, extreme unction and the commendation of the soul as contained in the Sarum Manual or Ritual.

The Sarum service opened with a procession of the priest and clerks reciting the seven penitential psalms with antiphons on their way to the sick man's house. Upon arrival a salutation was given and the sick man was sprinkled with holy water. After the *Kyrie eleison, Pater Noster,* versicles and responses, there followed nine prayers for the sick man's strengthening and recovery. The remainder of the office was intended to move the sick Christian to faith and repentance preparatory to unction and communion. Examined and instructed in the faith, motivated to acts of faith, hope and charity, the sick person was confessed and absolved, anointed, given communion and commended to God.[11]

The basic pattern of the Visitation Office of the first Prayer Book is as follows :

(1) Salutation: "Peace be in this house etc.".
(2) Ps. 143 (142) with antiphon: "Remember not".
(3) Lord have mercy, Our Father, versicles and responses.
(4) Prayers for strengthening: "O Lorde, looke downe from heauen"; "Heare vs almightie and most mercifull God, and Sauioure".
(5) Exhortation.
(6) Profession of faith.
(7) Examination of the sick person concerning repentance and charity.
(8) Confession and absolution.
(9) Prayer for the sick man's forgiveness: "O most merciful God".
(10) Ps. 71 (70) with antiphon: "O Saueour of the worlde".
(11) Benediction: "The almighty Lord, whiche is a moste strong tower".
(12) Unction of the sick.
(13) Ps. 13 (12).
(14) Communion of the sick.

The structure and sources of the Visitation Office of 1549 will now be considered in detail:[12]

(1) The Visitation Office opens with a shortened derivation of the Sarum salutation ("Pax huic domui et omnibus habitantibus in ea."). This greeting was enjoined by Christ upon his disciples when sending them forth on their missionary journey (Lk. 10:5).
(2) The introductory seven penitential psalms with antiphons from the Sarum service have been omitted. All that remains is Ps. 143 (142) with antiphon (Sarum: *Ne reminiscaris domine*), which is placed after the opening greeting.
(3) These prayers are taken over directly from the Sarum rite. The versicles and responses have been slightly altered by translation into attractive English prose.
(4) Of the nine Sarum prayers for recovery, alluding to Peter's raising of Tabitha, the healing of Tobias and Sarah, and of Hezekiah, only variations of the ninth and the third are retained:

O Lorde, looke downe from heauen, beholde, visite, and releue this thy seruaunte: Looke vpon hym with the iyes of thy mercy, geue him coumforte, and sure confidence in thee: Defende hym from the daunger of the enemy, and kepe hym in perpetuall peace, and safetie : through Iesus Christe our Lorde. Amen.

Heare vs, almightie and moste mercifull God, and Sauioure :
Extende thyne accustomed goodnesse to this thy seruaunte,
which is greved with sickenesse : Visite hym, o Lord, as thou
diddest visite Peters wyfes mother, and the Capitaynes seruaunte.
And as thou preseruedst Thobie and Sara by thy Aungell from
daunger : So restore vnto this sicke person his former health (if
it be thy will), or els geue hym grace so to take thy correccion,
that after this painfull lyfe ended, he may dwell with thee in
lyfe euerlastyng. Amen.[13]

Harris, who considers the Visitation Order a departure from the
positive spirit of the Sarum office, cites the compilers' choice of the
least confident of the nine Sarum collects as proof that the 1549
Prayer Book generally regarded sickness as a divine punishment for
sin. The sick person was expected to glorify God "by remaining
ill and suffering patiently, rather than by recovering quickly
through the ministrations of His Church".[14]
(5) In comparison with Sarum, the exhortation has been considerably expanded by incorporating matter taken from the "Homily
against the feare of Death" (1547). A suggested form only, the
exhortation is divided into two sections, the second of which may
be omitted if the sick person is very ill. The first section outlines
a reprehensible theology of the cause and purposes of sickness : a
a "visitacion" sent by God "to trye youre pacience", or "to correcte
and amende" whatever is displeasing to "our heauenly father". In
either case, by repentance, patient endurance, trust in God and
thanksgiving for "his fatherly visitacion", the sick man can look
forward to "euerlasting lyfe".

The second section, of a more hortatory nature, continues the
conception of sickness as a chastisement from God (Heb. 12 :
6-10). As our "carnall fathers" chastise us after their own pleasure,
so "our spirtuall father" chastises us for our own good, that we
may be "partakers of his holiness". Appropriating a paschal
insight found in "De cruce et afflictionibus" from the *Pia
deliberatio* of the Reformation Archbishop Hermann Wied of
Cologne (*d*.1547), the exhortation does, however, beautifully express
the baptismal implication of sharing in the sufferings of Christ in
order to enter into glory with him.[15] The exhortation then leads to
a rehearsal of the articles of faith.
(6) The profession of faith in the Sarum Manual consisted of

fourteen articles : seven pertaining to the Trinity, seven to the humanity of Christ. In the Visitation Office this profession is made through the Apostles' Creed in interrogatory form as at Baptism. (7) In the Sarum there follows as a preparation to confession a lengthy exhortation to faith, hope and charity, forgiveness of injuries and the obligation of restitution. In the event of recovery the sick person is admonished to almsgiving, good deeds and works of penance. More expediently, the Visitation Office replaces this with rubrics directing the priest to treat these topics. The minister is to examine whether the sick man *"bee in charitie with all the worlde"*, forgiving those who have offended him, as well as seeking the forgiveness of others he has wronged. He is to make amends as far as possible, to draw up a will disponsing of his goods, if this has not already been done, and to show *"lyberalytie to the poore"*.[16] The subject of hope emphasized in the Sarum is, as Brightman observes, omitted.[17]

(8) The Visitation Office, as in the Sarum Manual, here allows a place for auricular confession. The sick person is to confess his sins *"yf he fels his conscience troubled by any weightie matter"*. The form of absolution, which is also suggestetd for all private confessions, is adapted from the Sarum and the *Pia deliberatio*.

(9) The ensuing prayer, "O most merciful God", is from the Sarum form of absolution for dying penitents (*Deus misericors deus clemens*).

(10) During the administration of unction in the Sarum office, the clerks recited eight psalms with antiphons. The first of these, Ps. 71 (70), has been inserted at this point in the Visitation Order. The antiphon (Sarum : *Salvator mundi*) has the distinction of being the only recognizable antiphon in the Book of Common Prayer.[18]

(11) This form of benediction appears to have no liturgical precedent.

(12) The rite of unction has been vastly simplified in comparison with the Sarum seven-fold application of oil to different members, each with a formula of administration and an accompanying psalm. Similar to the rubric for confession, the anointing is optional : *"If the sicke person desyre to bee annoynted . . ."* The anointing, when requested, is to be administered by a single application of oil, either on the forehead or the breast, with a single sign of the cross. The formula for anointing, portions of which are derived from the Sarum, reads as follows :

As with thys visible oyle thy body outwardelye is annoynted : so our heauenly father, almightie god, graunt of his infinite goodnes, that thy soule inwardly may be annointed with the holy gost, who is the spirite of al strength, coumfort, reliefe, and gladnes. And vouchsafe for hys great mercie (if it be his blessed will) to restore vnto thee thy bodely health, and strength, to serue hym : and sende thee release of all thy paynes, troubles and diseases, both in bodye and mynd. And howsoeuer his goodness (by his diuyne and vnsearchable prouidence) shall dispose of thee : we his vnworthy ministers and seruauntes, humbly beseche the eternall maiestie, to doe with thee, according to the multitude of his innumerable mercies, and to pardone thee all thy synnes, and offences, committed by all thy bodely sences, passions, and carnall affeccions : who also vouchesafe mercifullye to graunt vnto thee gostly stregth, by his holy spirite, to withstand & ouercome al teptacions & assaultes of thyne aduersary, that in no wise he preuayle against thee, but that thou maist haue perfect victory & triumph against the deuil, sine, & deth, through Christ our lord : Who by his deth, hath ouercomed the prince of death, & with the father, & the holy gost euermore liueth & reigneth god, world without end. Amen.[19]

Considering the background in which it was formulated, both the general tone of the Visitation Office and the late medieval practice and theology of extreme unction, the rite for anointing the sick in the 1549 Prayer Book is remarkably avant-garde. The ceremony is simplified. The external anointing with oil symbolizes an internal unction of the Holy Spirit which conveys strength, comfort, relief and gladness. The prayer petitions God for the restoration of bodily health and release from all "paynes, troubles and diseases, both in bodye and mynd".

The healing literature regards the unction of the first Prayer Book as a return to the primitive usage, a sacrament of healing.[20] It is indeed the one element in the entire Visitation Office of which they speak kindly. Even the reference to pardon from sins is accepted as in accordance with early thought, although Harris regrets the mention of sins "committed by all thy bodely sences, passions, and carnall affeccions".[21]

(13) Ps. 13 (14) is the second of the original eight psalms retained from the Sarum office for extreme unction. This psalm furnishes a smooth transition to the Communion of the Sick.

(14) The 1549 Order for the Communion of the Sick consists largely of rubrics providing for the conveyance of the sacrament to

the sick person after the celebration of an "open communion" in a parish, or for the celebration of holy communion in the sick person's home.

2. Subsequent Changes

The 1549 Prayer Book was a compromise between conservative and reformed elements in the English Church. It satisfied neither group. The Book was soon revised according to the criticisms of continental Reformers such as Peter Martyr (d.1562) and Martin Bucer (d.1551). The Act of Uniformity of 1552 made the Second Prayer Book of Edward VI the law of the land.[22]

The changes in the Visitation Order consisted of various deletions from the first Prayer Book. The 1552 revision omitted Ps. 143 (142); only the antiphon "Remembre not" remained. The second of the two prayers for strengthening deleted the paradigmatic references to the healing of Tobias and Sarah. Upon the recommendation of Peter Martyr, the rubrics pertaining to the reservation of the eucharist from the parish communion ("extended communion") were likewise omitted; henceforth the only possibility for Communion of the Sick would be the celebration of the sacrament in the sick person's home. Most significant of all, the provision for anointing the sick, together with the accompanying Ps. 13 (12), was dropped.

The 1559 and 1604 revisions of the Prayer Book left the Visitation Office unaffected. Further changes occurred in the 1661/1662 Book of Common Prayer, which on the basis of an Act of Uniformity passed by Parliament, remains the official service book to this day.[23] The 1662 Book contains some notable improvements. The rubric for confession was strengthened: the sick person is to *"be moved"* to make a special confession of his sins, if his conscience is troubled. The Aaronic benediction (Num. 6:24-26) was introduced to fill the gap in the office created by the omission of unction. In an effort to make the Visitation Office more adaptable to the condition of those ministered to, an appendix of four prayers composed by Robert Sanderson was added: "A Prayer for a sick child", "A Prayer for a sick person when there appeareth small hope of recovery", "A commendatory Prayer for a sick person at the point of departure", and "A Prayer for persons troubled in Mind or in Conscience". Elsewhere in the revision, the insertion of a rubric into the communion service to the effect that the consecrated elements are not to be carried out of the church but are to be consumed by priest and communicants immediately after the parish communion made the possibility of reservation for purposes of communicating the sick seem even more remote.[24]

But the 1662 revision also removed whatever precious few references to healing and recovery that remained. In the second prayer for strengthening the reference to Peter's mother-in-law and the centurion's servant was omitted, and the prayer amended so as to stress the role of sickness as a "fatherly correction" from God. The last five verses of Ps. 71 (70), which included a promise of thanksgiving for expected recovery, were also deleted. As one commentator explains : ". . . they speak of the sick man as already delivered and restored to health, and are therefore not so suitable to the case of one still in affliction.[25] But the judgement of Harris on the Visitation Office is especially severe :

> In 1661 the whole of the references to healing were omitted, and the Visitation Services acquired that character and unrelieved gloom, which renders their use depressing and painful to both priest and patient. For more than three hundred years the Anglican Church abandoned all serious attempts to heal the sick by spiritual and sacramental ministrations.[26]

Perhaps one can best sum up by saying that "The Order for the Visitation of the Sick, and the Communion of the Sick" from the Book of Common Prayer is more important for the controversies induced by the provisions for auricular confession, unction of the sick (1549) and reservation of communion (1549), than it is in itself as an appealing pastoral ministration.

B. ANOINTING OF THE SICK

The provision for unction in the 1549 Prayer Book was removed in the 1552 revision and never restored. The background leading to this development and the tradition of unction in the Church of England will now be examined.

1. Henrician Period

The Church of England only gradually evolved its own doctrinal position in relation to the controversies of the sixteenth century. The initial attempt at formulating Anglican teaching was the Ten Articles of Religion, adopted by Convocation in 1536 at the bidding of Henry VIII. Of the sacraments, only three were expounded : baptism, the eucharist and penance; the other four were neither affirmed nor denied.[27]

The Ten Articles were superseded in 1537 by the "Bishops' Book", properly entitled *The Institution of a Christian Man,* which was a manual of Anglican belief compiled by a committee of bishops and scholars. In the section on the sacraments, special attention was once again given to baptism, the eucharist and penance; although this time all seven sacraments were treated. The exposition of unction of the sick in the Bishops' Book is particularly enlightening.[28] While the name "extreme unction" was retained, the term was understood to indicate that anointing of the sick was the last of the anointings previously conferred at baptism and confirmation. The Bishops' Book does not reflect the late medieval doctrine and practice of unction as a preparation for death.

The scriptural basis for the sacrament was the missionary charge of Christ, whereby the Apostles healed the sick by anointing them with oil, and the prescription of James 5 :14-16, although a new command from Christ to anoint the sick "be not expressed in scripture". The "holy fathers of the church" ordained that this "anointing of sick men" be continually observed in the Church as "a very godly and wholesome medicine or remedy to alleviate and mitigate the diseases and maladies, as well as of the soul as of the body of Christian men". The "holy fathers" therefore accepted the anointing of the sick with oil in the name of the Lord among the other sacraments, as "a visible sign of an invisible grace".

The grace of the sacrament was twofold : "the relief and recovery of the disease and sickness wherewith the sick person is then diseased and troubled", and "the remission of sins, if he be then in sin". For this reason the sick person was to prepare himself for the worthy reception of the sacrament by cultivating a spirit of trust and confidence in God regardless of the outcome of his illness, and by stirring up in his heart repentance for sin and forgiveness of others.

In the most revealing passage of all, the Bishops' Book spoke out against the abuse of delaying extreme unction until a single administration at the time of death. All "bishops and preachers" were to instruct the faithful :

> . . . first, that no man ought to think, that by the receiving of this sacrament of anointing the sick man's life shall be made shorter, but rather that the same shall be prolonged thereby;

considering the same is instituted for recovery of health both of the soul and body.

Second, that it is an evil custom to defer the administration of this sacrament unto such time as the sick persons be brought by sickness unto extreme peril and jeopardy of life, and be in manner in despair to live any longer.

Thirdly, that it is lawful and expedient to administer this said sacrament unto every good Christian man . . . so oft and whensoever any great and perilous sickness and malady shall fortune unto them.[29]

The Bishops' Book of 1537 thus understood extreme unction to be a sacrament not for the dying, but for the sick, ordained for the recovery of health both of body and soul, a sacrament of healing which could be repeated.

The Bishops' Book as a whole failed to win the approval of Henry VIII, who took it upon himself to revise and correct it. The result was the "King's Book", *The Necessary Doctrine and Erudition for any Christian Man,* which was issued in 1543. If the Bishops' Book reflected the more Protestant spirit of the Ten Articles, the King's Book followed the more Catholic mood of the Six Articles (1539). The treatment of extreme unction in the King's Book, however, was basically a shortened and condensed version of that in the Bishops' Book.[30]

According to the teaching of St. James and the use of the sacrament in "the catholic church of Christ", unction has been ordained for a sick man, that he "might be relieved of his bodily disease, and also attain pardon and remission of his sins". These two effects were further elaborated. The desired health of the body does not always follow; we must accept whatever be the will of God, who hears all prayers and disposes of all things for the good of man. The remission of sins, the other important result of extreme unction, should not be considered as an easy substitute for "true penance". Rather the fruitful ministration of extreme unction presupposes a prior reconciliation through the sacrament of penance. As in the Bishops' Book, the name extreme unction referred to the last of unctions previously administered at baptism, confirmation and orders. The King's Book outlined the pastoral practice :

And where it is called the extreme unction, that is to say, the

last unction, we must not so understand it, as though this sacrament might never be ministered but once, that is to say, in
extreme peril of death, when men be without hope of life; for
it should rather be ministered in the entry of sickness, and so
oftener, whensoever any great and perilous sickness and malady
shall come to any man.[31]

Despite the religious upheaval they provoked, the ecclesiastical
innovations introduced during the reign of Henry VIII (1509-
1547) were more of a political erastian nature than a doctrinal
one. The seven sacraments, including an updated teaching on
extreme unction, were maintained. At the time of Henry's death,
England still remained Catholic, although no longer Roman
Catholic.[32] Only in the brief reign of young Edward VI (1547-
1553) did the Reformation in England begin to assume a more
overt Calvinistic direction.

2. The Reformers

What was the real judgement of Archbishop Cranmer and the
other Reformers concerning unction of the sick? As noted above,
the simplified rite of anointing in the first Prayer Book was a
radical departure from the medieval tradition. The prayer for
anointing appears to have incorporated much of the theology
expounded in the Bishops' Book and King's Book. But there are
strong indications for believing that the English Reformers were
far from convinced about the inclusion of any form of unction at
all in the Visitation Office of the 1549 Book of Common Prayer.

Already in 1540, in his response to a questionnaire submitted on
the sacraments, Cranmer doubted the necessity of maintaining
that there were seven in number.[33] He found nothing in Scripture
concerning the "matter, nature, and effect" of confirmation, orders
and extreme unction which would seem to indicate they were sacraments. He likewise recognized no scriptural or patristic precedent
for the claim that unction of the sick, as then practiced, remitted
venial sins.

In the 1549 Visitation Office itself, the rite for unction of the
sick is included as an optional appendix. No provision was made in
the Prayer Book for the traditional consecration of the oil by a
bishop on Maundy Thursday.[34]

Two passages from the writings of the Reformers refer un-
enthusiastically to the usage of unction in the 1549 Book. In a

letter to Bishop John Hooper (*d*.1555) written in the year 1550, his confrere Bishop Nicholas Ridley (d.1555) acknowledged that the anointing of the sick was not unlawful. Together with the unction in baptism, anointing of the sick is not of scriptural necessity, but may be used "to teach the inward unction of the Holy Ghost".[35] In the records of the episcopal visitations undertaken by Hooper in 1551-1552, one of the questions posed was as follows :

> XXXIII. Item, when the sick man desire to be anointed before his death, whether the curate do give himself, or cause any other to give, any reverence to the oil, or else persuade and teach any man to put any trust in the oil, or use it as they did before time under the pope.[36]

The final decision on unction of the sick was pronounced by the German Reformer Martin Bucer in his *Censura,* a critical and detailed review of the 1549 Prayer Book. Although generally pleased with the Visitation Office, his judgement on the rite of unction was unequivocal :

> The entire ceremony has been written most in accordance with the norm of sacred scripture, with a single exception : the appended unction of the sick. For it is evident that this rite is neither ancient, nor commended by any precept of God or laudable example of the saints; but has been introduced by a distorted imitation of an apostolic act, of whose imitation the ministers have manifestly neither a mandate nor a faculty. The Apostles healed the sick by the anointing with oil, for the Lord conferred this gift upon them in Mark 6. From his very words, which Bede explains in the same sense, it is abundantly clear that the Apostle James speaks of this manner of unction as a symbol of healing, which by divine power was administered by the Apostles and by many others in the early Church.

> Not only therefore is this rite of no word of divine law, nor introduced by example, and was plainly unknown to many holy Fathers, but as all similar things devised after the manner of men it also accounts for much superstition today. Nor is it [used] as prescribed by James, that the sick may be healed, but is almost always administered when the recovery of the sick has been despaired of. To this [rite of unction] has been most unworthily associated the sacrament of the most holy Eucharist commended

by the Lord himself, by which the sick may be abundantly strengthened in health. For these reasons I hope this rite will be abolished.[37]

On the basis of Bucer's recommendation, the anointing of the sick was expunged from the revised Prayer Book of 1552.[38] On February 6, 1567 two English bishops could elatedly report to their Swiss colleagues:

The Church of England, too, has entirely given up the use of (prayers in) a foreign tongue, breathings, exorcism, *oil*, spittle, clay, lighted tapers, and other things of that kind, which, by the act of parliament, are never to be restored.[39]

Bucer's criticism of unction of the sick actually followed the same lines as that of John Calvin (*d*.1564) in his *Institutes* (1536), which was even more incisive, terming unction a "mere hypocritical stage play".[40] Calvin argued that the anointing of the sick with oil had belonged to the gift of healing of Apostolic times. These miraculous powers had not been communicated to subsequent generations. Even if the precept of unction had been applicable to the present age, it was scarcely the same unction advised by St. James. James urged that all the sick be anointed; the existing practice was confined to those *in extremis*. James referred to none other than common oil; the oil used for extreme unction was consecrated by a bishop amid much superstitious ceremony. James inferred that the prayer said over the sick man was what contributed to the remission of sin, and not the "abominable unction".

This manner of argument, first enunciated by John Calvin and confirmed by Martin Bucer, was adopted almost unanimously by the Anglican divines of the sixteenth century: Thomas Becon (*d*.1567), William Fulke (*d*.1589), Bishop John Jewel (*d*.1571), William Whitaker (*d*.1595), James Calfhill (*d*.1570), Bishop James Pilkington (*d*.1576), and Thomas Rogers (*d*.1616).[41] Their polemic against extreme unction may be reduced to two theses:

a. St. James' unction (Jas. 5 : 14-16) refers to the apostolic gift of healing, which no longer applies today. "As the gift of tongues was not to last for ever, but only for a time; so the gift of healing was not to continue ever, but for a time."[42]

b. Even granted the present relevance of the Jacobean method of healing through anointing with oil, such is not the current Roman practice, which has been encumbered with abuses concerning the anointing of the dying, the consecration of oil, and the claim to remit sins.

3. The Elizabethan Settlement

The unhappy reign of Mary Tudor (1553-1558) temporarily checked the progress of the Reformation in England and the country was formally reconciled to Rome by Reginald Cardinal Pole in 1555. The first Act of Repeal restored the liturgy and administration of the sacraments to that usage practised in the last year of Henry VIII; minor concessions were granted to the vernacular. In all likelihood the Latin service of extreme unction was revived.

With the accession to the throne of Elizabeth I (1558-1603), the Reformation continued. The 1559 Act of Uniformity prescribed once again the use of the 1552 Prayer Book, with small but important changes. The Queen chose a policy of comprehensiveness directed towards achieving the "via media" of the Elizabethan Settlement, which led to the emergence of the doctrinal system of Anglicanism.

The odyssey of the English Church in search of an acceptable formulae of doctrine ended with the adoption of the Thirty-nine Articles. At the time of their final revision in 1571, the fate of unction of the sick had long been sealed. The twenty-fifth Article presents the classical Anglican description of a sacrament, and explains why the other five sacraments do not fall under this definition to the same degree as do baptism and the eucharist.

Sacraments ordained of Christ be not only badges or tokens of Christian men's profession, but rather they be certain sure witnesses, and effectual signs of grace, and God's good will towards us, by the which he doth work invisibly in us, and doth not only quicken, but also strengthen and confirm our Faith in him.[43]

The twenty-fifth Article goes on to declare that the two sacraments "ordained of Christ our Lord in the Gospel" are Baptism and the Supper of the Lord, a teaching similarly stated in the "Homily of Common Prayer and the Sacraments" and in the Prayer Book

Catechism.[44] Only these two sacraments would appear to corres-
pond to the above definition.

What, then, is the status of the other traditional five sacraments?

> Those five commonly called Sacraments, that is to say, Con-
> firmation, Penance, Orders, Matrimony and extreme Unction,
> are not to be counted for Sacraments of the Gospel, being such
> as have grown partly of the corrupt following of the Apostles,
> partly are states of life allowed in the Scriptures; but yet have
> not like nature of Sacraments with Baptism, and the Lord's
> Supper, for that they have not any visible sign or ceremony
> ordained of God.[45]

The Homily adds some clarification on this point. The name
sacrament may be applied to "any thing whereby an holy thing
is signified". Ancient writers attributed the term sacrament not
only to the "other five commonly of late years taken and used
for supplying the number of the seven Sacraments", but also to
"divers and sundry other ceremonies" such as "oil, washing of feet
and such like". But none of these were reputed to be sacraments
in the same sense as baptism and the eucharist. Besides these
two sacraments, the Church of England likewise retains

> certain other rites and ceremonies about the Institution of
> Ministers in the Church, Matrimony, Confirmation of children
> by examining them of their knowledge in the Articles of the
> Faith and joining thereto the prayers of the Church for them,
> and likewise for Visitation of the Sick . . .[46]

Yet lacking the "signification and meaning" of baptism and the
eucharist, these "other rites and ceremonies" are either "for
godly states of life, necessary in Christ's Church", or else "such
ordinances as may make for the instruction, comfort and edifica-
tion of Christ's Church".

The teaching of the Church of England on the sacraments
as formulated during the Elizabethan Settlement has prevailed
until the present day. Taking the term sacrament in the strict
sense, an outward visible sign of grace instituted by Jesus Christ,
there are only two : baptism and the eucharist. Accepting a
broader concept of a sacrament, these are not necessarily limited
to the other five, but may be innumerable. Yet confirmation,

matrimony, orders and even absolution all find a place in the Book of Common Prayer; only unction of the sick has entirely vanished from the official liturgical book of the Church of England.

4. The Nonjurors and Unction

For the English Church in the seventeenth century, the case for unction of the sick remained closed. There is no record of anyone having been anointed; although this century witnessed the frequent royal ministration of another healing rite, the Touching for the King's Evil. Caroline divines such as Herbert Thorndike (d.1672), Bishop William Beveridge (d.1708), Hamon L'Estrange (d.1660) and John Gilbert (b.1659) reiterated what was becoming to be the classical Anglican critique of unction : the precept of James is no longer applicable today; even if it were, the Roman practice is so bound up with abuses so as to be a perversion of what St. James recommends.[47] Such was the state of affairs until the emergence of the Nonjurors, the High Church schism precipitated by the accession of William and Mary to the throne of England in 1688.[48]

a. The Nonjurors' Liturgy of 1718

The Nonjurors were at first content to use the liturgical services of the Established Church as found in the 1662 Prayer Book. In 1718, however, the quest to return to the primitive practices of the early Church led some of their number, under the leadership of Jeremy Collier (d.1726) and Thomas Brett (d.1744), to publish their own office, which included services for communion, confirmation and the visitation of the sick.[49]

The Visitation Office of the Nonjurors' Liturgy of 1718 followed the basic format of the 1662 Book of Common Prayer, with several notable additions—virtually all pertaining to unction of the sick as a means of recovery.[50] A brief paragraph in the preface of the book reveals the intention of the authors :

The Anointing with Oil in the *Office for the Sick* is not only supported by primitive practice, but commanded by the Apostle St. James. It is not here administered by way of *Extreme Unction*, but in order to recovery.[51]

In the Visitation Office itself the passage on anointing from James 5 :14-16 is inserted after the opening greeting. The 1549 rite of unction is restored to its original place at the close of the service. The Nonjurors also supplied something which had been entirely lacking in the first Prayer Book : a simple formula for blesing the oil, to be performed by the priest :

> *Then the Priest shall take some sweet oil of olives, and, putting it in a decent vessel, he shall stand and consecrate it according to the form following:*

O Almighty Lord God, who hast taught us by thy holy Apostle Saint James to anoint the sick with oil, that they may attain their bodily health, and render thanks unto thee for the same; look down, we beseech thee, and bless and sanctify this thy creature of oil, the juice of the olive : grant that those who shall be anointed therewith, may be delivered from all pains, troubles, and diseases both of body and mind, and from all the snares, temptations, and assaults of the powers of darkness, through our Lord Jesus Christ thy Son; who, with thee and the Holy Ghost, liveth and reigneth, ever one God, world without end. Amen.[52]

The Liturgy of 1718 unleashed a controversy among the Nonjurors between the "Usagers" (those who followed the revived ceremonies or "Usages") and those who rejected these as unlawful accretions, the "Non-Usagers".[53] A compromise solution on ritual unanimity was reached in 1732 by the "Instrument of Union". But this apparent unity was short lived. In 1734, the "Usagers" under Thomas Deacon (*d.*1753) published a new prayer book entitled *A Compleat Collection of Devotions* and the controversy broke out anew.

b. Nonjurors' Liturgy of 1734

The Visitation Office of Deacon's book is similar to that of the 1718 Liturgy.[54] The passage from James and the 1549 rite of anointing were again revived. Whereas the 1718 Office provided for the imposition of hands during the absolution, the Nonjurors' Liturgy of 1734 contained no explicit direction for confession, but suggests that the priest may lay his hands upon the sick person's head during the prayer "O Most merciful God". "The Form of Consecrating the Oil of the Sick" is included as an appendix to the

Visitation Office and foresees the consecration of oil by a bishop, assisted by a deacon, after the recitation of the Nicene Creed in the eucharist. The prayer of blessing is the same as in the 1718 Office. After the ceremony the deacon is to carry the consecrated oil *"into the Vestry, or some other convenient place"*. A special rubric advises priests to apply to their bishops for such consecrated oil.[55]

Thomas Deacon's largest work, *A Full, True, and Comprehensive View of Christianity* (1747), is a detailed commentary on the services contained in the Nonjurors' Liturgy of 1734, *A Compleat Collection of Devotions*. The two catechisms, a shorter and a longer, which comprise this study, represent the sacramental theology of the later "Usagers", who by this time must have constituted a very small community.

According to Deacon, the sacraments are divided into the "Greater Sacraments" and the "Lesser Sacraments". The "Greater Sacraments" are baptism and the eucharist, instituted by Christ himself. The "Lesser Sacraments" consist of "all the ceremonies of the Church"; they are ten in number and include unction of the sick.[56] A question and answer technique succinctly summarizes Deacon's theology of unction :

Q. What is the unction of the sick?
A. It is the outward ceremony of anointing the sick with oil.

Q. What is it joined with?
A. With the prayers of the Priest for the sick.

Q. What is the design of it?
A. To render those prayers effectual.

Q. What are the principal petitions put up for the sick person?
A. For his recovery, for the forgiveness of his sins, and for spiritual strength against the devil.

Q. Is anointing with oil a proper representation of these benefits?
A. Yes.

Q. Why is it so of recovery?
A. Because it was the custom to apply oil to persons, in order to give them strength or recover their health.

Q. And why of forgiveness and spiritual strength?

A.   Because, as the outward unctions of the Church are emblems
of the inward unction of the Holy Ghost, it is by his grace
alone that we are qualified for pardon, and enabled to withstand the wicked one.[57]

In the longer catechism of *A Full, True, and Comprehensive
View of Christianity* the author comes to terms with the common
objection that anointing the sick with oil pertains to the Apostolic
gift of healing.[58] He argues that were the anointing to pertain to the
miraculous gifts of healing, James would have given some assurance
that all sick Christians, when anointed, would certainly recover.
But such is not the case. Neither does James order the sick to call
for some gifted healer. Rather, the Apostle James' direction is stated
in general terms as "a standing order in the Christian Church". All
the sick are to call for the presbyters of the Church, who by virtue
of their office and not because of some special gift of healing, are to
pray over the sick and anoint them with oil.

From this exposition of unction of the sick as found in the Visitation Office of the Nonjurors' Liturgies of 1718 and 1734 and com-
mented upon by Thomas Deacon, one may conclude that the
"Usagers" attempted to restore the pristine significance of anointing of the sick as a sacrament of healing for the whole person.[59]

5.   Tractarians and Unction

The Nonjurors represented a High Church or Catholic tradition, a school of thought and practice always present in the Church
of England with varying degrees of influence.[60] This tradition
asserted itself most forcefully in the Tractarian Movement in the
nineteenth century, whose influence continues to this day. As the
High Church tradition stresses the historical continuity of the
Church of England with the Catholic Church and correspondingly
a "high" conception of the claims of the episcopate and the nature
of the sacraments, it is not surprising that the subject of unction of
the sick was once again voiced in the English Church during the
last century.[61] The two leading figures in the Tractarian Movement
both addressed themselves briefly to unction: J. H. Newman
(*d.*1890) indirectly in his discussion of the sacraments, and Edward
Pusey (*d.*1882) more directly.

In his controversial *Tract Ninety* on the Articles of Religion,
Newman speaks of the "five commonly called sacraments".[62] New-

man maintains that the twenty-fifth Article did not deny these five rites to be sacraments, but stated only that they are not sacraments in the same sense as baptism and the eucharist. These other sacraments—the number of which is left undetermined in the Anglican Church—fall under the wider conception of a sacrament. They also may each be considered as *"an outward sign of an invisible grace givén under it"*, for the Church is endowed with "the power of dispensing grace through rites of its own appointing".

Newman's consideration of the sacraments thus appeared to open the door to a renewed discussion on unction, which was taken up by Edward Pusey in his *Eirenicon* (1865), a voluminous letter to John Keble on the prospect of reunion with Rome.[63] Pusey saw the "custom of the Church" as the only reason why anointing of the sick was not practised in England. He had no difficulty accepting the use of unction in the Eastern Church. His principal problem lay with the statement of Trent that anointing of the sick remits sins, or the remains of sin.

Pusey observes that Robert Bellarmine admitted that theologians differed in their explanation of the remains of sin. Are these mortal sins, venial sins or something else? Bellarmine himself explained the "remains of sin" to mean either the "deadly sins into which a person may have fallen by ignorance", or the "torpor, sadness, anxiety which are wont to be left from sin, and which chiefly vex a man at the point of death".[64] Pusey finds the former explanation improbable, since deadly sins could scarcely be committed unknowingly by anyone with a well instructed conscience. Nor does the latter explanation of Bellarmine conform either to the words of St. James, "if any have committed sins", or to the definition of the Council of Trent that unction remits not merely the remains of sin, but sins themselves. And if sins are forgiven to a sincere penitent by absolution, what more does extreme unction provide?

The difficulty is, since sins are forgiven authoritatively upon true contrition through the absolution, what sins can remain afterwards to be remitted; and this the more, since the sick is to be anointed by the priests, and therefore, except in *extremis,* confession could be made, and the absolution pronounced.

Pusey concludes his discussion with a reasonable request for a fuller clarification of what is meant by the remission of sins effected by the anointing of the sick.

a. Theological

The second generation of the Tractarian Movement produced three forthright and impassioned appeals for the restoration of unction in the Church of England. The most prestigious of the three writers was Bishop Alexander P. Forbes of Brechin, an associate of Pusey, who considered anointing in his commentary on the Thirty-nine Articles published in 1867. In the same year the Rev. John Henry Pye penned a theological essay *Ought the Sick to be anointed?* And in 1881 appeared a catechism on anointing of the sick composed by Rev. Charles S. Grueber.

The three authors' common point of departure is that anointing of the sick is a Catholic rite which has the scriptural authority of the Apostle James (5 : 14-16). They refer to tradition, especially highlighting what was then considered to be the earliest source for unction, the celebrated letter of Innocent I (416). They note that unction is practised in both the Roman and Greek branches of the Catholic Church. The fact that the medieval abuse of deferring unction to the point of death marred the original meaning of the rite is no excuse for its present neglect in the Church of England.

After previously outlining a theology of the five other sacraments similar to that of Newman, Bishop Forbes poetically calls unction "the lost pleiad of the Anglican firmament". Despite the excuses made of a "corrupt following of the Apostles", he deplores the fact that the Church of England has lost "a distinctly Scriptural practice'. How does the bishop understand the anointing of the sick? He terms it

an Apostolic practice, whereby, in case of grievous sickness, the faithful were anointed and prayed for, for the forgiveness of their sins, and to restore them, if God so willed, or to give them spiritual support in their maladies.[66]

The monograph of J. H. Pye, a Prebendary of Lichfield, is a near desperate bid for the restoration of unction. The author tackles various objections that arise, in particular the opinion that St. James did not intend this rite to be practised by all Christians, but only by those living in his age.[67] Some would argue that in the East the anointing with oil was a bodily remedy for all kinds of disease. The elders were to pray for the sick man and to use this universal remedy for his physical recovery. To this Pye replies that the Apostles' use of oil in healing the sick (Mk. 6 : 13) was not an ordinary remedy for the cure of disease, but rather by means of the extraordinary gifts they had received in order to prove the divine mission of their Master. The more common objection is that the anointing was a sign of supernatural gifts which have since been abrogated. But Pye maintains that the prescription of St. James, "is any sick among you", is "a general rule". The temporal blessings of recovery in the early Church as well as now depend upon the "unsearchable will of God".

In his urgency Pye at no point goes into detail about the effects of anointing. One has the impression that he approaches the rite from an interest in a revived ceremonial, rather than from the standpoint of sacramental theology. Nowhere does the author use the word sacrament in reference to unction, although he calls it a "means of grace" which is "very dangerous to leave . . . undone".

As regards the necessity of blessing the oil, Pye considers such a ceremony as more in accordance with the Catholic tradition of the East and the West. Moreover, just as the Church of England usually consecrates the water before baptism, so an analogous procedure with olive oil would seem fitting prior to the anointing.

Charles S. Grueber, an incumbent in the diocese of Bath and Wells, presents the most systematic treatment of anointing. His catechism is probably a fair example of the direction in which the later Tractarian discussion of unction was proceeding. He describes the anointing of the sick as

a Rite or Ordinance of the Church instituted, in the first instance, for the purpose of impetrating the mercy of God for the recovery of persons in extreme sickness and in peril of death.[68]

The rite existed in the Church from the very beginning; the claim that unction belonged to the miraculous gifts of healing finds no support in the Epistle of St. James. This "Ordinance of Healing" is

a supernatural means vouchsafed in the goodness of God to all ages of the Church for recovery, where He sees fit, from sickness, or for obtaining ease in sickness.[69]

The anointing was instituted primarily for the healing of the body, but its effects extend also to the soul. The spiritual benefit is the imparting of "spiritual support and comfort to the sick one, whilst inspiring confidence and confirming his trust in God". The spiritual benefit especially singled out by James is the forgiveness of sin, which may include mortal or venial sin, or "the effects and relics of sin" previously remitted through the sacrament of penance.

Grueber explains the two-fold interpretation of the name "extreme unction" : the last of the anointings begun at baptism, or its administration in the extremity of sickness. But in any event the rite is reserved for any severe sickness and is not a viaticum. The proper minister of this healing ordinance is an ordained minister of the Church. The recipient of the anointing must be baptized, living in communion with the Church, endowed with the use of reason, and be seriously ill.

Anointing of the sick is a sacrament of the Eastern and Western Church. To the question as to whether anointing complies with the Anglican definition of a sacrament, Grueber answers affirmatively :

> There is in the Rite an Outward and Visible Sign and an Inward and Spiritual Gift, and being of Apostolical use, it cannot be said not to have been ordained by Christ; and further, there is expressly "annexed" to it the promise of free forgiveness of sin.[70]

The anointing may also be repeated as often as the sick person is afflicted with a "fresh disease", and during the same illness "at fit intervals".

The three authors—Bishop Forbes, Pye and Grueber—alike bemoan the absence of anointing of the sick in the Church of England; they all vigorously urged its restoration. As the rite was not contained in the official Prayer Book, did they find any sanction for the use of unction in their day? They did, and their justification of this practice delineates three different approaches.

Bishop Forbes considers the Visitation of the Sick to be a private office of the Book of Common Prayer. Since the Act of Uniformity pertained only to public offices, there is nothing to hinder the revival of the "Apostolic and Scriptural custom" of anointing the sick.[71] It is the privilege of the devout who may desire such a ministration.

J. H. Pye argues for the legality of unction on the basis of the Act of Uniformity of the 1552 Prayer Book itself.[72] Although anointing of the sick was deleted from this revision, the Act of Uniformity expressly praised the earlier 1549 Book as "a very Godly order . . . agreeable to the Word of God and the primitive Church". The only reason for any alterations was that "divers doubts *for the fashion and manner of the ministration of the same"* had arisen. Pye concludes somewhat unconvincingly that there was no doubt as to the fact that unction was intended to be administered; the only uncertainty was as to how it was to be administered. The "ultra-Reformers" took advantage of this situation by removing the rubric on anointing altogether from the 1552 Prayer Book. But in actual fact the omission of all mention of unction from the Prayer Book only proves that henceforth the manner of ministration is left to the discretion of the priest.

Charles Grueber finds a warrant for the practice of unction which is probably the most conclusive. He claims that the absence of unction in the Prayer Book does not imply a prohibition of its use any more than the omission of other offices employed in the Church of England which often vary from diocese to diocese; for example, "Laying the Foundation Stone of a Church or College", "the Consecration of Churches and Churchyards", "the Re-opening of a Church", "the Enthronization of a Bishop", "the Installation of a Dean", "the Institution of an Incumbent in the face of the congregation", "the Benediction of the Oil for the Coronation of the Sovereign", etc.[73] Grueber's argument was revived during the Canterbury Convocation debates which led to the approval of official services for unction and the laying on of hands in 1935.

b. Liturgical and Devotional

The Tractarian treatment of anointing of the sick was not confined to theological speculation. The renewed interest in unction also found expression in unofficial liturgical and private devotional forms.[74]

Pye included an appendix to his essay in which he printed an exhortation to unction and a short "Form of Consecration of the Oil, adapted from the Greek Office".[75] The exhortation is intended to introduce the subject of anointing to the sick person prior to the ministration of the Visitation Office. The exhortation begins with a reading from James 5.14-16. In the subsequent commentary on this passage, anointing is described as a "sacramental rite" signifying "the healing of infirmities" of both body and soul. Concerning the healing of the soul, "God has promised, by his holy Apostle St. James" the forgiveness of sins in answer to the prayer of faith together with the anointing. The exhortation terminates with a question pointedly directed to the sick person :

Wherefore forasmuch as thou hast called for me, in this thy

sickness, I demand, according to mine office, as an elder of the Church, Dost thou desire to be anointed with oil?[76]

Should the sick person so desire, the suggested formula for anointing would be from the First Prayer Book of Edward VI.

More Anglo-Catholic and less healing in tone is the *Manual for the Unction of the Sick* (1868), translated in part from Latin sources and arranged by Brother Cecil, a member of the Society of St. Joseph "in the Anglican Branch of the Holy Catholic Church".[77] In the preface Brother Cecil states his convictions about the use of the Manual. It has been drawn up for the benefit of "many Anglican Catholics, both clerical and lay, ready and anxious to revive the use of this precious but much-neglected sacrament". The compiler feels that St. James intended that the sick be anointed with oil in *"dangerous"* cases, as well as in *"hopeless"* illness". Unction is "for a miraculous cure of body as well as for a means of grace to the soul".

The Manual contains the following forms :

(1) "Directions for the Preservation, etc. of the Oil." Minute prescriptions are laid down regarding "the purest extract of the olive", the case of "pure silver" to contain the oil, which after "a most solemn benediction" is esteemed *"very holy"*. New oil should be blessed every year. If no bishop can be persuaded to perform this ceremony, the oil may be blessed by seven priests, according to the practice of the Eastern Church; although the blessing by a single priest would not appear to violate "the validity of its benediction".
(2) "The Benediction of the Oil", a translation from the *Rituale Romanum* of 1744, replete with exorcism.
(3) "Directions concerning the Sacrament of Extreme Unction", which fulfil the most exact ritual stipulations of the Roman Church, including a conditional clause : " 'If thou be still living, by this holy unction', etc.".
(4) "The Order for Administering the Sacrament of Extreme Unction", also translated from the 1744 Roman Ritual. The eyes, ears, nostrils, mouth, hands, feet and loins are anointed with the form : "Through this holy unction + and His most tender mercy, the Lord pardon thee whatever thou hast sinned . . . Amen."
(5) "The Order for the Unction of the Sick 'in periculo'." This form of anointing for persons "dangerously ill" is from the 1549 Prayer Book, selected in all probability because of its brevity.

Anointing of the sick also made its way into the devotional literature of the later Tractarian period. *The Priest's Book of Private Devotion* is a popular work, originally compiled by two Anglican clergymen, which has gone through seven editions from 1872 to as recently as 1960. The first edition contained two prayers to be said by the priest before and after administering unction. Both prayers were heavily coloured with a consciousness of sin and the thought of impending death.[78] The revised edition of 1877 replaced these prayers of the priest with two other prayers to be recited by the sick person himself before and after the anointing.[79] The prayer before the anointing paraphrased the teaching of St. James. The principal section petitioned God for patience in sickness, strength to resist temptation, pardon of sins, and "that true light by which I may be conducted through the shadow of death to eternal happiness". The possibility of recovery, however, if it be "expedient for thy Glory", was not neglected. The sick person's prayer after anointing was a verbose piece resembling a personal commendation of one's soul.

The Priest's Book of Private Devotion was further revised and expanded in 1884. The prayers before and after anointing of the previous edition were retained, although the wording of the first prayer was slightly modified; and for the first time the service of unction from the 1549 Prayer Book was reprinted. The later editions of 1891 and 1879 merely repeated the material and format of the 1884 edition.[80]

It is astounding how little notice has been taken by studies in the Oxford Movement and by the healing literature of the efforts of several Tractarians to revive the anointing of the sick. Motivated by their awareness of belonging to the universal Catholic Church, these men sought to restore to the Church of England the scriptural and Catholic sacrament of unction. But while Bishop Forbes, J. H. Pye and Charles Grueber regarded anointing as more than a preparation for death, their theology failed to find full expression in the liturgical and devotional forms of Brother Cecil and *The Priest's Book of Private Devotion*. Notwithstanding, the contribution of the Tractarians at least indirectly laid an important groundwork for the growth of the ministry of healing in the twentieth century.[81]

6. *Summary*

It is time to take stock of the findings of this section on the anointing of the sick, which has been traced in the Anglican tradition from Reformation times until the beginning of this century, when the cause for the revival of unction was taken up by the healing movement.

Two early Reformation documents, the Bishop's Book and the King's Book, attempted to transcend the medieval practice of extreme unction by restoring the earlier meaning of the sacrament as a means of anointing sick people for the healing of body and soul. This new approach was embodied in the simplified form of anointing in the Visitation Office of the First Prayer Book of Edward VI in 1549. But the streamlined rite was unable to withstand the ingrained prejudices of the Reformers, who deleted it from the 1552 revision. The doctrinal settlement under Elizabeth referred to unction only indirectly and ambiguously as one of the "five commonly called sacraments". And so was the case for unction decided, until the Nonjurors in the eighteenth and the Tractarians in the nineteenth century endeavoured to restore once again the primitive anointing of the sick as a sacrament in the English Church.

C. TOUCHING FOR THE KING'S EVIL

There was also in England another ministration to certain sick people of a more explicit healing character: the Touching for the King's Evil.[82] The history of this royal healing is at least loosely associated with the Book of Common Prayer, for services of this kind were reprinted—apparently without any authorization—in several editions of the Prayer Book between the reign of Charles I (1625-1649) and 1759.[83]

The King's Evil was a name given to scrofula. The sovereigns of France and England were supposedly invested with a royal touch, which by stroking the afflicted area of the sufferer was able to heal the glandular disease.[84] The special virtue of Touching for the King's Evil was commonly said to have originated with Edward the Confessor (d.1066).[85] In William Shakespeare's Macbeth (IV, iii), the words of Malcolm reflect the popular mentality of a later age which flourished about the saintly king:

'Tis called the evil:
A most miraculous work in this good king,
Which often since my here-remain in England
I have seen him do. How he solicits heaven

Himself best knows; but strangely-visited people,
All swollen and ulcerous, pitiful to the eye,
The mere despair of surgery he cures,
Hanging a golden stamp about their necks,
Put on with holy prayers, and 'tis spoken,
To the succeeding royalty he leaves
The healing benediction.

The "golden stamp about their necks" has reference to the Angel, a small gold or silver piece which was customarily bestowed by the generous sovereign upon his ailing subject.[86]

After Edward the Confessor the next extant record of the exercise of this unusual faculty is from a letter of Peter of Blois (c.1180), who attests to the Touching for the King's Evil performed by Henry II. The French cleric living in the English court attributed this marvellous power to the unction at a royal coronation, which was then considered to be a kind of sacrament making the sovereign a sacred personage.

I admit indeed that it is a sacred duty to attend upon the lord king; for he is holy and the Lord's Anointed; nor has he received the sacrament of regal unction in vain, for if its efficacy be not known or be in doubt, the disappearance of bubonic plague and the cure of scrofula will beget the fullest belief.[87]

Henry VII (1485-1509) was the first to introduce a fixed ceremony for the Touching for the King's Evil. The Latin service of his reign was reprinted in 1686 at the order of James II, who in publishing the pre-Reformation ceremony was striving to draw England closer to the Roman Church.[88] The service begins as the king, kneeling, makes the sign of the cross. After seeking and receiving a blessing from the chaplain, the monarch recites the *Confiteor*, to which the chaplain responds with the *Misereatur* and *Absolutionem*. The chaplain continues with a reading from the conclusion of the Gospel of Mark (16:14-20). While the chaplain repeats the clause from v.18, "Super aegros manus imponunt, et bene habebunt", the king lays his hand upon the sore of the sick person kneeling before him. After all the sick have been so treated, the chaplain ends the reading from Mark. There follows a second reading, from the Prologue to John's Gospel (1:1-14).[89] Once again the chaplain interrupts the reading to repeat v.9, "Erat lux vera etc.", until the king has completed crossing the sores of the sick persons with the Angel. The chaplain then finishes the reading. The prayer *Omnipotens sempiterne Deus, salus æterna credentium* concludes the public ceremony.[90] Another lengthy prayer, *Dominator Domine, Deus omnipotens,* is said quietly by the king after the sick have departed.

The Manual of Mary Tudor includes the service for Touching used by the Queen and most likely by her father, Henry VIII. There are only minor textual variations from the rite of Henry VII.[91]

In the reign of Elizabeth I there appeared the first systematic treatise on Touching for the King's Evil: *Charisma* (1597), composed by William Tooker. Tooker relates the story of one individual suffering from scrofula, who although a papist, went to the Queen to be touched. Being cured of his affliction, he became personally convinced that the Pope's excommunication of 1570 was of no consequence: no cure could be possible if Elizabeth was not the rightful queen. Tooker also describes the healing ceremony which Elizabeth was accustomed to perform at public prayers.[92] The *Confiteor,* with its petitions to the Virgin Mary and the saints, was expunged. After the Gospel of John, the *Kyrie eleison, Pater Noster* and various versicles and responses were inserted. The prayer *Omnipotens Deus, æterna salus omnium,* a rephrasing of the earlier prayer, concluded the service.

When James I (1603-1625) came from Scotland to ascend to the throne of England, his Puritan upbringing at first made him reluctant to touch for the King's Evil. Only when his English advisers convinced him of its political expediency for enhancing the Divine Right, did the sceptical king consent. The service of Touching for the King's Evil during the reigns of James I and Charles I was put into English and included in the 1633 folio edition of the Book of Common Prayer, between the Commination and the Ordinal.[93] The four parts of the ceremony were more sharply delineated:

(1) Gospel of Mark 16:14-20. The words "They shall lay their hands on the sicke and they shall recover" are repeated for as long as the king touches the sick person.
(2) Gospel of John 1:1-14. The words "That light was the true Light which lighteth every man that cometh into the world" are repeated while the king places the Angel around the neck of his sick subjects.
(3) Lord have mercy, Our Father, versicles and responses.

(4) The concluding prayer:

Almighty God the eternall health of all such as put their trust
in thee, heare us wee beseech thee on the behalfe of these thy
servants for whom wee call for thy mercifull helpe, that they
receiving health, may give thanks to thee in thy Holy Church,
through Jesus Christ our Lord, Amen.

and a blessing taken from the Prayer Book Order of Holy Communion: "The peace of God etc.".

The monarch of whose healings we are best informed is Charles
II (1660-1685). A member of his retinue, John Evelyn (d.1706),
described a healing ceremony which he witnessed on July 6, 1660.[94]
In another entry in his diary, for March 28, 1684, Evelyn indicated
the enormous popularity of the Touching when "six or seven were
crushed to death by pressing at the chirurgeon's door for tickets".[95]
Numerous public notices of the ceremony are still extant.[96] A copy
of a proclamation ordered to be published in all parishes during
January, 1683, announced a Touching for the King's Evil which
was to take place at Whitehall on January 9. Those of the sick
who planned to come were advised to bring a certificate from their
parishes showing that they had not been previously "touched by
his Majesty" and "to the intent to be healed of their disease".[97]

One of the royal physicians, John Browne, published a study
of this phenomenon in which he claimed that 92,107 people had
been touched for the King's Evil during the reign of Charles II,
many of whom were cured.[98] The service used by Charles was
reprinted in an edition of the Prayer Book in 1662, between the
Commination and the Psalms.[99] There were few changes from
the ceremony of 1634: a rephrasing of the concluding prayer, and
the substitution of the previous final blessing for the grace from
Morning and Evening Prayer: "The grace of our Lord Jesus
Christ etc.".

For the brief reign of James II (1685-1688), there exists the Latin
service of Henry VII and an English translation.[100] In exile the
Stuarts continued to touch for the King's Evil.[101] But there is no
evidence of William or Mary having used the ceremony, for as
Macaulay remarks: "William had too much sense to be duped,
and too much honesty to bear a part in what he knew to be an
imposture".[102] To one importunate patient pleading for the laying
on of hands, William replied: "God give you better health and
more sense".

The Touching for the King's Evil was revived in England for
the last time under Queen Anne (1712-1714). The young Samuel

Johnson (*d*.1784) was one of the subjects touched by the Queen, but to no avail.[103] The service used by Anne was published again in several editions of the Prayer Book, even during the reign of her successor, George I (1714-1727), who declined to perform the ceremony.[104] The revised "At the Healing" opens with a prayer from the Anglican Communion liturgy: "Prevent us, O Lord, etc.". The only scriptural reading is from Mark 16. After the Lord have mercy, Our Father, there follows a new rubric and form for the Touching:

> Then shall the infirm Persons, one by one, be presented to the Queen upon their knees; and as every one is presented and while the Queen is laying Her hands upon them, and putting the Gold about their Necks, the Chaplain that officiates, turning himself to Her Majesty, shall say these words following:
> God give a blessing to this Work; and grant that these sick Persons on whom the Queen lays her hands, may recover, through Jesus Christ our Lord.[105]

The versicles and responses and the prayer "O Almighty God, who art the giver of all health, etc." remain as in the previous healing services. Benedictions—"The Almighty God, who is a most strong tower, etc." (Visitation Office) and "The Grace of our Lord, etc." —bring the ceremony to a close.

Belief in the power of Touching for the King's Evil was held by such men of letters of the seventeenth and eighteenth centuries as Peter Heylyn (*d*.1662), Jeremy Collier (*d*.1726), William Whiston (*d*.1752) and Thomas Carte (*d*.1754).[106] Undoubtedly some cures did result, perhaps largely upon the use of psychological suggestion. Originally springing from the conception of the king as a sacred, almost priestly, person, the rite was later especially encouraged by the Stuarts on the throne of England, who sought to consolidate their political philosophy of the royal prerogative. While the practice did show some measure of concern for sick people in their infirmities, to say that the Touching for the King's Evil was a direct forerunner of the current healing ministry would be a gratuitous assumption. The liturgical impulses given to the ministry of healing are rather to be found in the dissatisfaction with the Visitation Office of the 1662 Prayer Book, and in the revival of anointing of the sick by the Tractarians in the nineteenth century.

CHAPTER IV

Unction of the Sick and the Laying on of Hands in the Church of England Today

As Horton Davies has remarked, the Church of England is "a *liturgical* Church", which "finds its nexus of unity, its spiritual regimen, its tradition and way of life in the Book of Common Prayer".[1] It follows that the ministry of healing would seek expression in liturgical services and that these services should find some measure of official approbation. This chapter first of all examines the liturgical services for unction and the laying on of hands used by the Church of England, and then attempts to systematize what is understood as sacramental healing.

A. *Liturgical Services*

1. Prayer Book Revision

a. Background

Already in 1904 F. W. Puller of the Society of St. John the Evangelist concluded his study *Anointing of the Sick in Scripture and Tradition* with a favourable judgement on the desirability of officially reviving unction in the Church of England as a supernatural means of healing. The reasons he adduced were the obligation of obeying a scriptural precept (Jas. 5 :14-15a); the stimulation unction of the sick would provide towards the recovery of the power of prayer, especially in times of sickness; and the negative argument that the practice of anointing stood in danger of being restored in the wrong way either by faith healing sects or by Anglo-Catholics emulating the Roman extreme unction. Puller further proposed that the bishops, either individually or collectively, should lead the way to recovering the apostolic and primitive use of unction.[2]

On a more pastoral and parochial level the cause for the restoration of anointing was widely promoted by Percy Dearmer. In the 1907 edition of his *The Parson's Handbook,* he regretted the loss of the scriptural practice of unction in the Reformed Church of England.[3] The author endorsed Puller's thesis that unction in primitive times was not a sacrament, but rather "one of the means of helping people to recover by the use of spiritual power". Any priest should comply with the request of a parishioner for either the anointing or the laying on of hands. The oil need not be blessed by the bishop; neither was the bishop's permission necessary for applying the oil with the prayer of faith. "The priest has just as much right to use prayer, the laying on of hands, or unction for a sick person as he has to read the Bible to him or to do any other Christian or charitable action."[4] Dearmer also reprinted in a footnote the form for unction from the First Prayer Book of 1549.

In his study of spiritual healing, *Body and Soul* (1909), Dearmer included an appendix with original forms for the laying on of hands and the anointing of the sick.[5] These forms, which first appeared in Dearmer, have been frequently reproduced both separately and in other publications; viz., *A Prayer Book Revised* (1913), a suggested model compiled by a team of liturgical scholars, with a foreword by Bishop Charles Gore; the *Lambeth Report on the Ministry of Healing* in 1924 (unction); *Psychology, Religion and Healing* (laying on of hands); *The Priest's Book of Private Devotion* (1960).[6] The influence of the Dearmer services is also evident in the rites of healing issued by the Guild of St. Raphael, the Convocation of York (unction), and the Guild of Health (unction).

The Dearmer "Forms for the Laying on of Hands and the Anointing of the Sick" convey a positive approach to illness and are orientated towards the recovery of the sick person : a concluding rubric states that *"Public Thanksgiving should be made in Church after recovery"*. Both services are interspersed with periods of silent meditation, and their basic pattern is simple and readily applicable to the pastoral situation : the recitation of an antiphon and psalm (at the discretion of the minister); confession and absolution; silent prayer, Lord have mercy, Our Father, versicles and responses, collect; silent prayer; the symbolic action of the laying on of hands or anointing; silent prayer, versicle and response, closing collect and benediction.

In the light of their importance as primordial forms, the Dearmer services deserve examination in greater detail. The structure of the rite for the laying on of hands is as follows :

(1) Antiphon, "O Saviour of the world", followed by either Ps. 91

(*Qui habitat*) or Ps. 71 (*In te, Domine, speravi*).

(2) Confession and absolution : either private or general.

(3) Silent prayer, Lord have mercy, Our Father, versicles and responses adapted largely from the Prayer Book Visitation Office. A collect derived from a Roman prayer for the sick, which also formed an integral part of the service of Touching for the King's Evil : "O Almighty God, who are the giver of all health, etc".[7]

(4) An acclamation by "the Clerk or one of the friends present", thus signifying the corporate concern of the members of the Church assembled together in the sick room or at church :

God give a blessing to this work; And grant that this sick Person, on whom thou dost lay thine hands may recover; through Jesus Christ our Lord.

(5) Silent prayer.

(6) The laying on of hands, administered together with the following prayer :

In the Name of God most High, may release from thy pain be given thee, and thy health be restored according to his holy will. In the Name of Jesus Christ, the Prince of life, may new life quicken thy mortal body. In the Name of the Holy Spirit, mayest thou receive inward health, and the peace which passeth all understanding.

And the God of all peace himself sanctify you wholly : and may your spirit and soul and body be preserved entire, without blame at the coming of our Lord Jesus Christ. Amen.

(7) Silent prayer; versicle and response from Ps. 117 (118):15; a collect from the Communion Service of the Prayer Book : "O Almighty Lord, and everlasting God, vouchsafe, we beseech thee, to direct, sanctify, and govern both our hearts and bodies, etc."; and a blessing from the Visitation Office : "Unto God's gracious mercy and protection, etc.".

The Dearmer service for anointing displays a similar pattern :

(1) Antiphon "O Saviour of the world", followed by either Ps. 23 (*Dominus regit me*) or Ps. 71.

(2) A short lesson from James 5 :14-15a, to be read by the minister.

(3) Confession and absolution : either private or general.

(4) Silent prayer, Lord have mercy, Our Father, versicles and responses, collect : all as in the form for the laying on of hands.

(5) Silent prayer.

(6) The consecration of oil by the priest, if not already blessed, modified from the Nonjurors' Liturgy :

> O Almighty Lord God, who hast taught us by thy holy Apostle James to anoint the sick with oil, that they may regain their bodily health, and render thanks unto thee for the same; look down, we beseech thee, and bless and sanctify this thy creature of oil; and grant that those who shall be anointed therewith, may be delivered from all sickness; through our Lord Jesus Christ thy Son, who, with thee and the Holy Ghost, liveth and reigneth, God, world without end. Amen.[8]

(7) The anointing of the sick person with oil. The priest makes the sign of the cross on the forehead of the patient, as he says a prayer adapted from the 1549 rite of unction :

> As with this visible oil thy body outwardly is anointed : so our heavenly Father, Almighty God, grant of his infinite goodness, that thy soul inwardly may be anointed with the Holy Ghost, who is the Spirit of all strength, comfort, relief, and gladness : and vouchsafe for his great mercy (if it be his blessed will) to restore unto thee thy bodily health, and strength, to serve him, and send thee release of all thy pains, troubles and diseases, both in body and mind; through Christ our Lord, who by his death hath overcome death, and with the Father and the Holy Ghost evermore liveth and reigneth, God, world without end. Amen.[9]

(8) Silent prayer, versicle and response as in the laying on of hands, and a collect derived from the Greek *Euchologion* :

> O Holy Father, physician of souls and bodies, who didst send thine only-begotten Son to heal the sicknesses of men and to save them from death; Deliver thy servant from all bodily and spiritual weakness, and quicken him by the grace of the same thy Son Jesus Christ our Lord, who liveth and reigneth with thee and the Holy Spirit, one God, world without end. Amen.[10]

The service terminates with the same closing benediction from the Visitation Office as in the Dearmer form for the laying on of hands.

The distinguished liturgical scholar W. H. Frere (*d.*1938) also addressed himself to the revision of the Prayer Book Visitation Office and the revival of unction. Writing in *Some Principles of*

Liturgical Reform (1911), he termed the services for the sick and
departed as "the least satisfactory of all the rites contained in the
Prayer Book".[11] Frere made the following suggestions towards revising the Visitation Office :

(a) Appropriate "short incisive prayers and sentences" to replace
the "long homiletic element . . . unsuited to most sick rooms".
(b) A greater opportunity for co-operation in prayer on the part of
the sick person's friends.
(c) A litany to be said on behalf of the sick person.
(d) The old form of the commendation of the dying.
(e) The inclusion of a rite of anointing which would balance the
petitions for the recovery of physical health with the benefits accru-
ing to the soul. The restriction of the consecration of oil in the
Western Church as the exclusive prerogative of the bishop need no
longer be maintained. Priests should be authorized to bless the oil
at the time of anointing according to a suitable form to be provided
in the Visitation Office.
(f) The possibility of communion from the Reserved Sacrament.

b. The Proposed Prayer Book of 1927/28

On April 29, 1920, the Convocations of Canterbury and York
at last presented a reply to the Crown on proposals for the revision
of the Book of Common Prayer. Only the most minute of changes
affected the Visitation Office.[12] In November of the same year the
Church Assembly, appointed a committee to examine the proposals
of the Convocations, and this presented its report (NA 60) in June,
1922; in October the Bishops incorporated these findings into the
Revised Prayer Book (Permissive Use) Measure (NA 84), which
received the general approval of the Church Assembly early in 1923.

"The Order for the Visitation of the Sick" embodied in NA 60
and NA 84 was entirely the work of W. H. Frere.[13] It met with the
final approval of the Church Assembly in 1927, and again in 1928,
virtually without amendment.[14] The Visitation Office incorporated
all of Frere's suggestions outlined some years earlier, with the notable
exception of anointing of the sick. But strong support for the
inclusion of unction was not wanting. On two occasions, on
November 27, 1924 and on February 25, 1927 the House of Clergy
petitioned the House of Bishops for some provision for anointing the
sick in the revised Prayer Book.[15] The various alternative revisions
and critical evaluations published unofficially during this period all

advocated unction of the sick : the "Green Book" of the English Church Union, the "Grey Book" representing a group of moderate Churchmen under the leadership of Bishop William Temple, and the "Orange Book" of the Alcuin Club.[16] Yet the House of Bishops, meeting often in closed sessions, appeared unwilling to commit itself to unction until the consideration of the *Lambeth Report on the Ministry of Healing* (1924) at the Lambeth Conference of 1930.[17] Until that time the laying on of hands was as far as the Bishops would go towards approving a symbolic action for ministering to the sick.

c. *"The Order for the Visitation of the Sick"*

The Proposed Prayer Book, as submitted in 1927 and again in 1928, was a composite work, consisting of the whole of the existing Prayer Book of 1662 together with the proposed additions and deviations approved by the Church Assembly. The Visitation Office, however, constituted an anomaly in this respect, as an introductory note explains : *"The Order in the Form of 1662 is not reprinted here, being, for the most part, contained in the Order following"*. Compared with the Visitation Office of the 1662 Prayer Book, the proposed revision of 1927/28 represents an improvement in structure, a correction of a misguided theology of sickness, and an enrichment of material. The 1927/28 Visitation Order consists of five sections or offices, which may be used either independently or as progressive stages during a pastoral visit :

    I.   Visitation.
    II.   Exhortation to Faith and Prayer.
  III.   Exhortation to Repentance.
  IV.   An Act of Prayer and Blessing.
   V.   Special Prayers to be Used as Occasion may serve.[18]

The first section, "Visitation", contains the opening prayers from the 1662 Visitation Order, with several alterations. One of the versicles and responses has been omitted :

Minister. Let the enemy have no advantage over *him.*
Answer. Nor the wicked approach to hurt *him.*

In the second of the prayers for strengthening, "Hear us, Almighty and most merciful God and Saviour", two interesting changes are

made : the word "trial" is substituted for the description of illness
as a "fatherly correction"; and the concluding portion of the same
prayer has been amended to read more hopefully :

> May it be thy good pleasure to restore *him* to *his* former health,
> that so *he* may live the rest of *his* life in thy fear, and to thy
> glory. *Amen.*
> And whatsoever the issue that thou shalt ordain for *him,* give
> *him* grace to be so conformed to thy will, that *he* may be made
> meet to dwell with thee in life everlasting; through Jesus Christ
> our Lord. *Amen.*

The second section, "Exhortation to Faith and Prayer", replaces
the verbose and dreary exhortation of the 1662 Order with a list
of subjects, in part suggested by the earlier exhortation, which the
priest can develop informally during the course of his visit. He may
also elect to choose *"some part of the Christian Faith"* which may
need clarification. The minister then says the relevant passages
from the 1662 exhortation pertaining to baptism and to the
rehearsal of the Articles of Faith, which is professed in the
Apostles' Creed. A new rubric directs that an instruction on prayer
may fittingly terminate this section :

> *Thereafter, as occasion serves, the Minister shall instruct the
> sick person so to order his rule of prayer, for himself and others,
> that his days of sickness may be a time of faithful and loving
> intercourse with God.*

The third section, "Exhortation to Repentance", repeats the first
and fourth rubrics of the exhortation to repentance in the 1662
Book. A special admonition to the sick person to examine his state
before God and man has been inserted. The opening antiphon of
the 1662 Visitation Order, "Remember not, Lord", has been effectively transposed to this section in the revised Order. There follows
an opportunity for sacramental confession, within the framework
of a modified *Confiteor,* together with the absolution and shortened
collect ("O most merciful God") from the 1662 Prayer Book.

The fourth section, "An Act of Prayer and Blessing", is a significant enrichment in that it provides for the laying on of hands. The
rite is introduced by the antiphon "O Saviour of the world", which
encloses Ps. 121 (*Levavi oculos*) or *"any other Psalm".* The procedure for the laying on of hands is as follows :

Then shall the Minister say (laying his hands upon the sick person if desired).

O Almighty God, who art the giver of all health, and the aid of them that see to thee for succour : We call upon thee for thy help and goodness mercifully to be shewed upon this thy servant, that being healed of *his* infirmities, he may give thanks unto thee in thy holy Church; through Jesus Christ our Lord. *Amen.*

The concluding benedictions are those of the 1662 Visitation Order: "The Almighty Lord who is a most strong tower", and "Unto God's gracious mercy and protection".

The fifth section, "Special Prayers to be Used as Occasion may serve", is a collection of prayers drawn largely from the 1662 Order and medieval sources, which are adaptable to the condition of the patient. There is a litany for the sick or dying, and prayers for healing, for a sick child, for one troubled in conscience, for a convalescent, for a dying child, and commendatory prayers.[19] An appended note to the Visitation Order suggests a rich assortment of collects from the Prayer Book and passages from Scripture arranged according to twenty different themes.

The Visitation Order of the Proposed Prayer Book was a vast improvement upon the 1662 Book. What was worthwhile from the earlier Order had been retained, and supplemented and enriched by the inclusion of new prayers, suggested passages from Scripture, and the rite of the laying on of hands. Both old and new elements had been neatly shaped into five sections which replaced the clumsiness of the one continuous previous Order. This new arrangement also rendered the Visitation Order more flexible to the situation and needs of the sick person. And while the earlier notion of sickness as a visitation and punishment for sin had not entirely disappeared,[20] an attitude of hope and healing predominated.

The fate of the Proposed Prayer Book is well known. On December 15, 1927 after having secured the approval of the House of Lords, the Proposed Prayer Book was rejected by the House of Commons (238-205). In the following year the Book was amended so as to allay Protestant objections, principally in regard to Reservation of Communion for the Sick—the Visitation Order remaining unchanged—only to be defeated once again in the House of Commons on June 13, 1928, by a slightly larger majority (260-220). In the wake of this crisis the Upper House of Canterbury in July, 1929, passed a resolution whereby the Bishops declared they would countenance the use of the 1928 Proposed Prayer Book if they are satisfied that such use would have the good will of the people represented in the Parochial Church Council, and that in the case of the Occasional Offices the consent of the parties concerned will always be obtained.[21]

2. *Official Services of Canterbury and York*

Although the revival of the ministry of healing in the Anglican Communion arose in the Church of England, it was not until the middle of the third decade of the twentieth century that the Mother Church gave official approval to services for unction and the laying on of hands.[22]

The long process of remedying this situation began in the Convocation of Canterbury on January 21, 1931, when Prebendary Charles Harris proposed and the Lower House agreed that some action be taken. The first of the four resolutions was the most important, outlining the background and need for official services of anointing of the sick and the laying on of hands :

That inasmuch as the primitive rites of anointing and laying hands upon the sick with a view to their spiritual benefit and bodily healing are in extensive and increasing use throughout this Province, for the most part with full episcopal approval, and favourable recognition has recently been accorded to them by the Lambeth Conference; and seeing that the parochial clergy greatly need guidance for the due and effective administration of these rites, this House respectfully petitions his Grace the President to appoint a Joint Committee to draw up and submit for approval a provisional service (or services) for Unction and Imposition of Hands, and for the Imposition of Hands without Unction, for temporary use in the Province until a permanent and fully authorized form can be issued under synodical sanction.[23]

The subsequent motions urged that the services should be drafted with due consideration for ancient precedent and for modern pastoral experience and therapeutic psychology, and that these rites should be tailored "not only to the physically infirm, but also to mental and nervous sufferers". On January 21, 1932 the Upper House of Bishops responded favourably to the suggestions of the Lower House and a joint committee from both Houses was appointed to draw up the services.

a. Province of Canterbury

(1) Background

The first report of the joint committee, Report 593, was completed on August 31, 1932. It bore the unmistakable stamp of Charles Harris, a member of the committee, who a short time previously had advocated in *Liturgy and Worship*:

> *One Principal Comprehensive Service of Visitation, containing the whole of the ministrations which a sick person normally requires, arranged in a carefully considered order, and containing a sufficient number of alternative scriptural readings and prayers to serve for at least a week without undue repetition.*[24]

There was material in superabundance in the forty-two page report: two orders for the consecration of oil; an order for holy communion on the day of anointing; an order for unction, the laying on of hands and communion of the sick; nine lessons from Scripture together with a response, prayer, antiphon and psalm; a confession of faith; communion of the sick; the laying on of hands and the anointing of the sick with three additional variants according to the condition of the patient; the commendation of the soul; five forms for the laying on of hands without unction; and a concluding introduction containing twenty points on pastoral care.[25]

The Preface to Report 593 explained the controlling factors in framing the services: ancient sources and the principles of modern psychology, especially the influence of the subconscious mind. The aim of unction was in keeping with the earlier tradition of both East and West, the healing of the whole person: "only through the strengthening and healing of the spirit or soul could benefit be expected to accrue to the mind or to the body". And while many of the ancient forms of unction were exorcistic in character, reference to exorcism had been carefully avoided in drafting the services.[26] The purpose of the laying on of hands was originally more of a personal benediction than a healing rite, "but such blessing, since it assures the individual of God's gracious favour and of the renewal of spiritual strength, gives joy and peace to the soul, a condition which reacts favourably on the physical and mental condition of the patient". The administration of holy communion was seen as an accompaniment to anointing from earliest times and was therefore encouraged. In all things the committee adhered to the principles set out in the *Lambeth Report on the Ministry of Healing* in 1924.

On May 31, 1933 Report 593 on unction and the laying on of hands was presented to the Upper House, and on the following day to the Lower House. The discussion in both Houses revealed a number of interesting facts.[27] The practice of unction had evidently been going on for a considerable time : e.g. in the diocese of London for some thirty years where the Bishop was already consecrating oil for the sick in his chapel every Maundy Thursday. The consecration of oil, however, was a sensitive topic in the Convocation debates, as fears of a superstitious property attached to the blessed oil were intense. The committee disclosed that the services in the Report drew their material from twenty ancient sources, one from the Nonjurors, one from the 1549 Prayer Book, and another from the South African Book of Common Prayer. The prayers were translated by Charles Harris, although F. E. Brightman had supplied numerous sources before his death.

In the Upper House two of the Bishops, Barnes of Birmingham and Whittingham of St. Edmundsbury and Ipswich, went on record as being categorically opposed to any form of unction, the former terming it a "retrograde step towards religious barbarism". Notwithstanding, the House of Bishops gave general approval to the forms contained in the Report. Most were in accord with the criticism of the Archbishop of Canterbury, who summed up the discussion : the services were needlessly elaborate, the numerous paradigmatic references to the Old Testament could be fruitfully omitted, and the services in their present format could not be used as a manual for the sick person. The Upper House moved that a special committee be appointed to revise the services, including the wording of the proposed Introduction where sacramental and psychological matters were not clearly distinguished. The House of Clergy followed a similar course of action, appointing a committee of its own to re-examine the services.

When the Upper House met on January 24, 1934, the special committee gave an interim report.[28] In the words of Bishop Frere of Truro, the committee was at work to find its own orientation in the "jungle" of the initial report and to produce a simpler service which could be put into the hands of the patient. On the same day the Lower House met to consider its own Report 598, which was a shortened version of Report 593. But the thirty-five page Report was not the drastic revision that had been called for, the principal alteration being an abridged pastoral Introduction now summarized in nine points. Several members of the House of Clergy were now reconsidering the advisability of any official rites at all for unction and the laying on of hands.[29] A crucial question was the authority with which the services would be issued. Charles Harris tried to explain that the forms would have the authority of Convocation, a procedure not at variance with the Parliamentary Act of Uniformity, for he maintained that services for the coronation of a monarch and for the consecration of churches and graveyards were used without being included in the Book of Common Prayer. As the debate in the Lower House was never completed, Report 598 lapsed, being superseded by a joint report of both Houses, Report 602.

On June 6, 1934 the Upper House committee produced its long-awaited Report 601, a revision of the original Report 593. The committee was fortunate in having the expert assistance of Bishop W. H. Frere, whose "Act of Prayer and Blessing" from the Proposed 1927/28 Prayer Book was incorporated into the service as the form for the laying on of hands without unction. The Report also co-ordinated the services of healing more felicitously with the Order of Holy Communion and made numerous stylistic changes. Report 601 was embodied into Report 602 of a joint committee from both Houses.[30] A new version of Report 602, Report 602A with appendix, prepared once again by a joint committee, was the final form approved by the Upper and Lower House of Canterbury on June 6, 1935 for "provisional use in the Province subject to due diocesan sanction".[31]

(2) Administration of Holy Unction and the Laying on of Hands (Canterbury)

The Canterbury services for the *Administration of Holy Unction and the Laying on of Hands* is an eighteen page booklet which has compressed much of the material first presented in Report 593. The services contain the following elements:

(1) Epistle and Gospel.
(2) The Order of the Holy Communion.
(3) The Order for the Hallowing of the Oil.
(4) The Anointing and the Laying-on of Hands.
(5) An Act of Prayer and Blessing.
(6) Intercessions and Lessons.
(7) Counsel to the Priest.

(1) The Epistle (Jas. 5:14-16) and Gospel (Mt. 8:5-13) for the rite of anointing or for the celebration of holy communion have been placed first, on the assumption that the service in the church was the normal procedure and that a private service was an exception. Should the service not take place in church, the minister upon entering the presence of the sick person is instructed to say an opening greeting ("The Lord be with you"), Lord have mercy, Our Father, versicles and responses, and a collect derived from the Sarum and York Manuals:

> Regard, O Lord, we beseech thee, this thy servant in *his* affliction, and cherish this soul whom thou hast created; that *he,* being purified by *his* suffering, may be relieved by the medicine of thy grace; through Jesus Christ our Lord. *Amen.*[32]

(2) "The Order of the Holy Communion" contains a collect, two brief readings—Epistle (1 Jn. 5:11-12) and Gospel (Jn. 6:51)—which may be used for the private administration of holy communion in lieu of the Prayer Book service for Communion of the Sick. After the communion, the following prayer is said:

> O Almighty God, our merciful Father, we pray for thy servant that thou wilt grant *him* health, raise *him* up from *his* sickness, and impart to *him* perfect health of body and soul; for thou art the Saviour and Benefactor, the Lord, and King of all. *Amen.*

A rubric notes that the anointing and laying on of hands is to take place ordinarily after communion but before the final blessing.
(3) Two forms are given in "The Order for the Hallowing of the Oil", which may be performed by either a bishop or a priest when the oil has not previously been blessed. The first form is derived from the Sarum Pontifical:

> Grant, we beseech thee, almighty Father, eternal God, that by the operation of the Holy Ghost, the Comforter, this oil may avail for the healing of all infirmities. To all who receive it, and put their trust in thy mercy, may this anointing be a heavenly medicine, a spiritual remedy, an inward and abiding unction, unto the strengthening and healing of soul and mind and body, and the renewal of the indwelling of the Holy Ghost in thy living temple. Hear us, O Father, for the sake of thy Son Jesus Christ

our Lord, who liveth and reigneth with thee and the same Holy Ghost, ever one God, world without end. *Amen.*

The alternative form is adapted from the Nonjurors' Liturgy :

O Almighty Lord God, who hast taught us by thy holy Apostle St. James to anoint the sick with oil for the restoration of bodily and spiritual health : vouchsafe to bless and sanctify this oil; grant that those who are anointed therewith may, by thy life-giving Spirit, be delivered from all sickness, whether of mind or body, and from all the crafts and assaults of the enemy; through our Lord Jesus Christ, thy Son, who with thee and the Holy Ghost liveth and reigneth one God world without end. *Amen.*

(4) "The Anointing and the Laying on of Hands" commences with a reading of comfortable words from Mark 16 :17-18. The response is from James 5 :15 : "The prayer of faith shall save the sick, and the Lord shall raise him up". At this point in the service one or more of the lessons or intercessions appended to the order may be inserted. The anointing is preceded and followed by the laying on of hands. The first imposition of hands occurs as the minister says the popular healing prayer : "O Almighty God, who art the giver of all health etc.". The actual anointing is to take place according to the following rite :

The Bishop (or Priest), dipping the thumb of his right hand in the holy oil, shall anoint the sick person on the brow in the form of a cross, saying thus: N., in the Name of our Lord Jesus Christ, I anoint thee with this holy oil, that thou mayest receive the anointing of the Holy Spirit, unto the healing of all thy infirmities of soul, and mind, and body. Amen.[34]

Hands are once again laid upon the sick person after the anointing, according to a shortened derivation from the 1549 rite of anointing, or, if there is small hope of recovery, according to the following prayer :

May the almighty Father, who by the glorious Resurrection of his Son, Jesus Christ, hath opened the kingdom of heaven to all believers : Vouchsafe to anoint thee with his life-giving Spirit; and, if it be his will to call thee to himself, give thee triumph over sin and death, and bring thee to everlasting life; through the same Jesus Christ our Lord. Amen.

The benedictions are from the Prayer Book : "The Almighty Lord who is a most strong tower" (Visitation Office); "The peace of God, which passeth all understanding" (Holy Communion). A concluding rubric mentions that if the person be at the point of death, then, *"according to ancient tradition"*, holy communion should be administered after unction.

(5) "An Act of Prayer and Blessing", taken directly from the Visitation Order of the 1928 Proposed Prayer Book, provides for the laying on of hands without unction.

(6) The "Intercessions and Lessons" are a spiritual treasury to which the minister can refer either in the private preparation of the sick person or in the course of the service itself. There are four intercessions : three are for the sick; the fourth, apparently a modern creation, is for doctors and nurses :

O Merciful Father, who hast created man in thine own image, and bestowed on him a body meet to be the temple of the Holy Ghost : Sanctify, we pray thee, all those whom thou hast called to study and practise the art of healing; that they may use the talent thou hast given them, to the promotion of thy glory, the well-being of those to whom they minister, and their own eternal salvation in Jesus Christ the Healer and Saviour of us all. *Amen.*[35]

Of the original nine lessons submitted in Report 593, only four have survived : "Christ Healing the Multitudes" (Mt. 4 :23-24), "The Healing of the Leper" (Mt. 8 :2-4), "Christ committeth the Healing Ministry to His Apostles" (Mk. 7 :7, 12-13), and "The Command to Anoint" (Jas. 5 :14-15). Their format consists of the reading itself; a response or acclamation : "Lord, I believe; help thou mine unbelief"; an antiphon and psalm; and a concluding collect for the most part derived from earlier sources. The readings from Scripture may be suitably terminated with the following prayer from the York Manual :

May our Lord Jesus Christ be near thee to defend thee, within thee to refresh thee, around thee to preserve thee, before thee to guide thee, behind thee to justify thee, beneath thee to support thee, above thee to bless thee; who liveth and reigneth with the Father and the Holy Spirit, ever one God, world without end. *Amen.*[36]

(7) The "Counsel to the Priest" is all that remains from the

original controversial six page Introduction in Report 593. The priest is urged to prepare the sick person for unction by preliminary pastoral visits. While a single visit a day or two prior to the anointing may suffice for simple cases of physical illness, moral, spiritual and nervous ailments require several preliminary visits "in order to diagnose accurately the nature and cause of the malady, and to determine in detail the spiritual treatment needed". This preparatory treatment should also include an opportunity for a special confession of sins and priestly absolution, although this need not be done in a formal manner.

Special emphasis was given to the preparation on the day before the administration of unction :

> The priest should visit the sick person in the afternoon or evening, read over and comment on the form of service to be used next day, and finally bid him sleep with his mind full of confident hope that on the following day he will receive a great blessing from God.

Persons seriously ill may be anointed and communicated daily, or at least frequently. Even those *in extremis* may be anointed and communicated, and encouraged to hope for recovery. Special emergencies would of course dictate a less extensive preliminary preparation. The priest should in all cases seek to co-operate closely with the medical profession.

The Canterbury services for unction and the laying on of hands endorse the content, if not the complete procedure, of a pastoral ministry to the sick as set forth by Charles Harris in *Liturgy and Worship*. All the prayers refer to the recovery of health, although the exigencies of a dying Christian are also taken into account. The envisaged restoration to health, however, is not merely physical, but rather the health and recovery of the whole person, as seen in such phrases as "medicine of thy grace", "perfect health of body and soul", "release from every defilement and infirmity of flesh and spirit", and "medicine of heavenly grace".

The role of the Holy Spirit in the sick man's restoration to wholeness is especially prominent in the symbolic actions of anointing and the laying on of hands. The forms for the hallowing of oil speak of "the operation of the Holy Ghost, the Comforter", "the renewal of the indwelling of the Holy Ghost in thy living temple", the "life-giving Spirit". The form for anointing prays that the patient may "receive the anointing of the Holy Spirit, unto the healing of all thy infirmities of soul, and mind, and body". The prayers for the laying on of hands after unction petition that "thy soul may inwardly be anointed with the Holy Ghost", that the sick person be "aided by his (God's) Holy Spirit". The Canterbury services thus disclose a theology of healing which looks towards the restoration of the entire person—body, mind and spirit— effected through the indwelling power of the Holy Spirit conferred by the anointing with oil and the prayer of faith.

b. Province of York

Not only are the services for unction and the laying on of hands authorized by the Convocation of York simpler and shorter than those of Canterbury, but also the events leading to their promulgation were less involved.

(1) Background

The procedure in the Convocation of York was marked by little actual discussion and by a desire to co-operate closely with the committee of the Convocation of Canterbury. The process began on June 2, 1932, when the Lower House of York petitioned for a joint committee to draw up services for unction of the sick and for the laying on of hands without unction.[37] On January 19, 1933 the Upper House concurred with this proposal.[38]

The first of three committee reports, Report 406, was presented on January 25, 1934.[39] Although the response was not unfavourable, final action on the matter was postponed until the forms of service adopted by Canterbury could be incorporated into the next report. Report 413, containing the Canterbury forms, was discussed on June 7, 1934.[40] The Lower House then moved that the York committee should attempt to meet with the corresponding Canterbury committee with a view towards a common form of service for unction.

The final report of the York committee, Report 428, was presented on May 28, 1936.[41] In light of the more frequent administration of unction and the laying on of hands in a sick room rather than in a church, as well as the needs of the busy parish priest, the York committee recommended simpler forms of service than those of Canterbury, such as submitted in the original York Report 406. On the same day both the Upper and Lower Houses of the York Convocation agreed with this assessment and approved the services "for provisional use in the Province subject to due diocesan sanction".

(2) The Administration of Holy Unction and the Laying on of Hands (York)

The York services consist of two parts: "An Act of Prayer and Blessing", and "The Administration of Holy Unction". The first part, taken from the 1928 Proposed Prayer Book, provides for the laying-on of hands without unction.

The second part is adapted from the earlier Dearmer form for unction, with the following alterations:

(a) The lesson (Jas. 5:14-15), versicles and responses, and the concluding prayer "O Holy Father, physician of souls and bodies, etc." have been omitted. Also missing is the rubric relating to confession and absolution.

(b) The Nonjurors' prayer for the blessing of oil has been rephrased:

> O Almighty Lord God, who hast taught us, by thy holy apostle Saint James, to anoint the sick with oil, that they may regain their bodily health; look down, we beseech thee, and bless and sanctify this oil, that *he* who shall be anointed therewith may be delivered from all sickness and give thanks to thee for thy mercy; through thy Son our Lord Jesus Christ, who with thee and the Holy Ghost liveth and reigneth, one God, world without end. *Amen.*

(c) The rite for anointing is as follows:

> *And dipping the thumb of his right hand in the holy oil, he shall anoint the sick person on the brow in the form of a cross, and say:* N., in the faith of Jesus Christ I anoint thee in the name of the Father, and of the Son, and of the Holy Ghost. Amen.

(d) The Dearmer prayer for anointing from the 1549 Prayer Book, "As with this visible oil etc.", has been reworded and is to be used for the laying on of hands after unction.

(e) A concluding note suggests that when the service for unction is

(2) Lesson from James 5:13-16.

(3) A short confession with absolution, when necessary.

coupled with Holy Communion, the anointing is to take place before the blessing. In this case also, the blessing from the Holy Communion Service may be used, together with a special Epistle (1 Jn. 5 :11-12) and Gospel (Jn. 6 :51).

3. Other Services of Healing

Side by side the official services for unction and the laying on of hands authorized by the Convocations of Canterbury and York, there also exist services issued by the various guilds and fellowships of healing. Not only do these unofficial forms complement the official services, but they also complement one another, as each reveals the particular approach to healing as advocated by the respective association.

a. Guild of St. Raphael

The Guild of St. Raphael has services for both the laying on of hands and anointing of the sick.[42] The Catholic principles espoused by the Guild are reflected in the high liturgical quality of the services. Both forms of service rely heavily upon the Dearmer forms : in fact, the "Form for the Laying on of Hands" deviates only in the omission of the acclamation before the symbolic action.

"The Order for the Anointing of the Sick" contains the following components :

(1) Antiphon, "O Saviour of the world", and a choice of Ps. 23, 31 or 71.
(2) A short lesson from James 5 :14-15.
(3) Confession and absolution. The confession is adapted from the *Confiteor*, the absolution from the Roman *Indulgentiam*.
(4) Lord have mercy, Our Father, versicles and responses.
(5) The blessing of oil, derived from the Nonjurors' Liturgy.
(6) The laying of hands upon the sick person's head, together with the prayer : "O Almighty God, who art the giver of all health etc."
(7) The rite of anointing :

Then the Priest, dipping his thumb in the holy oil, shall anoint the sick person on the forehead, in the form of a Cross, saying, N., I anoint thee with holy oil in the Name of the Father, and of the Son, and of the Holy Ghost. Amen.

There follows the prayer for anointing from the 1549 Prayer Book, as modified by the Dearmer form; an acclamation of thanksgiving by the priest: "Let us give thanks to God for the gift which He has bestowed upon this His servant"; and a period of silence.

(8) The Lord's Prayer, and the following prayer addressed to the Saviour:

O Christ our Lord, Redeemer of the souls and bodies of men: Be pleased, we pray Thee, to perfect the work of Thy healing grace in this Thy servant: that *his* bodily strength being renewed, if so it seem good unto Thee, *he* may be strengthened with might ever more and more in the inner man, and may be fitted at last for that life wherein there shall be no more sickness nor pain: for Thy Name and mercy's sake grant this, O Lord, who, with the Father and the Holy Spirit, livest and reignest, God over all, blessed for evermore. *Amen.*

(9) The closing benedictions, from the Visitation Order of the Prayer Book, and a dismissal:

Thanks be to God who giveth us the victory through our Lord Jesus Christ.
V. Let us depart in peace.
R. In the Name of Christ. Amen.

b.   Guild of Health

The strong psychological bent of the Guild of Health is manifested in its forms for the laying on of hands and the unction of the sick.[43]

The laying on of hands may take place at home or in church: directions are therefore given for the procedure in either case. "The Laying on of Hands in the House" is clearly designed to encourage the patient to relax and to find faith and confidence in the presence of God. Periods of silence are interspersed with points of meditation on the Life of God, revealed in Jesus Christ and offered to man. The following prayer is said during the actual imposition of hands:

Our Lord Jesus Christ, Who gave power and authority to His disciples to lay hands on the sick that they might recover, have mercy upon you and strengthen you in soul and mind and body

—and by His Authority committed unto me I now lay my hands upon you that you may be made whole through the power and in the name of Jesus Christ of Nazareth. Amen.

"The Laying on of Hands in Church" foresees the administration of this rite to persons who have been carefully prepared. It is to take place at the communion rail after the offertory during the service of holy communion. The minister bids the congregation to pray for the sick, "that in our prayers for them we may enter into His intercession and His love and concern for the healing of the members of His own Body, that His Body may be made whole to His glory". After a period of silence, the laying on of hands is administered according to the same prayer as at the sick person's home, or according to the following alternative form :

May the Holy Spirit, Who is the giver of all life and healing fill your soul, your mind and your body with His healing life-giving power and make you whole—in the name of Jesus Christ of Nazareth. Amen.

The "Service of Anointing the Sick with Oil", to be applied before or after the reception of Holy Communion, follows the basic lines of the corresponding Dearmer form :

(1) Antiphon, "O Saviour of the world", and Ps. 23, recited antiphonally between minister and people.
(4) Lord have mercy, Our Father, and collect : "O Almighty God, who art the giver of all health and healing etc.".
(5) Silence.
(6) The anointing on the forehead of the sick person, as the minister prays :
(The Christian Name) . . . In faith in the power and will of our Lord Jesus Christ to heal and to make you whole, I anoint you with this Holy Oil in the Name of the Father and of the Son and of the Holy Ghost. Amen.
or :
We anoint thee with oil in the name of the Father and the Son and of the Holy Ghost. May the Holy Spirit work in thee the good purpose of His perfect will and make thee whole, through Jesus Christ our Lord. Amen.
If the oil is not already blessed by the bishop, a prayer of blessing, derived from the Roman *Emitte,* is also supplied.

(7) The laying on of hands upon the head of the patient, with a prayer adapted from the 1549 rite of anointing.

(8) Silent thanksgiving, versicles and responses from the psalms, and a collect :

> Father, we thank Thee, that Thou hast heard us : and we know that Thou hearest us always. Therefore we praise Thee for Thy great love to us and to all men, beseeching Thee to increase our faith in the power of Thy Son to work His perfect will in us to Thy great glory, through Jesus Christ Our Lord. Amen.

(9) The service closes with a benediction from the Visitation Office, and a dismissal which includes a word of encouragement from the minister :

> And now as you go from here remember often to thank God for what He has begun in you. Healing does not often come suddenly, though it does sometimes. Healing is a symptom; it expresses the deeper healing which God has begun in you now. This may take time and time is nothing to God. So be at peace, knowing that God helpeth His anointed.

c. Dorothy Kerin Home of Healing (laying on of hands)

The Dorothy Kerin Home of Healing provides an order of service for the laying on of hands upon the sick which is conducted in the Church of Christ the Healer at Burrswood, Kent. The service is an elaborate one, imbued with the Prayer Book tradition and the spirituality of the foundress, Dorothy Kerin (d.1963), who in her lifetime laid on hands, assisted by a priest.[44]

The "Order of Service" is as follows :

(1) An introduction consisting of a hymn selected ad libitum; the comfortable words : "God is our Hope and Strength; a very present help in trouble"; and the Sursum Corda.

(2) Thanksgivings and Intercessions. Thanksgiving is offered for the blessings received by the members of the Burrswood Fellowship, for those "who have felt His Healing Touch upon them", for those "released from their fears", and for all "who have been saved from despair and have been given new hope". The intercessions pray for the revival of the Church's ministry of healing, the wider diffusion of this ministry among priests and ministers, the life and work of the Fellowship, the faithful departed, patients at homes and hospitals, especially at Burrswood, doctors and nurses, all those who have asked for prayers and particularly for children (pause for

silent prayer), and for all present who are "about to seek the Living Touch of our Lord Jesus Christ". The Fellowship Prayer concludes these thanksgivings and petitions :

O God, who has prepared for them that love Thee
Such good things as pass man's understanding,
Pour into our hearts such love towards Thee
That we, loving Thee above all things,
May obtain thy Promises, which exceed all that we can desire,
Through Jesus Christ our Lord.

(3) A lesson from Scripture selected ad libitum.

(4) An anthem or recorded music, followed by a versicle and response ("O Saviour of the world") and Ps. 91.

(5) General confession and absolution, introduced by a Sentence of Scripture from Morning and Evening Prayer of the Prayer Book (1 Jn. 1 :8-9). After a period of silent prayer follows the confession of sins : taken either from Morning Prayer, "Almighty and most merciful Father etc.", or an adaptation of the *Confiteor*. The absolution is from the Communion Service : "Almighty God, our heavenly Father etc."

(6) A series of prayers : Lord have mercy, Lord's Prayer, versicles and responses from the Visitation Office, and a type of intercessory prayer which refers to the saintly foundress :

O God of the spirits of all flesh, we praise and magnify Thy Holy Name for all Thy servants who have finished their course in Thy faith and fear, especially Thy Servant, DOROTHY, and we beseech Thee that encouraged by their examples, strengthened by their fellowship, and aided by their prayers, we may at the last enter with them into the fulness of thine unending joy, through Jesus Christ our Lord. Amen.

(7) An acclamation, similar to the one found in the Dearmer form for the laying on of hands, to be said by a member of the congregation : "God give a blessing to this work, etc.".

(8) Hymn 153 in the English Hymnal : "Come, Holy Ghost" (*Veni Creator*).

(9) Prayers said by the priest preparatory to the laying on of hands, of which the central passage reads as follows :

And, now, O God, I give myself to Thee,
Empty me of all that is not of Thee;
Cleanse me from all unrighteousness,
And if it be Thy Will,
Take my hands and use them for Thy glory,
Be it unto us according to Thy Will. Amen.

(10) The laying on of hands. Placing his hands upon the sick person's head, the priest says:

> In the Name of God most High, and through His infinite love and power, may release from all sickness be given thee.
> In the Name of the Holy Spirit, may new life quicken thy mortal body, and mayest thou be made whole, and kept entire, to the glory of our Lord and Saviour Jesus Christ.

One of the practising physicians frequently assists the priest and also lays on hands as an expression of the medical profession's authority to heal.

(11) A hymn, ad libitum, followed by a collect: "Remember, O Lord, what Thou hast wrought in us, etc.".

(12) The concluding blessing, consisting of versicles and responses, to be sung alternatively between choir and congregation.

d. Divine Healing Mission

Every week at the Crowhurst Home of Healing the Divine Healing Mission conducts a service consisting of a liturgy of the Word, a liturgy of prayer with intercessions, and the laying on of hands. Only the form for the laying on of hands has been published:

> The Healing Mercies of the risen Lord, Jesus Christ, Who is present here, with us, now, enter into your soul, your mind, your body, and heal you from all that harms you, and give you His peace.[45]

The imposition of hands is also sometimes interposed between the Comfortable Words and the Prayer of Humble Access in the Communion Service. Holy unction is more frequently used as a culmination of one ministration which contains elements of deliverance (exorcism — absolution) and healing (laying on of hands (unction).

4. Summary and Outlook

The ministry of healing in the Church of England exhibits a variegated spectrum of services, both of official and grass roots origin. This phenomenon points to the organic development of liturgy within the life of the Church: a development which springs from the witness of the faithful and is confirmed by the authorities in the Church.

In all the services the symbolic actions of the laying on of hands and the anointing of the sick are encompassed by passages from Scripture, prayers for healing, and periods of meditative silence. The scriptural portions consist of psalms, and in the case of anointing, a reading of the pertinent passage from James 5.

The sources for the prayers are almost exclusively derived from earlier liturgical forms, either the Book of Common Prayer or ancient prayers. The Communion Service of the Prayer Book has contributed several prayers, as also Morning and Evening Prayer. But the Visitation Order itself has been the office most heavily drawn upon: the antiphon "O Saviour of the world"; the sequence of Lord have mercy, Lord's Prayer, versicles and responses; and the closing benedictions: "The Almighty Lord who is a most strong tower", "Unto God's gracious mercy and protection". The prayer for anointing from the 1549 Prayer Book has in various adaptations been used either for the anointing itself, or for the laying on of hands after the anointing. The Nonjurors' prayer for blessing the oil is likewise a recurring form.

The Canterbury services have made the greatest use of ancient precedent, with collects translated largely from the Sarum and York Manuals. The Greek rite of unction from the *Euchologion* is also represented. A Roman prayer for the sick which is found in every healing service is "O Almighty God, who art the giver of all health" (*Omnipotens sempiterne deus, salus æterna credentium*), a prayer employed earlier in the service of Touching for the King's Evil.

Is it possible to predict about the future development of the liturgical services of healing? The Archbishops' Commission reporting in 1958 on the Church's ministry of healing offered a suggested pattern of service for the laying on of hands and/or the anointing of the sick for use in the sick room, after the patient has been sufficiently prepared beforehand.[46]

(1) The priest upon entering the sick room is to say: "Peace be to this house. In the name of the Father, and of the Son and of the Holy Ghost".
(2) Antiphon: "O Saviour of the world", and a psalm.
(3) A short lesson.
(4) Confession, a brief period of silence, absolution.
(5) Lord have mercy, Our Father, versicles and responses from

the Visitation Office, "Lord I am not worthy that thou shouldest come under my roof, etc".

(6) The anointing or the laying on of hands. Suggested prayers for anointing are taken from the First Prayer Book of Edward VI : "The Almighty Lord, who is a most strong tower", "As with this visible oil". For both the laying on of hands or the anointing there are three alternatives : "O God of all grace and blessing, etc.". (Visitation Office); "In the name of God most high, etc.". (Dearmer forms); and a prayer :

> Our Lord Jesus Christ, who gave commandment to his Church to heal the sick, of his great mercy make thee whole : and by his authority committed unto me I (lay my hand on) (anoint) thee, that thou mayest be healed of thy infirmities, in the name of the Father, and of the Son and of the Holy Ghost.

On October 7, 1958 and January 13, 1959 both Houses of the Canterbury Convocation, in accepting and commending the Report of the Archbishops' Commission, requested the Archbishop to refer the 1935 Canterbury service of unction to the Liturgical Commission for possible revision.[47]

At the Lambeth Conference of 1958 the Committee Report on Prayer Book Revision also made some suggestions about the reform of the Visitation Office. The name of the order should be altered to the "Ministry to the Sick". The service should minister to the whole person : body, mind and soul. It should seek to strengthen the hope and faith of the sufferer, and to assist him in putting his affairs in order and finding peace with all men and Almighty God. The Committee felt that the following elements should be included in the "Ministry to the Sick" :

(i) Passages of Scripture for reading and meditation.
(ii) A form for the Laying-on of Hands.
(iii) A form for Anointing.
(iv) A form for the Communion of the Sick.
(v) A form for Confession and Absolution of the Sick.
(vi) A Commendation of the Dying.
(vii) Various prayers and short litanies appropriate to different types of suffering.[48]

On the basis of the Prayer Book (Alternative and Other Services) Measure of 1965, liturgical revision is once again in official progress within the Church of England : and there is hope that

the ministry of healing, together with the sacramental rites of
the laying on of hands and unction, will eventually find expression in the future revised Book of Common Prayer.[49]

B. SACRAMENTAL HEALING

We must now attempt to set out a statement on what is understood and practised in the Church of England as sacramental
healing. This is no easy task. Few official sources supply any
kind of extended consideration of unction and the laying on of
hands. Almost all the major commentaries on the Thirty-Nine
Articles, which treat unction in the discussion of the sacraments,
were written before the present revival of the ministry of healing.
In this century Anglican studies on the sacraments tend to con-
centrate on the sacramental principle, baptism and the eucharist;[50]
although there is a noticeable trend in recent years towards a
teaching of the other five sacraments not unlike that of the Roman
Catholic Communion.[51] The best sources for understanding the
theology and practice of sacramental healings are the healing
services themselves and the healing literature; but even the
advocates of the healing ministry often present such a variety of
approaches so as to make only the widest consensus possible.[52]
Furthermore, the healing movement could be strengthened by a
more substantial theological reflection.

With these preliminary observations in mind, the most commonly acceptable definition of sacramental healing is found in the
Revised Catechism :

> The sacramental ministry of healing is the ministry by which
> God's grace is given for the healing of spirit, mind and body,
> in response to faith and prayer, by the laying on of hands, or
> by anointing with oil.[53]

Some of the authors have briefly noted the sacramental or incar-
national implications of all healing, insofar as the ministry of
healing presses towards visible expression in either the laying
on of hands or unction.[54] By "sacramental" the Lambeth Report
of 1924 understood that "a blessing is sought and received through
the performance of outward and visible actions".[55] The healing
envisaged by the sacramental rites is nowadays generally considered to extend to the whole person : body, mind and spirit. In
fact, where the spiritual dimension of man has been insufficiently

respected, no genuine healing can result : the healing of the spirit is primary.[56]

What is the distinction between unction and the laying on of hands? While some authors recognize no distinction in efficacy between the two rites,[57] most consider unction to be more definitely sacramental.[58] The heightened sacramentality of unction is indicated in both the minister and the recipient. The minister of unction is an ordained priest or bishop; virtually no one suggests that a layman should anoint the sick. The laying on of hands, however, may be performed by either a layman or a priest. In the former case the imposition of hands would be a charismatic ministration, executed by one endowed with the gift of healing; whereas in the latter instance, it would be a sacramental or ministerial act, although the priest may also possess a special gift.[59] As regards the recipient, unction is restricted to a baptized member of the Church, understanding and using the sacramental life. Unction is also usually considered a more potent ministration to be used more sparingly than the laying on of hands.

1. The Laying on of Hands

In the liturgical tradition of the Church of England the laying on of hands is witnessed in the Prayer Book rite of Confirmation, in the Ordinal, and in the earlier ceremony of Touching for the King's Evil. Supported by ancient precedent, it has reappeared in this century as a sacramental act of the ministry of healing to be performed by a priest.

Upon closer scrutiny, the term "sacramental" can be variously interpreted. Charles Harris considers the imposition of hands primarily as a blessing conveying peace and confidence to the sick person, an opinion in practice borne out by "An Act of Prayer and Blessing" from the Visitation Order of the 1928 Proposed Prayer Book, which is also reprinted in the Canterbury and York services.[60] J. Wilson, on the other hand, regards the laying on of hands a sacrament, and applies to the rite the traditional Anglican definition from the Catechism.[61]

The manner of ministration may be either formal, according to one of the liturgical services, or informal, in the course of a pastoral visitation. In either case the minister is advised to lay both hands firmly upon the head of the sick person while saying the corresponding prayer. When performed in a more formal manner, a small group of intercessors should be on hand to show the corporate concern of the Church for her ailing members and to prevent the sacramental act from becoming too "person-centred".[62] The acclamation by one of the faithful provided for in the Dearmer forms and in the Dorothy Kerin service is one such gesture of corporate concern.

As the laying on of hands is the sacramental rite which lends itself to a congregational setting more than unction, the question of private or public healing services may best be considered at this point. A private healing service is generally deemed to be one conducted in the parish church from time to time in the presence of the priest, the sick person or persons, and a small number of friends and relatives. The patient is known to the priest and has been prepared in advance for the service. A public healing service is one to which sick people are invited indiscriminately, often through advertisements in church bulletins, with little or no previous preparation.

The healing literature in general, and the Archbishops' Report of 1958 in particular, is severely critical of public healing services.[63] Not only are public healing services without any primitive precedent in the tradition of the Church's ministry to the sick, but they are also open to a number of dangers. These dangers include a false emphasis in worship which seeks first of all to receive, rather than to submit and offer; and a lack of sufficient preparation of the sufferer which often leads to unjustifiable claims of healing, a failure to recognize the highly emotional component of psychogenic cases, and a disappointment approaching despair when the expected cure has not been forthcoming.

In an effort to obviate the innate perils of public healing services, the Archbishops' Report made the following recommendations :

(1) The Church's ministry of healing should closely coincide with its regular worship and pastoral care. The parish priest, upon whom the ministry to the sick devolves as part of his pastoral office, bears the prime responsibility for the healing services, as well as for the preparation and subsequent care of the participants.

(2) When at all possible, the sacramental rites should be administered within the context of Holy Communion, so as to relate the ministry of healing to Christ's saving work and to the strength communicated to the members of his Body in the sacrament. The objectivity of eucharistic worship may at the same time prove a wholesome corrective to possible subjective and emotional excesses.

(3) Only those sick persons known to the conductor of the healing services and prepared in advance should be ministered to publicly.

(4) Clergy should endeavour to obtain the advice and cooperation of those members of the medical profession who attend to their parishioners, especially in the case of emotional and psychological disorders.

(5) The publicity and advertisement given to healing services should be prudent and restricted.

(6) Any minister of a church not in communion with the Church of England or a layman ministering at a healing service should first secure the permission of the bishop of the diocese.

(7) A panel of priests and doctors to advise the clergy on the conduct of the healing services should be established under the authority of the bishops.

2. Holy Unction

Unction of the sick, included in the Visitation Office of the First Book of Common Prayer of 1549, was expunged in the 1552 revision and never restored. The twenty-fifth of the Thirty-Nine Articles of Religion refers to unction as one of the "five commonly called Sacraments", and rejects the medieval extreme unction as a "corrupt following of the Apostles".[64] Now that the Convocation of Canterbury (1935) and York (1936) have officially approved services for unction, the Church of England has restored what must be considered one of the lesser sacraments.

On one point, however, the healing literature is unanimous : no Anglican should consider unction to be extreme unction or a sacrament exclusively orientated towards the dying. The recovery of unction in the Church of England is a return to primitive usage : a rite of healing for Christians who are seriously ill. The Report on Doctrine in the Church of England defines unction as

an outward and visible rite, having a background both in the New Testament and in Church tradition, which, expressing the Church's pastoral care for the sick and dying, is, in the context of faith and of the Church's ministration, a symbol of the grace of God for the strengthening of the body and soul in their weakness.[65]

In its treatment of the sacraments, the Church Catechism speaks

of "an outward and visible sign of an inward and spiritual grace".
One may apply, as some writers have done, this schema to unction
of the sick.[66]

a.   Outward visible sign

The outward visible sign of unction is the anointing of the sick
person on the forehead with oil in the sign of the cross, together
with the prayer of faith and healing.

In the development leading to the restoration of unction, the oil
of anointing has been a controversial subject. The controversy stems
from two factors : what is the meaning of the blessed oil; and by
whom should the oil be blessed, by the bishop or by the priest?
The debates on unction of the Canterbury and York Convocations reveal an abhorrence of any insinuation that the oil, when
blessed, assumed a special physical property rendering it more
effective.[67] The emphasis was laid not so much on the hallowing of
oil, which was a matter of religious propriety, as on its use as a
suggestive medium influencing both body and soul, an outward
way of expressing the love and blessing of God. In an effort to
allay any misunderstanding, J. R. Pridie and Purcell Fox draw an
analogy between the blessing of the oil of the sick for unction and
the blessing of the water before Baptism.[68]

As regards the second question, who is to bless the oil, all of the
healing services for unction allow for the hallowing of oil by either
the bishop or a priest.[69] Charles Harris recommends that priests
ordinarily use oil supplied by their bishops out of respect for the
bishop's office as "the chief minister of the sacrament", and in view
of the psychological consideration that oil with an episcopal blessing would have more prestige in the eyes of the faithful.[70] Most
bishops in the Church of England today consecrate oil every
Maundy Thursday for the use of their diocesan clergy in ministering to the sick.[71]

b.   Inward spiritual grace

Purcell Fox calls unction a "covenanted 'means of grace' ".[72]
Charles Harris considers it "a sacrament conveying sanctifying
grace to the soul of the worthy recipient".[73] Marjory Wight defines
the essence of any sacrament, including unction, as "God's gift to
us of His own life".[74] But what is the specific effect of the inward
spiritual grace of unction? What is the sacramental grace? The

key to understanding the special grace of unction is found in the symbolic meaning of anointing itself. Just as the other anointings —of kings, prophets and priests—all have a consecratory signifcance in tradition, so the unction of the sick is a re-hallowing or re-dedication to God of a Christian who has been afflicted by disease or illness.[75] And further, as the prayer of anointing from the 1549 Prayer Book indicates, a form adopted with variations for all of the healing services for unction, the outward anointing with oil symbolizes an inward anointing of the soul by the Holy Spirit. This intensification of the indwelling of the Holy Spirit in the soul of the sick person affects the whole man : body, mind and spirit.[76] This inward anointing is a strengthening against the evils often oppressing the body, mind and spirit of the sick person in his illness; viz. strain and fatigue of mind, tribulation of spirit.[77] Unction is the sacrament whereby the Holy Spirit is conferred for the restoration to wholeness of body, mind and spirit.[78] The results which may therefore be expected from unction include three possibilities : immediate or gradual recovery of health, a happy and peaceful death, or a non-physical healing by which the patient is invited to share more deeply in the sufferings of the cross of Christ.[79]

3. Minister

What sanction is there for a priest to lay on hands and to anoint the sick? Evidence for a ministry of healing inherent in the Church and exercized by those in ministerial office is found in the New Testament and in the Book of Common Prayer.

In the New Testament Christ sent forth his apostles to preach the kingdom and to heal the sick (Mk. 6 : 7ff; Lk. 10 : 1ff).[80] Jesus' usual method of healing was the laying on of hands, a gesture in turn adopted by his disciples.[81] The Apostle James prescribes the anointing with oil by the presbyters with the prayer of faith as a means of healing (Jas. 5 : 14-15), a passage reproduced in all the healing forms but the York service for unction.

The Prayer Book rite for the consecration of a bishop contains the charge : "Hold up the weak, *heal the sick*, bind up the broken, bring again the out-casts, seek the lost". At his ordination the priest is urged to be a "faithful Dispenser of the Word of God and of his holy Sacraments". In the formula for administering Holy Communion, the Body and Blood of Jesus Christ is given to "preserve thy body and soul unto everlasting life".

As early as 1920 a Lambeth Conference Committee Report recommended that candidates for Holy Orders receive a suitable training in the principles and methods of the ministry of healing.[82] Today the Hospital Chaplaincies Council offers a programme of training courses for clergy and theological students who will be undertaking chaplaincy duties on either a full- or part-time basis.

4. Recipient

Both the laying on of hands and unction are sacramental expressions of the Church's ministry of healing to the sick. While the laying on of hands may be the more frequent ministration, unction of the sick is a sacrament generally reserved for one who is seriously ill, but by no means necessarily dying. Not only adults, but also children may be anointed. The illness need not be solely physical, but may also have a mental or moral origin. Charles Harris advocates the use of unction for the treatment of insanity and neurosis, and even in sexual cases such as sterility, impotence and frigidity.[82] Henry Cooper of the Guild of St. Raphael, however, wisely cautions that the sacrament should not be cheapened by indiscriminate administration and should be restricted to crisis situations in a patient's deteriorating condition or to a single application during a serious illness.[84]

a. Preparation

A constant theme in the healing literature has been the need for a thoroughgoing preparation of the sick person before the use of the sacramental rites.[85] This preparation may begin with pastoral visits some days previous to the actual ministration. Especially where moral or psychological disorders exist, the priest, in co-operation with the medical doctor, should endeavour to reach the deeper-lying causes of evil. The Visitation Order of the 1928 Proposed Prayer Book, the Canterbury services, the Archbishops' Report and *The Priest's Vade Mecum* each contain scriptural lessons and prayers which may be used to prepare the patient. The three qualifications for the fruitful reception of the sacramental rites, especially in the case of unction, are faith, repentance and charity.[86]

The desired response of faith is an attitude of complete trust and confidence in a loving God, a conformity to the will of God regardless of the outcome of the sickness. It should be an active faith whereby the recipient deepens the fellowship he shares with God through Jesus Christ. By this faith the sick person is brought to realize that "nothing can separate him from the love of God, in whose mighty power all evil is transfigured through the victory of the Cross".[87] In the motivation of the recipient's faith the friends, relatives and members of the parish congregation through their intercessory prayer play an important role. It is this "corporate, vicarious faith of the Church" which is particularly invoked in situations where the sick person has lapsed into unconsciousness.[88] Doctors, nurses and all associated with the care of the patient may also be invited to participate in the healing service.

The necessary repentance prior to unction would seem to imply confession and absolution—auricular or general—which is provided for in most of the healing services. This reconciliation is necessary for two reasons : theologically, as the sins of the sick man may be objectively grave; psychologically, for his troubled conscience may need to be assuaged.[89] Penance, not unction, is the sacrament instituted for the remission of post-baptismal sins.[90] The remission of sins can be considered only a secondary and indirect result of unction, affecting the secondary consequences of sin which remain after the theological guilt has been pardoned in the sacrament of penance. These relics of sin which remain after the forgiveness of penance consist of spiritual weaknesses such as anxiety and tension, bad habits and evil tendencies. Through unction the sick person experiences something different from the pardon of sins; namely, an *"inward liberation from the power of evil"*.[91] To quote Charles Harris, "the specific effect of unction is not to pardon sin, but to destroy it at its root, by healing the morbid condition of the soul from which it springs—in short, Unction is rather a *remedial* than an absolving rite". To this end both the Canterbury and York services have a prayer for the laying on of hands after unction which contains the petition : "May he pardon thee all thy sins and offences . . ."

The charity required of the sick person for the fruitful reception of unction strives to break through the selfish confines of an excessive preoccupation with self in order to open out to those who care for him and to engender a concern for other sufferers. On the highest level, the patient can see himself as one with the Lord, crucified with Jesus, "making up what is lacking in his sufferings *for his Body's sake, which is the Church"*.[92]

b. Actual Administration of Unction

The actual ministration of unction provided for in the healing services is simple : a single anointing with oil on the forehead in the sign of the cross, together with the form or prayer of anointing. The oil should be pure olive oil, contained in a decent vessel, and previously blessed by either the bishop of the diocese or the officiating priest within the healing service itself. After the anointing, the oil is removed from the sick person's forehead with a piece of fabric or wool which is later burnt.

The anointing may take place in church, or more likely, at the hospital or in a sick room. In either case unction is preferably celebrated within the framework of holy communion. The Lambeth Report of 1924 recommends the ancient sequence of reconciliation, anointing, communion. For psychological reasons Charles Harris suggests that unction should be administered after communion as the climax of the service, since unction is "more definitely and exclusively" a sacrament of healing than the eucharist. An exception to this rule would be when the patient is at the point of death, in which case it would be more appropriate to administer holy communion last of all as viaticum. The Canterbury and York services follow Harris : unction is to be applied after holy communion and before the final blessing.

c. Subsequent Pastoral Care

The subsequent pastoral care may be considered as important as the preparation for unction.[93] The recipient of unction will often immediately experience a period of peace and tranquillity, although such a feeling is not indispensable. The priest should visit the patient the next day, or shortly thereafter, to offer thanksgiving with him. Through Scripture reading, instruction and prayer the sick man should be encouraged to live his life more effectively in the service of God and the Church. To this end, the anointed Christian can perform acts of charity, such as praying for others. The treasures of the sacramental life should continue to be made available : frequent holy communion, the laying on of hands. Charles Harris and the Canterbury services recommend the frequent repetition of unction within the same illness until recovery or death occur. Some writers, in view of St. Paul's threefold entreaty that the thorn in the flesh be removed (2 Cor. 12 :7-9), maintain that unction be administered no more than three times during the same illness.[94] No hard and fast rule exists : the repetition of unction is a matter of pastoral prudence.

CHAPTER V

CONCLUSION

It remains to evaluate the results of this study and to examine the ecumenical possibilities which present themselves on the basis of recent developments in the Roman Catholic theology and liturgy of the sacrament of anointing of the sick.

A. THE MINISTRY OF HEALING IN THE CHURCH OF ENGLAND

1. *Anglican Healing in General*

The emergence of the ministry of healing in this century represents the recovery of a Gospel insight and primitive practice that the Church has indeed a ministry to her sick members qua sick. The ministry of healing is not the exclusive concern of sects such as Pentecostalism, Spiritualism and Christian Science, but is an integral part of the mission committed to the Church by her founder : to preach the Kingdom and to heal the sick. The scriptural conception of man and modern psychology both demonstrate that in illness and disease it is the whole man who is sick; the whole man—body, mind and spirit—must be ministered to. The desired goal of this ministry is a wholeness or healing of body, mind and spirit, which, however, can only find relative fulfilment in this life. Healing is a sign of the Kingdom of God already inaugurated, but the Kingdom will be fully revealed only when Christ comes again at the end of time.

The healing ministry is also an ecumenical endeavour. Associations such as the Churches' Council for Health and Healing, the Guild of Health and the Divine Healing Mission consist of both Anglican and Free Church members. In recent years there has also been increasing contact with Roman Catholic clergy. One could say that a healing Church goes a long way towards becoming a healed Church.

Finally, the healing ministry in the Church of England has earnestly sought out the co-operation of the medical profession, thus striving to effect a rapprochement between the Church and modern medicine.

But the shortcomings of this ministry should not be overlooked. The subject of healing is a topic which easily lends itself to extremism, cultism. There exists a subtle danger of distorting the ministry of healing out of context, so as to make of Christianity a therapeutic means for the restoration of health. The ministry of healing, therefore, and ultimately the Church, could profit from more effective episcopal leadership, guidance and encouragement. The healing ministry would also do well to attract the interest of theologians who could provide a firmer biblical foundation and examine questions as yet unanswered such as the relationship of sickness to the original fall of man and the inherent connection between sickness and death. The paschal mystery of the passion, death and resurrection of Jesus Christ and the participation therein of every Christian is another central truth which deserves a fuller consideration.

2. *Liturgical—Sacramental*

It would seem that sacramental healing is the soundest and most enduring achievement of the Anglican healing ministry.

The rites for the laying on of hands and anointing of the sick are the liturgical expressions of a diversified ministry of healing. The sacrament of unction signifies the inward unction by the Holy Spirit of the entire personality. The recipient of both the laying on of hands and unction is a sick person, who may be either physically or mentally ill. The use of unction is a return to the primitive meaning of the sacrament as a rite of healing for sick Christians. The danger of death need not necessarily be present, and the anointing may be repeated.

In addition, the practice of sacramental healing is marked by the following pastoral characteristics :

(a) A genuine personal concern in the preparation, sacramental administration and subsequent pastoral care of the sick. To quote the Report of the Archbishops' Commission : "Each patient must be dealt with individually".[1]

(b) A flexibility and variety manifested in the choice and manner of ministration. The choice of ministration may be either the laying on of hands or unction or both. The manner of ministration may be either informal or formal, according to one of the official (Canterbury and York) or "unofficial" liturgical services.

(c) The involvement of the local Church, supporting the sick person by its faith and prayers of intercession.

B. ECUMENICAL POSSIBILITIES

The Eastern Orthodox and the Roman Catholic Churches are the other Christian confessions which regularly practise the anointing of the sick. Roman Catholics have thus far taken little notice of the revival of the ministry of healing in the Church of England.[2] Reciprocally, Anglican writers, while adamant in deploring the practice of extreme unction as a sacrament of the dying, do admire the selection of prayers and readings in the Roman Ritual for ministering to the sick.[3] But already twenty-five years ago one theologian, T. W. Crafer, commenting on a conference held at Vanves, France, in April, 1948, on *La Liturgie des Malades,* drew attention to the fact that a development in the theology of unction was in progress in the Roman Church :

> It is not known to all that a desire for a return to the earlier use of Unction for the healing of the sick is taking place within the Roman Communion, which is following in the wake of the Anglican Communion in this revival, in the same way as in the encouragement of frequency of Communion.

What is this newer development in Roman Catholic circles on the theology of unction? Until a few years ago the prevailing theology of unction was that of an anointing unto glory which remitted all the temporal punishment due to sin, so that the dying Christian would be immediately received into heaven. This opinion, based on the practice of unction as a preparation for death, was first formulated by the Scholastics and revived in 1907 in the learned treatise of J. Kern.[5]

More recently, however, there has been a growing consensus of theologians who from scriptural, liturgical and pastoral considerations challenge the very premise upon which Kern's thesis stands; viz., that unction is a sacrament of the dying. This school can claim the support of most exegetes, who recognize that the beneficiary of the anointing in James 5 :14-15 is a sick, not a dying, Christian. It can point to the tradition of the first 800 years of the Church until the Carolingian reform, of which many liturgical traces remain in the prayer for the consecration of oil in the Roman

Pontifical and the prayers for recovery in the *Ordo ministrandi Sacramentum Extremæ Unctionis* of the Roman Ritual. Unction is a sacrament of the sick; the sacrament of the dying is viaticum.[6]

This newer theology of unction steers a middle course between the Scylla of a one-sided emphasis on bodily healing possibly exaggerated in earlier times prior to the systematization of sacramental theology, and the Charybdis of an excessive spiritualization of the sacrament as has been the case at least since the Schoolmen. The grace of the sacrament effects the sick person as a whole : a strengthening of the whole man to live intensely the supernatural life, notwithstanding the special difficulty of sickness. The restoration effected by the anointing has repercussions on the whole man throughout his faculties, both spiritual and corporeal. The sacramental grace is thus an aid to the recovery of the integrity and harmony of the entire human person; it may sometimes result in the complete restoration to health.

As is readily apparent, the newer Roman Catholic orientation on unction runs parallel to the sacramental theology of the Anglican healing movement. But is it at conflict with the defined teaching of the Roman Church on unction as set forth at the Council of Trent (1551)? Upon closer examination it is clear that the Council of Trent was primarily concerned with refuting the attacks of the Reformers regarding unction. Many questions pertaining to anointing were deliberately left open, as may be seen in the following observations.

The Council of Trent deliberately did not define unction as a sacrament to be restricted exclusively to the dying. The final draft, substituting the word "especially" (*praesertim*) for "only if" (*dumtaxat*) was considerably more positive than the original schema :

> The Synod declares, moreover, that this anointing is to be used for the sick, but especially for those who are so dangerously ill as to appear at the point of departing this life; hence, it is also called a sacrament of the departing.[7]

What is defined is that unction is a sacrament for Christians who are seriously ill. The time of application as stipulated in the Code of Canon Law, whereby the sick person must be in danger of death from sickness or old age, would seem to be a matter of Church discipline and not dogma.[8] If anything, papal documents of this century have encouraged an earlier rather than later administration of unction, as soon as there be "a prudent or probable judge-ment of danger".[9]

Trent also refrained from defining the primary effect of unction. The Council stressed most of all the grace of the Holy Spirit: the outward anointing with oil was understood to symbolize the inward anointing by the Holy Spirit. Following the James' passage, the grace or reality (res) of the sacrament includes not only spiritual results, but psychological and physical ones as well:

> To continue, the reality and effect of this sacrament is explained in these words: "And the prayer of faith will save the sick man, and the Lord will raise him up; and if he be in sins, they will be forgiven him" (Jas. 5:15). For this reality is the grace of the Holy Spirit, whose anointing wipes away sins, provided there are still some to be expiated, as well as the remnants of sin, and comforts and strengthens the soul of the sick person, by arousing in him great confidence in the divine mercy; encouraged there-by, the sick person bears more easily the difficulties and trials of his illness, and resists more readily the temptations of the demon who *lies in wait for the heel* (Gen. 3:15), and, where it is expedient for the health of the soul, he receives, at times, health of body.[10]

These expected results of unction listed by the Council point to the strengthening of the entire human person in time of sickness.

The discreet approach of the Council of Trent and the newer theology of unction as a sacrament of the sick prepared the way for a breakthrough in the Church's teaching and practice of unction at the Second Vatican Council (1963). Three of the articles in the Constitution on the Sacred Liturgy (*Sacrosanctum Concilium*) dealt with the anointing of the sick. Although not defined doctrine, the documents of Vatican II represent the highest teaching authority of the Church, that of an ecumenical Council.

Art. 73 discussed the nature of unction, its name and the proper time of ministration:

> "Extreme unction", which may also and more fittingly be called "anointing of the sick", is not a sacrament for those only who are at the point of death. Hence, as soon as any one of the faith-ful begins to be in danger of death from sickness or old age, the fitting time for him to receive this sacrament has certainly already arrived.[11]

The substance of unction as a sacrament of the sick has always been preserved in the Roman Church : the sacrament has always been denied to those in danger of death from some cause other than sickness or old age; e.g. prisoners facing execution, soldiers going forth to battle. But ever since anointing became associated with the practice of death-bed penance in the ninth century, the Church, itself the primordial sacrament, in her economy of the dispensation of the sacraments had restricted unction to those sick persons in danger of death. The Council Fathers, wishing to obviate the pastoral abuse which often resulted from delaying the sacrament, cautiously discouraged the ambiguity of the term "extreme unction" and deemed "anointing of the sick" a better name. The time of ministration was not in extreme danger of death (*articulum mortis*), but rather at the beginning of the danger of death in sickness or old age.

Art. 74 restored the ancient sequence of reconciliation, anointing and viaticum :

> In addition to the separate rites for anointing of the sick and for Viaticum, a continuous rite shall be prepared according to which the sick man is anointed after he has made his confession and before he receives Viaticum.[12]

All sacraments are ordered ultimately to the eucharist. The use of the term viaticum indicates that the Council Fathers were here concerned with the sacramental ministration to one who is actually dying. The position of viaticum ("food for the journey"), and not unction, as a sacrament of the dying was thus put into greater prominence. Art. 75 contained some recommendations for revising the rite of anointing :

> The number of the anointings is to be adapted to the occasion, and the prayers which belong to the rite of anointing are to be revised so as to correspond with the varying conditions of the sick who receive the sacrament.

In November 1969 the Congregation for Divine Worship considered the initial draft for the revision of the rites for the sick. During the period of further deliberation and refinement, permission was extended to local churches to experiment with these provisional rites. This experimentation met with great success, notably at Lourdes in France where anointing is administered in a communal celebration, and in several English speaking dioceses, which have used a translation prepared in 1971 by the International Committee on English in the Liturgy (ICEL).[13] The Latin text of the finalized version, together with the Apostolic Letter of Pope Paul VI on the Sacrament of Anointing, was published by decree of the Congregation for Divine Worship, dated December 7, 1972. This model ritual for the universal Latin Church has now been translated into the vernacular and adapted to local needs by the national episcopal conferences, and was officially implemented on January 1, 1974.

The most important single change is stated in the Apostolic Constitution, where Paul VI uses his apostolic authority to determine the essential rite of the sacrament, the liturgical action and prayer (matter and form).

> The sacrament of the anointing of the sick is administered to those who are dangerously ill, by anointing them on the forehead and hands with properly blessed olive oil or, if opportune, with another vegetable oil and saying once only the following words:
> "Through this holy anointing and his great love for you, may the Lord help you by the power of his Holy Spirit. Amen. May the Lord who freed you from sin heal you and extend his saving grace to you. Amen". (*Per istam sanctam unctionem et suam piissimam misericordiam adiuvet te Dominus gratia Spiritus Sancti, ut a peccatis liberatum te salvet atque propitius allevet.*)

The revised prayer of anointing thus contains a fuller theology of the sacrament than was expressed in the previous form for anointing, which stressed solely the penitential aspect of the rite. The grace of this as in all sacraments is the action of the Holy Spirit which benefits the whole person, body and soul (freedom from sin, healing, saving grace). The previous rite specified the anointing of the five senses, a remnant of the medieval penitential understanding of the sacrament, with a single anointing sufficient in case of necessity. The revised rite normally includes only two anointings, on the forehead and hands, to be accompanied by the sacramental form. Particular rituals may retain or introduce more or different applications of oil, as well as the kind of oil employed, provided it be of vegetable origin. The change in the sacramental form and matter thereby results in a prayer which expresses a richer meaning of the sacrament that brings the grace of salvation, comfort and consolation to the sick and in an action whereby the healing properties of the oil of the sick may be more properly released.

The title — "Anointing and Pastoral Care of the Sick" (*Ordo Unctionis Infirmorum eorumque Pastoralis Curae*) — and the order of chapters also emphasize anointing as a sacrament of the sick. The emphasis is on the normal ministry to the sick, beginning with the excellent pastoral theological introductory notes (*Prænotanda*), the Visitation and Communion of the Sick (Ch. I) and the Rite of Anointing (Ch. II). The later chapters treat of more urgent cases when the sick Christian may actually be dying : Viaticum (Ch. III), the Rite for Administering the Sacraments to Those Near Death (Ch. IV), Confirmation in Danger of Death (Ch. V), and the Rite for Commendation of the Dying (Ch. VI). Chapter VII contains a rich assortment of optional texts and readings. A major breakthrough has been the fortunate omission of the danger of death as a condition for the reception of anointing. In accordance with the teaching of St. James, Christians seriously ill (*periculose aegrotant*) from sickness or old age are the proper recipients. A prudent or probable judgement regarding the seriousness of the illness suffices; scrupulosity should be avoided.

The "Offices and Ministries for the Sick" call for a total community involvement. All men and women, even non-Christian doctors and nurses, all baptized Christians, the local community with its priests, and the family and friends of the sick, share in Christ's healing ministry as it is continued in His Body, the Church. No fixed ritual for visiting the sick is prescribed; rather all Christians are urged to share their faith by strengthening and praying with the sick. Priests, who are to be especially assiduous in this regard, are called upon to lay on hands when visiting the sick as well as during the course of the anointing ceremony. The preparation and subsequent pastoral care of the sick person and his family are essential if this sacrament is to be the "prayer of faith" suggested by James.

One of the most significant changes of the revised rite is the encouragement given to communal celebrations of anointing—the anointing of several sick persons within the same ceremony—which may even take place in church. The anointing may be celebrated within mass after the liturgy of the Word, or with a communion service. Directions are also provided for the celebration of anointing with a large congregation and for some measure of concelebration. In all cases except absolute necessity, the sacrament is to be administered within a more proper liturgical service which presumes the presence of at least the family and friends of the sick.

The revised Roman Catholic *Rite of Anointing and the Pastoral Care of the Sick* is thus one of the most radical of the post-Conciliar liturgical revisions, comparable to the revised rite of infant baptism. In order to be fully implemented it will require a massive catechesis, perhaps similar to the encouragement Pius X gave to frequent communion at the beginning of this century.

In conclusion, the Church of England has come to the sacramental rites of the laying on of hands and unction as liturgical expressions of an overall ministry to the sick. Hopefully the renewed awareness of the substance of unction as a sacrament of the sick with its revised liturgy may lead to the development of a similar ministry of healing in the Roman Catholic Church. And maybe the day will come when both the Roman and Anglican Communions will be working closely together in ministering to the needs of the sick.

BIBLIOGRAPHY

(Unless otherwise stated, books and pamphlets are published in London.)

1. Source Works

Anglican Liturgies of the Seventeenth and Eighteenth Centuries, ed. W. J. Grisbrooke. Alcuin Club Collections No. 40, 1958.

Archbishops' Report, 1958: The Church's Ministry of Healing. Report of the Archbishops' Commission. (Church Information Office), 1958.

The Book of Common Prayer with the Additions and Deviations Proposed in 1928. Oxford edition.

Canterbury Services: Administration of Holy Unction and the Laying on of Hands. 1935.

A Communion Office Taken Partly from Primitive Liturgies, And Partly from the First English Reformed Common-Prayer-Book: together with Offices for Confirmation and the Visitation of the Sick. 1718. Reprinted in Peter Hall, ed., *Fragmenta Liturgica. V. Nonjurors' and Scottish Offices.* Bath, 1848.

A Compleat Collection of Devotions: taken from the Apostolical Constitutions, the Ancient Liturgies, and the Common Prayer Book of the Church of England. Part I. Comprehending the Publick Offices of the Church. 1734. Reprinted in Peter Hall, ed., *Fragmenta Liturgica. VI. Deacon's Devotions.* Bath, 1848.

Dorothy Kerin Service: Church of Christ the Healer. Order of Service for the Laying on of Hands of the Sick. Burrswood, Kent (Dorothy Kerin Home of Healing).

The English Rite, ed. F. E. Brightman. 2 vols., 1915.

Euchologion sive Rituale Graecorum, ed. Jacobus Goar. 2nd ed., Venice, 1730.

Formularies of Faith put forth by authority during the reign of Henry VIII, ed. Charles Lloyd. 2nd ed., Oxford, 1856.

"The Green Book": A Suggested Prayer Book: being the text of the English rite, altered and enlarged in accordance with the

Prayer Book Revision proposals made by the English Church Union. Oxford, 1923.

"The Grey Book": A New Prayer Book. Proposals for the Revision of the Book of Common Prayer and for additional services and prayers, drawn up by a Group of Clergy. 1923.

Guild of Health Forms: Forms for the Laying on of Hands, Anointing with Oil, Exorcism of Evil Spirits, Confession and Absolution. rev. ed. (Guild of Health), 1961.

Guilds and Fellowships of Healing. (Churches' Council of Healing), 1967.

Lambeth Conference 1908: Conference of Bishops of the Anglican Communion Holden at Lambeth Palace, July 27 to Aug. 5, 1908. 1908.

The Lambeth Conferences (1867-1930). The Reports of the 1920 and 1930 Conferences, with selected Resolutions from the Conferences of 1867, 1878, 1888, 1897 and 1908. 1948.

The Lambeth Conference 1958. The Encyclical Letter from the Bishops together with the Resolutions and Reports. 1958.

Lambeth Report, 1924: The Ministry of Healing. Report of the Committee appointed in accordance with Resolution 63 of the Lambeth Conference, 1920. 1924.

Liber Sacramentorum Romane Aeclesiae Ordinis Anni Circuli (Sacramentarium Gelasianum), ed. L. C. Mohlberg. Rerum Ecclesiasticarum Documenta, Fontes IV. Rome, 1960.

Manual for the Unction of the Sick containing instructions for the Preservation, Benediction, and Use of the Holy Oil, ed. Brother Cecil, S.S.J. 1868.

Monumenta Ritualia Ecclesiæ Anglicanæ, or occasional Offices of the Church of England according to the old use of Salisbury, the Prymer in English, and other prayers and forms with dissertations and notes, ed. William Maskell. 3 vols., 1846-47.

"The Orange Book": A Survey of the Proposals for the Alternative Prayer Book. II. Occasional Offices. (Alcuin Club), 1924.

Ordo Unctionis Infirmorum eorumque Pastoralis Curae. Typis Polyglottis Vaticanis, 1972.

Pontificale Romanum. Editio prima post typicam. New York, 1891.

A Prayer-Book Revised. Being the Services of the Book of Common Prayer, with Sundry Alterations and Additions offered to the Reader. 1913.

The Priest's Book of Private Devotion, edd. Joseph Oldknow and Augustine Crake. Oxford, 1872; 1st rev. ed., 1877; 2nd rev. ed., 1884. Rev. John Stobbart, 1960.

Rituale Romanum. Editio juxta typicam. Rome, 1952.

Sarum Manual: Manuale ad usum percelebris ecclesia Sarisburiensis, ed. Jeffries A. Collins. HBS, 91. 1960.

St. Raphael's Forms: The Order for the Anointing of the Sick. Form for the Laying on of Hands. (Guild of St. Raphael), n.d.

York Manual: Manuale et Processionale ad usum insignis Ecclesiae Eboracensis, ed. W. G. Henderson. Surtees Society, vol. 63, 1875.

York Services: The Administration of Holy Unction and the Laying on of Hands (York). 1957.

2. A Select Bibliography of Literature Promoting the Ministry of Healing

Arnold, Dorothy Musgrave. *Dorothy Kerin. Called by Christ to Heal.* 1965.

Autton, Norman. *Pastoral Care in Hospitals.* Library of Pastoral Care. 1968.

    ed. *A Manual of Prayers and Readings with the Sick.* 1970.

    ed. *From Fear to Faith.* Studies of Suffering and Wholeness. 1971.

Bennett, George. *Miracle at Crowhurst.* Evesham, Worcs. 1970.

Child, Kenneth. *Sick Call. A Book on the Pastoral Care of the Physically Ill.* Library of Pastoral Care. 1965.

Cobb, E. Howard. *Christ Healing.* 1933, reprinted 1964.

Cooper, Henry. *Holy Unction.* (Church Union), 1961.

    Holy Unction. A Practical Guide to its Administration. (Guild of St. Raphael), 1966.

Crafer, T. W., ed. *The Church and the Ministry of Healing.* 1934.

            The Priest's Vade Mecum. A Manual for the Visiting of the Sick. 1945, reprinted 1961.

Dawson, George G. *Healing: Pagan and Christian.* 1935.

Dearmer, Percy. *The Parson's Handbook.* 2nd rev. ed., 1907. 13th ed. rev., C. E. Pocknee.

            Body and Soul. An Enquiry into the Effect of Religion upon Health, with a Description of Christian Works of Healing from the New Testament to the Present Day. 1909.

Fox, A. H. Purcell. *The Church's Ministry of Healing.* 1959.

            A Little Book about Holy Unction. (Guild of St. Raphael), 1938, reprinted 1962.

Frost, Evelyn. *Christian Healing. A Consideration of the Place of Spiritual Healing in the Church of To-day in the Light of the Doctrine and Practice of the Ante-Nicene Church.* 1940, reprinted 1954.

Garlick, Phyllis L. *Man's Search for Health. A Study in the Inter-Relation of Religion and Medicine.* 1952.

Grueber, Charles S. *The Anointing of the Sick, commonly known as Extreme Unction: a catechism.* Oxford, 1881.

Harris, Charles. "Visitation of the Sick. Unction, Imposition of Hands, and Exorcism". *Liturgy and Worship,* ed. W. K. Lowther Clarke, 1932, pp. 472-540.

            "The Communion of the Sick, Viaticum, and Reservation". *Liturgy and Worship,* pp. 541-615.

Hickson, James M. *The Healing of Christ in His Church.* 1908.

            Heal the Sick. London, 1924.

Hoch, Dorothee. *Healing and Salvation,* tr. John Hoad. Studies in Ministry and Worship, ed. G. W. H. Lampe. 1958.

Ikin, A. Graham. *New Concepts of Healing: Medical, Psychological and Religious.* 1955.

Kelsey, Morton T. *Healing and Christianity.* New York, 1973.

Kerin, Dorothy. *The Living Touch.* Tunbridge Wells, 1914, reprinted 1961.

            Fulfilling. A Sequel to the Living Touch. 4th rev. ed., 1963.

King, Archdale A. *Holy Unction. A Dogmatic Treatise on the Unction of the Sick.* (Society of SS. Peter & Paul), 1921.

Lang, Cosmo Gordon. *Divine Healing. Its place in the normal Ministry of the Church of England.* (Guild of St. Raphael), 1949.

Langford-James, R. Ll. *The Church and Bodily Healing.* London, 1929.

Lambourne, R. A. *Community, Church and Healing. A study of some of the corporate aspects of the Church's Ministry to the Sick.* 1963.

Loxley, Arthur Percival. *Holy Unction. A Plea for its Restoration.* Oxford, 1904.

Martin, Bernard. *The Healing Ministry in the Church,* tr. Mark Clement. 1960.

Morgan, Edmund R. *The Ordeal of Wonder. Thoughts on Healing.* 1964.

Pridie, J. R. *The Church's Ministry of Healing.* 1926.

Puller, F. W. *Anointing of the Sick in Scripture and Tradition, with some Considerations on the Numbering of the Sacraments.* 1904.

Pye, John H. *Ought the Sick to be anointed? A theological essay.* 1867.

Reade, Robert C. L. *Spiritual Healing and the Anointing of the Sick. A simple explanation.* 1911.

Robins, H. C. *A Guide to Spiritual Healing,* 1953.

Robinson, John A. T. "The Gospel and Health", *On Being the Church in the World.* 1960, pp. 121-128.

Spencer, Malcomb and H. W. Workman. *Spiritual Healing: A Critical Appreciation.* 1934.

Weatherhead, Leslie. *Psychology, Religion and Health.* rev. ed., 1963.

Wight, Marjory. "Spiritual Healing: Towards an Interpretation", *Theology* 10 (1925), 90-96.

Wilson, Jim. *Go Preach the Kingdom. Heal the Sick.* 1962.

Wilson, Michael. *The Church is Healing.* 1966.

Woolley, Reginald M. *Exorcism and Healing of the Sick.* 1932.

3. Studies Commissioned by the World Council of Churches

The Healing Church. World Council Studies, No. 3. Geneva, 1965.

Health: Medical-Theological Perspectives. World Council of Churches and Lutheran World Federation. Tübingen, 1967.

Hellberg, J. H. *Community, Health and Church.* World Council of Churches, Geneva, 1971.

NOTES

CHAPTER I

1. John Wordsworth, *Teaching of the Church of England on some points of Religion set forth for the Information of Orthodox Christians in the East* (Arabic-English ed., 1904), p. 19.

2. *The Canons of the Church of England* (1969). Canon B37, sc 3.

3. *The Revised Catechism* (1962), p. 13.

4. These associations are represented on the Churches' Council for Health and Healing, the co-ordinating body of the ministry of healing in Britain. See Churches' Council of Healing, *Guilds and Fellowships of Healing* (1967), hereafter cited as *Guilds and Fellowships*.

5. Percy Dearmer, *Body and Soul. An Enquiry into the Effect of Religion upon Health, with a Description of Christian Works of Healing from the New Testament to the Present Day* (London, 1909; New York, 1923).

6. As quoted in Nan Dearmer, *The Life of Percy Dearmer* (1941), p. 187.

7. Malcomb Spencer and H. W. Workman, *Spiritual Healing: A Critical Appreciation.* (1934).

8. *Guild of Health Handbook* (1967), pp. 4-5.

9. Reprinted on the back cover of *Chrism,* the quarterly periodical of the Guild of St. Raphael.

10. See Cosmo Gordon Lang, *Divine Healing. Its place in the normal Ministry of the Church of England* (1949), pp. 6-8.

11. *St. Raphael Prayer Book for the Use of the Sick* (1964); T. W. Crafer, ed., *The Priest's Vade Mecum. A Manual for the Visiting of the Sick* (1961); Henry Cooper, *Holy Unction* (Church Union, 1961); A. H. Purcell Fox, *A Little Book about Holy Unction* (Guild of St. Raphael, 1962); Henry Cooper, *Holy Unction. A Practical Guide to its Administration* (Guild of St. Raphael, 1966).

12. J. M. Hickson, *Heal the Sick* (1924). For the more recent history of the Divine Healing Mission see George Bennett, *Miracle at Crowhurst* (Evesham, Worcs., Arthur James, 1970).

13. See the two books by Dorothy Kerin: *The Living Touch* (Tunbridge Wells, 1914; 1961); and *Fulfilling. A Sequel to the Living Touch* (1952; 4th rev. ed., 1963). See also the biography by Dorothy Musgrave Arnold, *Dorothy Kerin. Called by Christ to Heal* (1965).

142

14. "Report of the Committee Appointed to Consider and Report upon the Subject of the Ministries of Healing: (a) the Unction of the Sick; (b) Faith Healing and 'Christian Science'," in: *Conference of Bishops of the Anglican Communion Holden at Lambeth Palace, July 27 to Aug. 5, 1908* (1908), pp. 133-138.

15. The principal tenets of this sect, founded by the American Mary Baker Eddy (1821-1910), are summarized in a book by the foundress, *Science and Health, with Key to the Scriptures* (Boston, 1875), p. 113:
    1. God is All-in all.
    2. God is good. Good is Mind.
    3. God, Spirit, being all, nothing is matter.
    4. Life, God omnipotent good, deny death, evil, sin, disease.— Disease, sin, evil, death, deny good, omnipotent God, Life.
For a critical evaluation of Christian Science see Horton Davies, *Christian Deviations. The Challenge of New Spiritual Movements* (1954; 2nd rev. ed., 1965), pp. 86-95.

16. *Lambeth Conference, 1908*, pp. 54-55.

17. "Report of the Committee Appointed to Consider and Report upon the Christian Faith in Relation to (a) Spiritualism; (b) Christian Science; and (c) Theosophy," in: *The Lambeth Conferences (1867-1930). The Reports of the 1920 and 1930 Conferences, with selected Resolutions from the Conferences of 1867, 1878, 1888, 1897 and 1908* (1948), pp. 106-117.

18. *Ibid.*, p. 49.

19. *The Ministry of Healing. Report of the Committee appointed in accordance with Resolution 63 of the Lambeth Conference, 1920* (1924), hereafter cited as *Lambeth Report 1924*. Two valuable appendices were also included in the Report: "Historical Evidence for a Ministry of Healing," pp. 22-37; and "Forms of Service Suggested for Use at the Anointing of the Sick," pp. 38-43. The following is a condensation of pp. 9-21.

20. R. Ll. Langford-James, *The Church and Bodily Healing* (1929), p. 31, considered unfortunate the Report's description of devotional and sacramental healing as excluding "the use of material means", for such a statement was inconsistent with the Committee's encouragement of unction.

21. *Lambeth Report, 1924*, p. 14.

22. *Ibid.*, pp. 18-19.

23. *Ibid.*, p. 20.

24. *The Lambeth Conferences (1867-1930)*, p. 178. The findings of the *Lambeth Report, 1924* were also incorporated into a committee report at the 1930 Lambeth Conference entitled "The Ministry of the Church," pp. 267-268. W. W. Hough, "The Revival of the Ministry of Healing in our Church," in: *The Church and the Ministry of Healing*, p. 24, tells of the overwhelming consensus the *Lambeth Report, 1924* found at the Lambeth Conference of 1930.

25. *The Lambeth Conference, 1958. The Encyclical Letter from the*

Bishops together with the Resolutions and Reports (1958), 2. pp. 91-92.

26. See *The Book of Common Prayer with the Additions and Deviations proposed in 1928*. No. 33, "The Order for the Visitation of the Sick, and Communion of the Sick".

27. For the Lower House debate see *Chronicle of Convocation*, 1931, 75-81, 98-104; for the Upper House: *Chronicle of Convocation*, 1932, 92. The committee reports considered were Nos. 593, 598, 601, 602 and 602A. For the final approval of Report 602A see *Chronicle of Convocation*, 1935, 351-354, 427-429.

28. See *Journal of Convocation*, 1936, 34-35, 69-70. The forms for unction and the laying on of hands for both the Canterbury and York Convocations are published by SPCK.

29. See F. A. Iremonger, *William Temple, Archbishop of Canterbury. His Life and Letters*. (1948), pp. 612-613.

30. Baptists, Churches of Christ, Congregationalists, Methodists, Presbyterians and Friends are included among the thirty-seven bodies from Great Britain and Ireland represented on the Churches' Council of Healing. Also represented are virtually all the prestigious medical and nursing associations such as the British Medical Association, Royal College of Surgeons, Royal College of Nursing, etc. See the complete listing in *Guilds and Fellowships*, p. 1.

31. As quoted in Leslie Weatherhead, *Psychology, Religion and Healing* (1951; 3rd rev. ed., 1963), pp. 232-233.

32. "Medicine and the Church. Statement approved by the Council of the British Medical Association," Supplement to the *British Medical Journal*, Nov. 8, 1947, ii, 112. Reprinted in *Guilds and Fellowships*, pp. 21-23.

33. British Medical Association, *Divine Healing and Co-operation between Doctors and Clergy* (1956), p. 15.

34. See Church Information Office, *Clergy-Doctor Co-operation. A Report* (1963).

35. Institute of Religion and Medicine, *Annual Report, 1968* (1968).

36. *Chronicle of Convocation*, 1952, xxxix. Both motions were proposed by the Dean of Salisbury, the Very Rev. H. C. Robins, author of *A Guide to Spiritual Healing* (1953).

37. Church Information Office, *The Church's Ministry of Healing. Report of the Archbishops' Commission* (1958), hereafter cited as *Archbishops' Report, 1958*, p. 3.

38. The following is a condensation from Chap. I, "The Meaning of Terms", of the *Archbishops' Report, 1958*, pp. 11-14.

39. The word "healthy", together with "whole" and "hale", is derived from the Old English "háelp". At one time "health" could be used to denote spiritual, moral or mental soundness, even salvation. Morning Prayer from the BCP has retained this archaic meaning: "We have left undone those things which we ought to have done;

And we have done those things which we ought not to have done; And there is no health in us". See *The Oxford English Dictionary.* V (Oxford, 1933), pp. 153-154; James Hastings, ed., *Dictionary of the Bible, II* (Edinburgh, 4th ed., 1903), p. 317.

40. Percy Dearmer, *Body and Soul,* frequently referred to "faith healing". But the usual nomenclature had been "spiritual healing"; e.g. Lambeth Conferences of 1908, 1920 and 1930, and the *Lambeth Report, 1924.*

41. *Archbishops' Report, 1958,* p. 14.

CHAPTER II

1. *Archbishops' Report, 1958,* p. 15. See the sixth article of the Articles of Religion: "Of the Sufficiency of the holy Scriptures for Salvation", reprinted in the BCP.

2. These general principles are briefly summarized in the *Archbishops' Report, 1958,* pp. 15-16.

3. *Lambeth Conference, 1908,* p. 134.

4. Phyllis L. Garlick, *Man's Search for Health. A Study in the Inter-Relation of Religion and Medicine* (1952), p. 153.

5. See Leslie Weatherhead, *Psychology, Religion and Healing,* p. 193. See also Jim Wilson, *Go Preach the Kingdom, Heal the Sick* (1962), pp. 87-90; Edmund R. Morgan, *The Ordeal of Wonder: Thoughts on Healing* (1964), pp. 29-34.

6. *Archbishops' Report, 1958,* pp. 15-16.

7. Garlick, p. 142. George Dawson, *Healing: Pagan and Christian* (1935), p. 114 concurs: Christ came to give "fullness of life in fellowship with God". Physical healing was secondary to this spiritual purpose. See also A. H. Purcell Fox, *The Church's Ministry of Healing* (1959), pp. 108-109.

8. *Archbishops' Report, 1958,* p. 16. See also Evelyn Frost, *Christian Healing* (1940; 1954), pp. 20-25, et passim.

9. R. A. Lambourne, *Community, Church and Healing* (1963), pp. 90-111, esp. p. 93.

10. *Ibid.,* p. 101. This viewpoint is shared by A. Richardson, *A Theological Word Book of the Bible* (1950), p. 103: "The crude but widespread view that all sickness is punishment for sin is rejected by Job and by Jesus himself (Lk. 13:1-5; Jn. 9:1-3); but this must not be taken as a denial of any relationship between sickness and sin".

11. Lambourne, p. 102.

12. See *Lambeth Report, 1924,* p. 14.

13. Charles Harris, "Visitation of the Sick", in *Liturgy and Worship,* ed. W. K. Lowther Clarke (1932; 1964), p. 513.

14. Reginald M. Woolley. *Exorcism and the Healing of the Sick* (1932), p. 1.

15. Percy Dearmer, *Body and Soul,* pp. 150-153.

16. Weatherhead, pp. 49-77. Weatherhead, p. 77, does qualify this approach by asserting that "while the mental mechanisms which He used can sometimes be identified through our modern psychological knowledge, the miracles certainly cannot be regarded merely as psychotherapeutic treatments".

17. Lambourne, vi. He is particularly critical (p. 92) of the fact that much of the literature fails to consider the place of the healing miracles in the life-situation of the early Church, where they were a source of instruction for catechumens preparing for baptism.

18. See Lambourne's chapter, "The New Testament and the Community", pp. 33-44, where the author incorporates into his study the findings of exegetes such as C. H. Dodd, *The Parables of the Kingdom* (1936); A. Richardson, *The Miracle Stories of the Gospels* (1941); and V. Taylor, *The Life and Ministry of Jesus* (New York, 1954). A recent study on the miraculous element in religion, Louis Monden, *Signs and Wonders* (New York, 1966), would seem to support Lambourne's thesis.

19. Lambourne, p. 39.

20. *Ibid.*

21. *Ibid.,* p. 41.

22. *Ibid.,* p. 42.

23. *Ibid.,* pp. 53-58. The framework of a "representative" cast of the New Testament healings serves to enhance Lambourne's argument for a more corporative involvement of all Christians in the ministry of healing.

24. For an analysis of the Greek verb *splagknizomai,* "to have compassion", Lambourne, p. 53 n. 1, refers his readers to A. Richardson, *The Miracle Stories of the Gospels,* p. 33.

25. Lambourne, p. 55.

26. *Ibid.*

27. The corporate concept of sin, found in the Deuteronomic tradition, later modified by Jeremiah and Ezekiel and the Wisdom literature, persisted into Jesus' day. "The same can be said of the relationship between sin and disease, which the Old Testament always assumes to be very close". Lambourne, p. 56. Lambourne also challenges Weatherhead's contention (Weatherhead, p. 33) that Christ exploded "the heresy which attributes illness to personal or family sin".

28. *Archbishops' Report, 1958,* p. 17.

29. See Garlick, pp. 183-185; Weatherhead, pp. 78-83; Lambourne, pp. 64-73.

30. *Archbishops' Report, 1958,* p. 20. For a scientific study of the charismatic gift of healing see Joseph Brosch, *Charismen und Amster in der Urkirche* (Bonn, 1951), pp. 50-58.

31. The James' passage on unction was treated at the *Lambeth Conference, 1908,* pp. 137-138; and more extensively in the *Lambeth Report, 1924,* pp. 22-29. Two other important considerations of Jas. 5:14-16 in the healing literature are found in F. W. Puller, *Anointing of the Sick in Scripture and Tradition* (1904), pp. 8-41; Harris, *Liturgy and Worship,* pp. 508-510. In the non-Catholic commentaries and exegetical studies on the Epistle of James by English speaking scholars, little importance has been attached to Jas. 5:14-16 as support for the unction of the sick as a sacramental rite of the Church. See Joseph B. Mayor, *The Epistle of St. James* (3rd rev. ed., 1913), pp. 169-179, 232-238; James H. Ropes, *A Critical and Exegetical Commentary on the Epistle of St. James,* The International Critical Commentary (Edinburgh, 1916), pp. 304-310; James Moffatt, *The General Epistles of James, Peter and Judas,* The Moffatt New Testament Commentary (1953), pp. 76-82; Alexander Ross, *The Epistles of James and John,* The New International Commentary (Grand Rapids, Michigan, 1954), pp. 98-101. But a notable exception is one of the most recent commentaries: Burton S. Easton and Gordon Poteat, *The Epistle of James,* The Interpreter's Bible, XII (New York, 1957), pp. 16-18, 70-72. The commentators understand the James' passage on anointing as a basis for the "ministry of healing", and refer to unction as a "quasi-sacramental" rite.

32. From the Revised Version, as quoted in Puller, pp. 9-10.

33. *Lambeth Conference, 1908,* p. 137.

34. *Lambeth Report, 1924,* p. 23. Canon Mason makes reference to the first of four canons of Trent on extreme unction: "a Christo Domino institutum (cf. Mc 6,13) et a beato Iacobo Apostolo promulgatum (Iac. 5.14)". See CT, VII. IV/1. *Acta Concilii iterum Tridentinum congregati a Massarello conscripta (1651-1552)* (Freiburg, Herder, 1961), p. 359.

35. *Lambeth Report, 1924,* p. 26. See Is. 38:21; Ecclus. 38:5; Wis. 7:20, 16:12; Ecclus. 38:14. Harris, *Liturgy and Worship,* pp. 510-512, refers to a Jewish non-medical use of unction employed by healers who prayed in a whispered voice. Such a remedy for curing skin disease is mentioned in *The Jewish Encyclopedia,* I (New York, 1916), p. 613. See also Dawson, p. 99; and Hermann Strack and Paul Billerbeck, *Kommentar zum Neuen Testament aus Talmud und Midrasch, III* (Munich, 1926), pp. 759-760.

36. *Lambeth Report, 1924,* p. 27. Mason's definition of a sacrament corresponds closely to the concept of *ex opere operatum* as defined by Trent. See CT, V. II. *Acta post sessionem tertiam usque ad Concilium Bononiam translatum* (Freiburg, 1911), p. 995.

37. *Lambeth Report, 1924,* p. 28.

38. *Ibid.*

39. F. W. Puller, *Anointing of the Sick in Scripture and Tradition, with some Considerations on the Numbering of the Sacraments.*

Puller's thesis, as outlined here, is presented on pp. 8-41, and thereafter supported by an exhaustive analysis from the Fathers, the ancient liturgies, and historical instances of the administration of unction.

40. Puller regards the Vulgate *alleviabit* an unfortunate rendering of *egerei*. The older Latin version cited by Pope Innocent in his letter to Decentius read *suscitabit* (PL 20, 559). Puller, p. 20, remarks: "If St. Jerome had retained 'suscitabit' in the Vulgate, or if the medieval copyists had refrained from changing 'allevabit' into 'alleviabit', a good deal of very doubtful Latin teaching about the effect of Unction would probably never have been written". See also a similar assessment by Otto Bardenhewer, *Der Brief des hl. Jakobus* (Freiburg, 1928), p. 151.

   The opinion that the effect of the anointing in James is essentially an aid for the soul is shared by such Roman Catholic scholars as J. Bord, *L'extrême onction dans L'Epître de S. Jacques (v. 14-16), examinée dans la tradition* (Bruges, 1923), pp. 25-28; Max Meinertz, *Der Jakobusbrief*, Bonner NT, IX (Bonn, 4th ed., 1932); *idem*. "Die Krankensalbung, Jak. 5, 14f", *Biblische Zeitschrift*, 20 (1932), 23-26; and P. de Ambroggi, *Le Epistole cattoliche di Giacomo*, Garofalo, La Sacra Biblia, XIV/1 (Turin-Rome, 2nd ed., 1949). An eschatological interpretation has been advanced by the Protestant exegete Hans von Soden, *Der Brief des Jakobus*, Hand Kommentar zum Neuen Testament, III/2 (Freiburg, 3rd ed., 1899), pp. 201-202.

   But the majority of modern exegetes—Protestant and Catholic—opt for a more literal meaning of *sōsei* and *egerei*, and see therein the healing of a sick Christian. See Friedrich Hauck, *Der Brief des Jakobus*, Kommentar zum Neuen Testament, XVI (Leipzig, 1926), pp. 232-237; Joseph Chaine, *L'Epître de Saint Jacques*, Etudes Bibliques (Paris, 2nd ed., 1927), pp. 126-133; Bardenhewer, pp. 148-157; Peter Ketter, *Der Jakobusbrief*, Die heilige Schrift für das Leben erklärt, XVI/1 (Freiburg, Herder, 1950), pp. 182-186; Hans Windisch, *Die katholischen Briefe*, Handbuch zum Neuen Testament, XV (Tübingen, 3rd ed., 1951), p. 33; Kevin Condon, "The Sacrament of Healing", *Scripture*, 14 (1959), 33-42; Conleth Kearns, "Christ and the Sick in the New Testament", *Furrow*, 11 (1960), pp. 566-571; Johannes Schneider, *Die katholischen Briefe*, Das Neue Testament Deutsch, 10 (Göttingen, 1961), pp. 36-38; Martin Dibelius, *Der Brief des Jakobus*, Meyer Kommentar, XV (Göttingen, 11th rev. ed., 1964), pp. 299-305; Franz Mussner, *Der Jakobusbrief* (Freiburg, Herder, 1964), pp. 218-229; Johann Michl, *Die katholischen Briefe*, Regensburger Neues Testament 8/2 (Regensburg, Pustet, 2nd rev. ed., 1968), pp. 62-68; Bo Reicke, *The Epistles of James, Peter and Jude*, Anchor Bible (New York, 1964), pp. 57-62; *The Jerome Biblical Commentary* (Englewood Cliffs, N.J., 1968), II, pp. 376-377.

41. Puller, p. 20.

42. Harris, p. 508.

43. *Ibid.* Bardenhewer, p. 151, also points out this liberty taken by the Vulgate version.

44. Harris claims this interpretation of *aphethēsetai* as referring to absolution (penance) has the support of the majority of the Fathers

(Origen, GCS, 29, 295ff; Chrysostum, PG, 48, 643f; Bede, PL, 93, 39); the Roman Catholic Estius, *In omnes St. Pauli et septem catholicas Epp. Commentarii,* VII (Munich, 1845), pp. 125-127; and many Anglican theologians: A. Sparrow, *A Rationale of the Book of Common Prayer* (1657), pp. 347-348; Herbert Thorndike, *Theological Works,* Library of Anglo-Catholic Theology (Oxford 1852), IV, pp. 263-280; Puller and others.

But Augustine, *Tract. 58 in Jo.* (CC. 36, 475), saw no basis for the sacrament of penance in Jas. 5:16. Neither do the majority of modern exegetes: Bardenhewer, Windisch, Dibelius, Hauck, Meinertz, Michl, Schneider, Mussner. But Chaine, Ropes, Ketter and Michael Schmaus, *Katholische Dogmatik,* IV/1 (Munich, 6th rev. ed., 1964), p. 702, admit the possibility of an interpretation such as Harris'. For the history of the exegesis of Jas. 5:16, see Paul Althaus, " 'Bekkenne einer dem andern seine Sünden'. Zur Geschichte von Jak 5,16 seit Augustin", in *Festgabe für Theodor Zahn* (Leipzig, 1928), pp. 165-194.

45. Harris, p. 507.

46. Dearmer, pp. 242-250; Garlick, pp. 183-191; Weatherhead, pp. 84-86; Fox, p. 12; Wilson, pp. 25-33.

47. See Frost, pp. 20-70, of which a synopsis appears on pp. 17-19.

48. An interesting study on this point is Heinrich Weinel, *Die Wirkungen des Geistes und der Geister im nachapostolischen Zeitalter bis auf Irenaeus* (Freiburg, 1899).

49. Frost, pp. 56-70. See also the appendix to Part I, pp. 99-110, where the patristical passages are translated. But the author gives no reference to critical textual editions.

50. EP, 109, as cited in Dearmer, pp. 242-243; Frost, p. 64.

51. *Dialogue with Trypho,* xxx 3 (Goodspeed, 124); see Frost, pp. 58, 99. See also *Apology* II, vi (Goodspeed, 83): Dearmer, p. 244; Frost, pp. 58, 99; Garlick, p. 186. *Dialogue with Trypho,* lxxvi (Goodspeed, 186-187): Frost, pp. 58, 99. *Dialogue with Trypho,* lxxxv (Goodspeed, 197): Dearmer, p. 243; Frost, pp. 58, 99-100.

52. *Dialogue with Trypho,* xxxix (Goodspeed, 135-136): Dearmer, p. 243; Frost, pp. 64, 103.

53. *To Autolycus,* I, 13 (Sch. 20, 88): Frost, pp. 65, 103.

54. *Oration to the Greeks,* xvii, xviii, xx (Goodspeed, 284-288): Frost, pp. 65, 104.

55. *Against Heresies,* II, xxxi, 2 (PG, 7, 824): II xxxii, 4 (PG, 7, 828-829); II, xxxii, 5 (PG, 7, 830): cited by Dearmer, pp. 244-246; Frost, pp. 65-66, 105-106.

56. *Against Heresies,* III, v, 2 (SCh 34, 124): Frost, pp. 66-67, 106.

57. *De Testimonio Animae,* iii (CC, i, 178): Frost, pp. 58, 100-101. *De Anima,* lvii (CC, ii, 867): Frost, pp. 67, 106-107.

58. *Apologeticum,* xxiii (CC, i, 131): Frost, pp. 58-59.

59. *Ad Scapulam,* iv (CC, ii, 1130-1131): Frost, pp. 58, 100.

60. *Against Celsus,* I, vi (GCS, 2, 59): Frost, pp. 59, 101; I, lxvii (GCS, 2, 121): Frost, pp. 68, 107.

61. *Against Celsus,* I, xlvi (GCS, 2, 96): Dearmer, p. 247; Frost, pp. 68, 107.

62. *Against Celsus,* III, xxiv (GCS, 2, 220): Dearmer, p. 248; Frost, pp. 68, 108; Garlick, p. 186.

63. *Against Celsus,* II, viii (GCS, 2, 134): Dearmer, p. 247; Frost, pp. 68, 107.

64. *De lapsis,* vi (FIP, 21, 13-14): Frost, pp. 68, 108.

65. *Divinae Institutiones,* V, xxi (CSEL, 19, 471): Frost, pp. 61, 102.

66. Frost, p. 69.

67. Garlick, p. 190.

68. Frost, pp. 180-181. A similar thesis had recently been advanced by R. Hernegger, *Macht ohne Auftrag. Die Entstehung der Staats- und Volkskirche* (Olden, 1963): With Constantine's conversion to Christianity, the Church became a "Power Church" (*Machtkirche*). Hugo Rahner, "Die konstantinische Wende", in *Abendland* (Freiburg, Herder, 1966), pp. 186-198, rejects this interpretation as an oversimplification.

69. *De Civitate Dei,* xxii, 8 (CC, 48, 815f): as cited by Weatherhead, p. 85.

70. Adolf Harnack spoke of Christ as a healer, a doctor, whose foremost function was to heal a sick human race. This mission of Christ was further reflected in the healing activity and the conflict with demons of the early Church. See A. Harnack, *Medicinisches aus der ältesten Kirchengeschichte,* Texte und Untersuchungen, 8/4 (Leipzig, 1892), pp. 37-152; *The Mission and Expansion of Christianity in the first three centuries,* tr. James Moffatt (2nd rev. ed., 1908), I, pp. 101-146. Franz Dölger, "Der Heiland", in *Antike und Christentum,* vi, 4 (Münster, 1950), 241-272, likewise refers to the altercation between Christ and Asclepius, the Greek god of medicine. Most recently, Morton T. Kelsey, *Healing and Christianity* (New York, 1973)—a comprehensive history of sacramental healing in the Christian Church from biblical times to the present—supports the patristic interpretation of the Anglican healing literature. But Th. Trede, *Wunderglaube im Heidentum und in der alten Kirche* (Gotha, 1901), pp. 262-264, considers the interest in healing of the early Church a remnant from the pagan world. Another less-convinced scholar is J. S. McEwen, "The Ministry of Healing", *Scottish Journal of Theology,* 7 (1954), 133-152.

71. Puller, pp. 149-198.

72. Dearmer, pp. 353-400.

73. R. Ll. Langford-James, *The Church and Bodily Healing,* pp. 15-26; Garlick, pp. 192-208.

74. Other healing writers, e.g. G. Dawson, pp. 146-150, appear to have largely appropriated Harris' findings. The following is a condensation of Harris, pp. 475-479.

75. Hans Archelis, ed., *Die ältesten Quellen des orientalischen Kirchen-rechts. Die Canones Hippolyti,* Texte und Untersuchungen, 6/4 (Leipzig, 1891), p. 74:

> 53. Si quis petitionem porrigit, quae ad ipsius ordinationem pertinet, quod dicit: Nactus sum charisma sanationis, non prius ordinetur, quam clarescat ea res.
> 54. Imprimis inquirendum est, num sanationes, quae per eum fiunt, revera a Deo deriventur.

Harris, p. 475 n.1, regarded the *Canons of Hippolytus* as dating from the fourth century. The present state of research generally considers the Canons as a later redaction in Syria c. 500 of Hippolytus' *Apostolic Tradition.* See Johannes Quasten, *Patrology,* II (Westminster, Maryland, 1953), p. 186; Berthold Altaner, *Patrology,* tr. Hilda Graef (New York, Herder, 1961), p. 60. Harris supplies no text edition for the *Canones Hippolyti:* the Archelis edition will hereafter be cited as CH.

76. Canon 18 as translated by Harris, p. 477. CH, p. 46:

> et tribue illi facultatem ad dissolvendi omnia vincula iniquitatis daemonum, et ad sanados omnes morbos, et contere satanum sub pedibus ejus velociter . . .

77. Canon 40 as translated by Harris, p. 477. CH, p. 66:

> "utque illi concedas vim vincendi omnem potestatem dolosi signo crucis tuae, quo ipse signatur."

78. *Apostolic Constitutions,* viii, 16, as translated by Harris, p. 477. See F. X. Funk, ed., *Didascalia et Constitutiones apostolorum* (Paderborn, 1905), I, p. 522: *plēstheis energēmatōn iatikōn.*

Puller, pp. 291-294, likewise discerns in the liturgies a close connection between the charism of healing and the ministerial office.

79. See Funk, II, pp. 164-167.

80. CH, p. 123:

> 219. Ceterum quod ad infirmos pertinent, medicina ipsis in eo posita est, ut frequentent ecclesiam, ut fruantur oratione, excepto eo, qui morbo periculoso laborat talis a *klērō* visitetur quotidie, qui certiorem reddunt eum.

81. Harris, p. 476. A curious practice originating in pagan temples and adopted by some of the churches of the East and West was incubation or "temple sleep". The patient would seek out a Christian church renowned for its cures. After engaging in his devotions, he would fall into a deep sleep in which he envisioned the apparition of a saint who would touch him. The patient would then expect to awaken healed. See Dearmer, pp. 278-279. Joseph Coppens, *L'imposition des mains et les rites connexes dans le nouveau testament et dans l'église ancienne* (Paris, 1925), p. 82, considers this practice an abuse. The subject has been extensively examined by L. Deubner, *De Incubatione* (Leipzig, 1900); and Mary Hamilton, *Incubation or the Cure of Diseases in Pagan Temples and Christian Churches* (London, 1906).

82 Harris, p. 476 (PL, 78, 235):

> Moreover, the priests and ministers of Holy Church ought to chant daily to the sick, with the utmost reverence, Vespers

and Matins, with the hymn, *Christ cœlestis medicina Patris,* etc., with antiphons and responses, also the lections and prayers appertaining thereto.
The hymn *Christe cœlestis medicina Patris* is of Mozarabic origin, and may be found in H. A. Daniel, *Thesaurus Hymnologicus,* I (Leipzig, 1855), n. 163. See also John Julian, ed., *A Dictionary of Hymnology* (New York, 2nd rev. ed., 1907), I, p. 226.

83. CH, p. 117:
200. Magna enim res est infirmo a principe sacerdotum visitari; reconvalescit a morbo, quando episcopus ad eum venit, imprimis si super eo orat; quia umbra Petri sanavit infirmum.

84. Harris, p. 478. See Ambrose, *A Paulino ad Beatum Augustinum Conscripta* (PL, 14: 36-37, 42).

85. Heinrich Schlier, *Theological Dictionary of the New Testament,* ed. G. Kittel (Grand Rapids, Michigan, 1964), I, pp. 229-232, notes that the anointing with oil (*aleiphō*) as a method of healing in Hellenistic and Jewish circles had a medicinal-exorcistic meaning which was reflected in the New Testament (Mk. 6:13; Jas. 5.14f) and in the early prayers for blessing the oil. Franz J. Dölger, *Der Exorzismus im altchristlichen Taufritual* (Paderborn, 1909), pp. 142-148, likewise attests to the exorcismal character of many of the primitive prayers for the blessing and application of oil. The exorcismal anointing in the baptismal liturgy had been taken over from the rite for the unction of the sick.

86. Funk, II, p. 166: *epitimēson tois nosēmasin.*

87. Harris, p. 478 n. 1.

88. Harris, pp. 477-478. See M. Magistretti, ed., *Pontificale in usum Ecclesiae Mediolanensis,* Monumenta veteris liturgiae Ambrosianae, I (Milan, 1897), pp. 68-71; F. E. Warren, ed., *The Leofric Missal* (Oxford, 1883).

89. Harris, p. 477.

90. *Sacramentarium Serapionis* (Funk, II, pp. 178-181, 190-193); *Constitutiones Apostolorum,* viii, 29 (Funk, I, pp. 532-533).

91. Harris, p. 477. Puller, pp. 87-88, on the contrary, holds that the holy oil and holy water were put on the same level of supernatural efficacy.

92. Harris, p. 475. See also pp. 482-484. A contrary hypothesis —rejected by Harris, p. 484—has been advanced by Reginald M. Woolley, *Exorcism and the Healing of the Sick,* who claims that the healing ministry was originally lay and charismatic, and only in the fourth and fifth centuries was gradually assumed by the clergy and annexed to the pastoral office.

93. PL, 20, 560-561. See also Puller, pp. 54-57.

94. *Super Divi Jacobi Epistolam* (PL, 93, 39-40). See also Puller, pp. 48-51.

95. Harris, pp. 483-484.

96. *Lambeth Report, 1924,* p. 20.

97. *Ibid.,* p. 15.

98. See *Ibid.,* p. 29; Harris, p. 500.

99. Harris, p. 501. Harris, p. 500, also reproduces the Latin version from Hugh Connolly, *The So-called Egyptian Church Order and Derived Documents,* Texts and Studies, 8/4 (Cambridge, 1916), p. 176:

> Si quis oleum offert, secundum panis oblationem et vini, et non ad sermonem dicat, sed simili virtute gratias referat dicens, "Ut oleum hoc sanctificans das, Deus, sanitatem utentibus et percipientibus, unde uncxisti reges, sacerdotes, et profetas, sic et omnibus gustantibus comfortationem et sanitatem utentibus præbeat."

For the most recent edition, see B. Botte, ed., *La Tradition apostolique de Saint Hippolyte,* Liturgiegeschichtliche Quellen und Forschungen, 39 (Münster, Aschendorf, 1963), p. 18. See also G. Dix, *The treatise on the Apostolic tradition of St. Hippolytus of Rome* (revised H. Chadwick, 1968).

100. Harris, p. 501.

101. Harris, p. 486 et passim. See also J. R. Pridie, *The Church's Ministry of Healing* (1926), pp. 67-86; Langford-James, pp. 67-86; Fox, pp. 51-60; and the literature from the Guild of St. Raphael.

102. Harris, pp. 487-489. See also Puller, pp. 124-126. Antoine Chavasse, *Etude sur l'onction des infirmes dans l'église latine du IIIe au XIe siècle,* t. I: *Du IIe siècle à la reforme carolingienne* (Lyon, 1942), pp. 40-51, has examined the origins of the *Emitte.*

103. Harris provides neither the Latin text nor the English translation. He does, however, translate some of the phrases of the *Emitte,* which have been incorporated into this English translation of the text in the *Pontificale Romanum,* Editio prima post typicam (New York, 1891), pp. 237-238:

> Emitte, quaesumus, Domine, Spiritum sanctum tuum Paraclitum de coelis in hanc pinguedinem olivae, quam de viridi ligno producere dignatus es, ad refectionem mentis, et corporis; ut tua sancta benedictione sit omni hoc unguento coelestis medicinae peruncto, tutamen mentis, et corporis, ad evacuandos omnes dolores, omnes infirmitates, omnemque aegritudinem mentis et corporis, unde unxisti Sacerdotes, Reges, Prophetas, et Martyres; sit Chrisma tuum perfectum, Domine, nobis a te benedictum, permanens in visceribus nostris: In nomine Domini nostri Jesu Christi.

104. Harris, p. 488.

105. *Lambeth Report, 1924,* p. 33. Canon Mason's observation has been verified by A. Chavasse, p. 28: the only liturgical documents relative to the unction of the sick before the Carolingian reform are the forms for the blessing of the oil.

106. Harris, p. 495. Harris likewise recognizes that this office for unction is absent in H. A. Wilson, ed., *The Gregorian Sacramentary,* HBS, 49 (1915), as it is also missing in the most recent critical textual

edition of Jean Deshusses, ed., *Le sacramentaire gregorien* (Fribourg, Editions Universitaires, 1971). H. B. Porter, "The Origin of the Medieval Rite for Anointing the Sick or Dying", *Journal of Theological Studies,* 7 (1956), 223, agreeing basically with Harris' evaluation, considers Menard's "Gregorian" service a Carolingian compilation from Roman, Gallican and Mozarabic sources dating between 815-845. See PL, 78, 231-236.

107. Harris, p. 495. He observes (p. 495 n. 3) that both oil and water were not only applied externally, but also sometimes internally. The term *gustantibus* occurs in the Verona Latin fragment, *gustanti* in the Gelasian form for consecrating the oil.

108. As translated by Harris, p. 496, from PL 78, 234:
Et sic flectat genu vel genua qui est languidus, et stet ad dexteram sacerdotis, et sic decantetur haec Antiphona: "Dominus locutus est discipulis suis: In nomine meo daemonia ejicite; et super infirmos manus vestras imponite, et bene habebunt."

109. As translated by Harris, pp. 496-497, from PL 78, 235:
Et sic perungat infirmum de oleo sanctificato, cruces faciendo in collo et gutture, et inter scapulas, et in pectore, seu in loco ubi plus dolor imminet amplius perungatur; et supplicando, dum ungitur infirmus, dicat unus ex sacerdotibus hanc Orationem: "Inungo te de oleo sancto in nomine Patris et Filii et Spiritus sancti, ut non lateat in te spiritus immundus, neque in membris, neque in medullis, neque in ulla compagine membrorum, sed in te habitet virtus Christi altissimi, et Spiritus sancti . . ."

110. As translated by Harris, p. 497, from PL 78, 235:
". . . sed fiat illi haec olei sacra perunctio morbi et languoris praesentis expulsio, atque peccatorum omnium optata remissio."

111. As translated by Harris, p. 498, from PL 78, 235:
Et sic faciant illi per septem dies, si necessitas fuerit, tam de communione, quam de alio officio; et suscitabit eum Dominus, et, si in peccatis fuerit, dimittentur ei.

112. As translated by Harris, p. 498, from PL 78, 236:
Multi enim sacerdotum infirmos perunguent insuper in quinque sensus corporis . . . Hoc enim faciant, ut si in quique sensus mentis et corporis aliqua macula inhaesit, hac medicina Dei sanetur.

113. As translated by Harris, p. 503. See Funk, II, p. 180.

114. As translated by Harris, p. 504. See Funk, II, p. 192.

115. Puller, pp. 95-97.

116. F. E. Brightman, "The Sacramentary of Serapion of Thmuis", *Journal of Theological Studies,* 1 (1900), 88-113, 247-277; *Lambeth Report, 1924,* p. 31; Harris, pp. 504-505.

117. Harris, p. 505. See F. E. Warren, *The Liturgy and Ritual of the Celtic Church* (Oxford, 1881), p. 169, for the anointing formula in

the Book of Dimna: "Ungo te de oleo sanctificato in nomine trinitatis, ut salveris in saecula saeculorum". See also George F. Warner, ed., *The Stowe Missal,* HBS, 32 (1915), II, p. 35: "Ungo te de oleo sanctificato ut salveris in nonomine patris et filii et spiritu(s) sancti in saecula etc."

118. Jacobus Goar, ed., *Euchologion sive Rituale Græcorum* (Venice, 2nd ed., 1730), pp. 322-357. See also Theophilus Spáčil, "Doctrina theologiae orientis separati de sacra infirmorum unctione", *Orientalia Christiana,* 24 (1931), 45-259.

119. As translated by Harris, p. 502, from *Euchologion,* p. 335: "Ut oleum hoc virtute, et operatione, et adventu Spiritus Sancti benedicatur; Dominum precemur".

120. As translated by Harris, p. 502, from *Euchologion,* p. 337:
. . . emitte sanctum tuum Spiritum, oleumque hoc sanctifica: et unguendo huic fervo tuo illud in perfectam liberationem peccatorum ejus, et in regni caelorum haereditatem percipiendam effice.

121. See Harris, p. 503; Puller, pp. 136-139. Puller also discusses other Eastern rites associated with the oil of the sick: the form for the blessing of oil in the *Testamentum Domini,* pp. 103-123; and the East Syrian or Nestorian service for blessing oil mixed with dust from the tomb of a saint, pp. 140-145, which has preserved a tradition independent of the *Euchologion.*

122. *Lambeth Report, 1924,* p. 25; Harris, pp. 476, 478, 483, 496. See also A. Malvy, "Extrême Onction et imposition des mains", *Recherches de science religieuse,* 7 (1917), 519-523; 22 (1932), 320-324; F. Cabrol, "Imposition des mains", *Dictionnaire d'archéologie chrétienne et de liturgie,* VII/1 (1926), 406; P. Galtier, "Imposition des mains", *Dictionnaire de théologie catholique,* VII (1927), 1329-1331.

123. *Lambeth Report, 1924,* p. 25. See Origen, *In Levit.,* hom. II, 4 (GCS, 29, 296-297): "In quo impletur et illud, quod Iacobus Apostolus dicit: si qui autem infirmatur, vocet presbyteros ecclesiae, et imponant ei manus ungentes eum oleo in nomine Domini". But this passage may have reference to penance, and not to unction. See Puller, pp. 42-44; Paul F. Palmer, ed., *Sacraments and Forgiveness,* Sources of Christian Theology, II (Westminster, Maryland, 1959), pp. 277-278.

124. Harris, p. 512 n. 1. See M. Magistretti, ed., *Manuale Ambrosianum* (Milan, 1905), I, pp. 79ff., 94ff., 147ff.

125. *Lambeth Report, 1924,* p. 25.

126. See Langford-James, pp. 86-112; James Moore Hickson, "The Laying on of Hands", in *The Church and the Ministry of Healing,* ed. T. W. Crafer (1934), pp. 44-54. For the laying on of hands as a healing rite see also J. Behm, *Die Handauflegung im Urchristentum nach Verwendung, Herkunft und Bedeutung in religionsgeschichtlichem Zusammenhang untersucht* (Leipzig, 1911), pp. 16-18, 62-69, 102-116; Joseph Coppens, pp. 28-109; Luc. DeBruyne, "L'imposition de mains dans l'art chrétien ancien", *Rivista di archeologia cristiana,* 20 (1943), 173-174. The laying on

of hands has also figured prominently in the rites of ordination, confirmation and reconciliation.

127. A. Chavasse, pp. 163-202, reaches a similar conclusion in his monumental study of anointing of the sick before the Carolingian reform.

128. See Puller, pp. 77-78, 217-219; *Lambeth Report, 1942,* p. 33.

129. *Lambeth Report, 1924,* p. 33.

130. See Puller, pp. 201-210.

131. Placid Murray, "The Liturgical History of Extreme Unction", *Furrow,* 11 (1960), 572-593, relying on the unpublished manuscript of the second part of Chavasse's projected study, sees the change in unction as resulting from the Carolingian liturgical reforms. "The disappearance of lay-anointing and the association of Anointing by priests with two other rites already being conferred by priests, viz. Viaticum and death-bed Penance, proved the decisive factor in the later history of Anointing" (p. 591). For an informative study of the practice of unction in the middle ages, see also Peter Browe, "Die letzte Ölung in der abendländischen Kirche des Mittelalters", *Zeitschrift für katholische Theologie,* 55 (1931), 515-561; F. Lehr, *Die Sakramenale Krankenölung im ausgehenden Altertum und im früh-Mittelalter* (Freiburg, 1934). For the debate among Scholastic theologians regarding the effects of extreme unction, a systematic reflection which *followed* the change in pastoral liturgical practice, see Paul F. Palmer, "The Purpose of Anointing the Sick: A Reappraisal", *Theological Studies* 19 (1958), 309-344. The Francisan school of Bonaventure and Scotus held that the principal effect of unction was the forgiveness of venial sins; the Dominican school of Albert the Great and Thomas Aquinas argued that it was the remission of the remnants of sin.

132. Harris, pp. 489-495, where the author also makes some practical recommendations for reconstructing the Ritual service. See *Rituale Romanum,* Editio juxta typicam (Rome, 1952), tit. VI, cap. ii.

133. As translated by Harris, p. 491: "Per istam sanctam unctionem et suam piissimam misericordiam indulgeat tibi Dominus quidquid per visum deliquisti, etc."

134. Harris, p. 492. While Harris refers to "the Council of Metz", the council in question was that of Mainz. See J. D. Mansi, *Sacrorum Conciliorum nova et amplissima collectio,* XIV (Florence, 1759), 910. For the text of *Capitulaire,* see PL 105, 220ff. The authorship of the *Second Capitulaire* by Theodulf of Orleans has been recently disputed. H. B. Porter, "Rites for the Dying in the Early Middle Ages", *Journal of Theological Studies,* 10 (1959), 43-62, argues persuasively that the *Second Capitulaire* has been falsely attributed to Theodulf and was actually compiled 150 years after his death.

135. Pridie, p. 79. See the pertinent passages in *Decretum pro Armenis,* DS 1311, 1324.

136. Pridie, p. 79. See *Decretum de pœnitentia et unctione extrema,* CT VII. IV/1, pp. 355-357, esp. p. 356. Actually the final document from Trent was considerably more positive than the

initial schema, which saw the administration of unction only to those in the agony of death. See Andre Duval, "L'Extrême-Onction au Concile de Trent", *Maison Dieu* 101 (1970), 127-172.

137. Pridie, pp. 85-86.

138. *Archbishops' Report, 1958,* pp. 31-39. The Report, pp. 39-44, also considers "Misconceptions about Medical Factors in Healing".

139. See Harris, pp. 487, 493, 497 n. 1; Dawson, pp. 117, 133.

140. Harris, p. 487.

141. *Archbishops' Report, 1958,* pp. 31-32. See also Pridie, p. 101.

142. E. Howard Cobb, *Christ Healing* (1933; 1964), p. 92: "If surrender is absolutely complete, the only reason that can prevent instantaneous healing is our inability to expect it . . ."; pp. 98-99: "Though I do not pretend to be able to explain anything like all the cases in which the healing has not been manifested, I am perfectly convinced that the failure is not on God's side, but on the side of humanity".

143. See Frost, esp. pp. 362-363, 368-370.

143. Weatherhead, p. 429.

145. See Cobb, pp. 7-8; H. C. Robins, *A Guide to Spiritual Healing,* pp. 20-27.

146. *Lambeth Conferences (1867-1930),* p. 268.

147. See *Lambeth Report, 1924,* p. 14; Fox, p. 82; and esp. Weatherhead, p. 460.

148. See Pridie, pp. 96-97; Garlick, p. 156.

149. Garlick, p. 156. But this view, if pursued to its logical conclusion, manifests an inadequate theology of death. See *Archbishops' Report, 1958,* pp. 32-33, for a further discussion on this point.

150. See J. Wilson, pp. 107-109.

151. Frost, p. 202.

152. *Ibid.,* p. 248.

153. Lambourne, p. 108.

154. *Archbishops' Report, 1958,* p. 32.

155. Weatherhead, p. 247; see also pp. 193-194, 231.

156. Fox, p. 89.

157. Garlick, p. 163.

158. Pridie, p. 102.

159. M. Wilson, *The Church is Healing* (1966), p. 85. See Pierre Teilhard de Chardin, *Le Milieu Divin* (Fontana, 1964), p. 92.

160. John A. T. Robinson, "The Gospel and Health", in *On Being the Church in the World* (1960), pp. 121-128, esp. p. 126, which is a

sermon preached at the annual service of the Guild of Health on October 2, 1958.

161. Fox, p. 82. See also *Lambeth Report, 1924,* p. 14; Weatherhead, p. 33, who regards disease and sickness as a result of "ignorance, folly, or sin". The relationship of the Fall of man (original sin) to evil and sickness in the world is a point which could be more thoroughly developed in the healing literature.

162. *Archbishops' Report, 1958,* p. 33.

163. See Fox, pp. 103-107. Garlick, pp. 209-220, shows that a repressive attitude by Church authorities contributed to the present separation between medicine and religion. M. Wilson, pp. 55-83, attempts to find once again a place for the Church in the world of modern medicine.

164. A. Graham Ikin, *New Concepts of Healing* (1955), p. 39.

165. *Archbishops' Report, 1958,* pp. 33-35.

166. *Ibid.,* p. 36.

167. Pridie, pp. 105-106; Fox, pp. 26-34; M. Wilson, pp. 20-54.

168. Lambourne, vii.

169. *Lambeth Conferences (1867-1930),* pp. 267-268.

170. *Archbishops' Report, 1958,* p. 37.

171. M. Wilson, p. 93.

172. *Lambeth Report, 1924,* pp. 15, 18.

173. Weatherhead, p. 189.

174. See W. W. Hough, "The Revival of the Ministry of Healing in our Church", p. 26, and H. Pakenham-Walsh, "Spiritual Healing in the Mission Field", p. 135 in *The Church and the Ministry of Healing;* Pridie, p. 96; Cobb, p. 70.

175. Fox, pp. 44-45.

176. Weatherhead, p. 141.

177. *Lambeth Report, 1924,* p. 14; Wilson, p. 86.

178. *Archbishops' Report 1958,* p. 37.

178. *Ibid.,* p. 12.

180. *Lambeth Conference, 1908,* p. 138: "Care must be taken that no return be made to the later custom of anointing as a preparation for death".

181. Harris, p. 537.

182. Harris, "The Communion of the Sick, Viaticum, and Reservation", in *Liturgy and Worship,* pp. 599-603.

183. *Archbishops' Report, 1958,* pp. 37-38.

184. Weatherhead, p. 141.

158

185. *Lambeth Report, 1924,* pp. 14-15, 18.

186. See Hough, p. 26; Garlick, p. 155.

187. *Archbishops' Report, 1958,* pp. 38-39.

188. *Ibid.,* pp. 22-30.

189. *Ibid.,* pp. 28-29.

190. *Ibid.,* p. 39.

CHAPTER III

1. See John H. Blunt, *Annotated Book of Common Prayer* (1866; rev. ed. 1899), p. 460.

2. Charles Wheatley, *A Rational Illustration of the Book of Common Prayer* (3rd ed., 1720), p. 421, notes the deficiency of the Visitation Office and its supplementation by private forms. See also Percy Dearmer, *Body and Soul,* p. 306; J. R. Pridie, *The Church's Ministry of Healing,* p. 118.

3. J. V. Bullard, ed., *Constitutions and Canons Ecclesiastical 1604* (1934), p. 29.

4. A modern edition of this masterpiece is F. E. Brightman, ed., *The Manual for the Sick of Lancelot Andrewes* (1909).

5. F. E. Brightman, "New Prayer Book examined", *Church Quarterly Review* ccviii (1927), p. 248.

6. H. E. Scott, "Sick, Order for the Visitation", in *Prayer Book Dictionary,* edd. G. Harford, M. Stevenson, J. W. Tyrer (1912), p. 753.

7. See Pridie, pp. 80-81, 118-119; Charles Harris, "Visitation of the Sick", in *Liturgy and Worship,* pp. 513-515; H. C. Robins, *A Guide to Spiritual Healing,* p. 48; R. A. Lambourne, *Community Religion and Health,* p. 140. But Lambourne, p. 140, notes "an inalienable connection between sin, suffering, love, sacrifice and redemption in Christ".

8. See Pridie, pp. 80-81. An equally lamentable approach to sickness from the same era is found in the devotions of the English Reformer Thomas Becon (*d.*1567), *The Sick Man's Salve.* See Thomas Becon, *Prayers and Other Pieces,* Parker Society (Cambridge, 1844) III, pp. 87-191.

9. See *Lambeth Conference, 1908,* Resolution 35, p. 54; *Lambeth Conferences (1867-1930),* Committee Report, p. 113; *Lambeth Conference, 1958,* Committee Report, 2. 92.

10. See Henry B. Swete, *Church Services and Service-books before the Reformation* (1896; rev. ed., 1930).

11. See Jeffries A. Collins, ed., *Manuale ad usum percelebris ecclesie*

Sarisburiensis, HBS, 91 (1960), pp. 97-132. Hereafter cited as *Sarum Manual.*

12. The following observations are based on F. E. Brightman, ed., *The English Rite* (1915), II, pp. 818-847, where the author reproduces in parallel columns the sources together with the Visitation and Communion Offices from the 1549 BCP and the revisions of 1552 and 1661/1662. For the sake of clarity this present study will adhere to the Hebrew numeration of the psalms as followed in the Anglican liturgies.

   For the background and history of the compilation of the 1549 BCP, see F. A. Gasquet and Edmund Bishop, *Edward VI and the Book of Common Prayer* (1891; 3rd rev. ed., 1928); F. Proctor and H. Frere, *A New History of the Book of Common Prayer* (3rd rev. ed., 1908), pp. 45-64; 622-629; F. E. Brightman and K. D. MacKenzie, "The History of the Book of Common Prayer down to 1662", in *Liturgy and Worship,* pp. 130-169; E. C. Ratcliff, *The Booke of Common Prayer of the Churche of England: Its Making and Revisions,* Alcuin Club, 37 (1949), pp. 9-15; Horton Davies, *Worship and Theology in England. I. From Cranmer to Hooker 1534-1603* (Princeton Univ. Press, 1970). G. J. Cuming, *A History of Anglican Liturgy* (1969).

13. *English Rite,* II, p. 822. See *Sarum Manual,* pp. 99-100.

14. Harris, p. 514.

15. Brightman, *English Rite* I, cxxv, II, pp. 824, 826, quotes from f. 44 of the Latin edition (1545). The *Pia deliberatio* was also translated into English by J. Daye, *A Simple and Religious Consultation of us, Hermann, by the grace of God, Archbishop of Cologne . . .* (1548), and exercised considerable influence upon the compilers of the first BCP.

16. William Maskell, *Monumenta Ritualia Ecclesiæ Anglicanæ* (1846-47) I, pp. 101-104, has reproduced several medieval texts which illustrate the parish priest's obligation to inquire whether the sick person has drawn up a will.

17. *English Rite* I, cxxv.

18. See Blunt, p. 469.

19. *English Rite* II, p. 834-836.

20. See Pridie, p. 81; R. Ll. Langford-James, *The Church and Bodily Healing,* pp. 82-83; Harris, p. 514; T. W. Crafer, ed., *The Priest's Vade Mecum,* p. 20.

21. Harris, p. 514.

22. For the background of the 1552 revision see Proctor and Frere, pp. 66-90; Brightman and MacKenzie, pp. 171-185; Ratcliff, pp. 15-17; Cuming, pp. 96-116.

23. For the background of the 1661/62 revision, occasioned by the Restoration of Charles II in 1660, see Proctor and Frere, pp. 163-205; Brightman and MacKenzie, pp. 190-197; Ratcliff, pp. 19-21; Cuming, pp. 136-167.

24. W. H. Freestone, *The Sacrament Reserved. A Survey of the Practice of Reserving the Eucharist, with Special Reference to the Communion of the Sick, during the First Twelve Centuries.* Alcuin Club 21 (1917), has demonstrated that the original purpose of the eucharistic reservation — prior to the formulated doctrine of trans-substantiation and ensuing eucharistic cult — was for purposes of viaticum and communion of the sick. J. Wickham Legg, *English Church Life. From the Restoration to the Tractarian Movement (1660-1833) considered in some of its neglected or forgotten features* (1914), pp. 64-66, cites instances of eucharistic reservation for the sick even after 1662, although the author admits the difficulty in ascertaining how widespread this practice was.

25. Blunt, p. 469.

26. Harris, p. 515.

27. See the text of the Ten Articles in C. Hardwick, *A History of the Articles of Religion* (1851), pp. 231-248. For recent background material on the Henrician period, see G. Constant, *The Reformation in England. I. The English Schism. Henry VIII (1509-1547)*, tr. R. E. Schantlebury (1934); H. Maynard Smith, *Henry VIII and the Reformation* (1962); A. G. Dickens, *The English Reformation* (1964).

28. See the pertinent text on unction in the Bishops' Book in Charles Lloyd, ed., *Formularies of Faith put forth by authority during the reign of Henry VIII* (Oxford, 1825; 2nd ed., 1856), pp. 123-129.

29. *Ibid.,* p. 127.

30. See the pertinent text in Lloyd, *Formularies of Faith,* pp. 290-293.

31. *Ibid.,* p. 292.

32. See C. H. Smyth, *Cranmer and the Reformation under Edward VI* (Cambridge, 1926), p. 7.

33. See Thomas Cranmer, *Miscellaneous Writings and Letters,* Parker Society (Cambridge, 1846), p. 115. The questionnaire was most probably drawn up by Cranmer himself. See Jasper Ridley, *Thomas Cranmer* (Oxford, 1962; 1966), pp. 207-208.

34. William Maskell, *Monumenta Ritualia* I, p. 100, found no evidence for the consecration of oil by English bishops during 1550-1551, although he suggests this probably did take place.

35. *The Writings of John Bradford,* Parker Society (Cambridge, 1853) II, p. 385.

36. *Later Writings of Bishop Hooper,* Parker Society (Cambridge, 1852) II, p. 147. This question also seems to indicate that the newer approach of the Bishops' and King's Book and the 1549 rite of anointing was in actual practice unable to dislodge the prevalent notion of unction as a sacrament of the dying.

37. Martin Bucer, *Censura super libro sacrorum, seu ordinationis Ecclesiæ atqui ministerii ecclesiastici in regne Angliæ,* in *Scripta Anglicana* (Basel, 1577), p. 489:

    Haec tota ceremonia scripta est ad divinarum Scripturarum

regulam quam convenientissime: eo solo excepto, quod est annexum de unctione aegrotorum. Constat enim ritum hunc nec vetustum esse, nec ullo Dei praecepto, vel laudate Sanctorum exemplo comendatum: sed praepostera invectum Apostolici facti imitatione: cuius imitationis ministri vulgo non habent nec mandatum, nec facultatem. Apostoli aegrotos unctione ex oleo sanabant: id enim doni Dominus eis detulerat Marci 6. Atqui de huiusmodi unctione symbolo sanationis, quae divina vi administrabatur ab Apostolis, atqui aliis plerisque in prima Ecclesia, loqui Iacobum in sua Epistola, ex ipsiusmet verbis abunde constat, quae etiam in eundem sensum Beda explicat.

Cum itaque hic ritus nullo sit negis divinae vel verbo, vel exemplo invectus, primisque sanctissimis Patribus fuerit plane ignoratus, tum etiam ut similes omnes humanitus excogitati, multae hodie quoque serviat superstitioni: neque ut a Iacobo praescribitur, ut sanentur aegroti: sed tum fere adhibeatur, cum de aegrotorum restitutione est desperatum. Ad haec indignissime iungitur sanctissimae Eucharistiae sacramento a Domino ipso commendato, quo sane aegroti abunde confirmantur. Hisce de causis optarem hunc ritum aboleri.

38. See *English Rite* I, cxxv.

39. "Letter LXXV. Bishops Grindal and Horn to Henry Bullinger and Rudolph Gualter", in *The Zurich Letters,* Parker Society (Cambridge, 1842), p. 178 (Italics mine). Until the Convocations of Canterbury (1935) and York (1936) gave their approval to the services for unction of the sick and the laying on of hands, the only official ceremony in the Church of England involving unction was in the Coronation Service. See E. C. Ratcliff, *The Coronation Service of her Majesty Queen Elizabeth II* (1953), pp. 42-45.

40. Petrus Barth and Guilelmus Niesel, edd., *Joannis Calvini Opera Selecta* V (Munich, Chr. Kaiser, 2nd rev. ed., 1962), pp. 452-455. For an English translation of this passage, see Paul F. Palmer, *Sacraments and Forgiveness,* pp. 307-309. See also the canons on extreme unction defined at Trent in 1551, the same year in which the Anglican anointing rite was in the process of being deleted from the 1552 revision, CT, VII. IV/1, p. 359.

Martin Luther (*d.*1546), while refusing to accept extreme unction to be a sacrament instituted by Christ, nonetheless did not condemn its use. See *De captivitate Babyonica ecclesiæ præludium* (1520) in *D. Martin Luthers Werke, Kritische Gesamtausgabe* VI (Weimar, 1888), pp. 567-571. Later in life Luther wrote a remarkable letter (1545) to an Ern. Schulzen, a pastor in Belgern, in which he advised his friend on how to minister to a parishioner suffering from melancholy. Such as disturbance was a *tentatio diaboli* which called for *orationes fidei in virtute Christi.* After briefly referring to a successful healing ministration of his own, Luther suggests that the pastor, together with an assistant and two or three good men, proceed to the sick person, lay on hands and pray over him. This treatment should be repeated two or three times a day, along with prayers of intercession for the sick man during the public services in church. See Heinz Doebert, *Das Charisma der Krankenheilung.*

Eine biblisch-theologische Untersuchung über eine vergessene Grundfunktion de Kirche (Hamburg, Furche Verlag, 1960), pp. 88-89 (German tr.), 127-128 (Latin text), where this letter is reproduced from *WA Briefwechsel,* Bd. 11, Nr. 4120, pp. 111-112.

41. See Thomas Becon, *Prayers and Other Pieces,* Parker Society (Cambridge, 1844) III, p. 619; William Fulke, *A Rejoinder to John Martiall's Reply,* Parker Society (Cambridge, 1848) II, p. 170; John Jewel, *Works,* Parker Society (Cambridge, 1847) II, pp. 1135-1137; *idem* (Cambridge, 1848) III, p. 243; William Whitaker, *A Disputation on Holy Scripture,* Parker Society (Cambridge, 1849), p. 199; James Calfhill, *An Answer to John Martiall's Treatise of the Cross,* Parker Society (Cambridge, 1846), pp. 245-248; James Pilkington, *Works,* Parker Society (Cambridge, 1842), pp. 524-527; Thomas Rogers, *The Catholic Doctrine of the Church of England,* Parker Society (Cambridge, 1854), pp. 263-264.

42. Jewel II, p. 1136.

43. As reprinted in the BCP. See also the commentaries: E. C. S. Gibson, *The Thirty-Nine Articles* (London, 1896-97) II, pp. 584-614; Edward H. Browne, *An Exposition of the Thirty-Nine Articles* (London, 11th ed., 1878), pp. 580-590; E. J. Bicknell, *A Theological Introduction to the Thirty-Nine Articles,* rev. H. J. Carpenter (London, 1955), pp. 444-462.

44. See J. Griffiths, ed., *Homilies Books I and II* (Oxford, 1859), p. 355. "The Homily of Common Prayer and Sacraments" is from the Second Book of Homilies, authorized in 1571. The pertinent section on the sacraments from the Catechism, reprinted in the BCP, was added in 1604 at the Hampton Court Conference.

45. Browne, p. 588, comments:

> *Extreme Unction* is an ordinance, concerning which we differ from the Church of Rome more than the other four. We admit the proper use of confirmation, confession, orders and matrimony, but extreme unction we neither esteem to be a Sacrament, nor an ordinance of the Church at all.

It should be noted that the number of sacraments was first claimed as seven in the twelfth century by Peter Lombard in his *Sententiae.*

46. Griffiths, *Homilies,* p. 356.

47. See Herbert Thorndike, *Theological Works,* Library of Anglo-Catholic Theology (Oxford, 1852) IV, pp. 263-280; William Beveridge, *Ecclesia Anglicana Ecclesia Catholica,* Library of Anglo-Catholic Theology (Oxford, 1851), pp. 439-440; Hamon L'Estrange, *The Alliance of Divine Offices,* Library of Anglo-Catholic Theology (Oxford, 1846), pp. 449-450. For John Gilbert, see Paul E. Moore and Frank L. Cross, edd., *Anglicanism. The Thought and Practice of the Church of England, Illustrated from Religious Literature of the Seventeenth Century* (1935; 1962), pp. 522-523.

48. For background on the Nonjurors see Thomas Lathbury, *A History of the Nonjurors* (1845); J. H. Overton, *The Nonjurors: their Lives, Principles and Writings* (1902), esp. pp. 280-308; Henry Broxap,

The Later Nonjurors (Cambridge, 1924); J. W. C. Wand, *The High Church Schism* (1951). For the Nonjurors' Liturgies see W. J. Grisbrooke, ed., *Anglican Liturgies of the Seventeenth and Eighteenth Centuries,* Alcuin Club 40 (1958), pp. 71-135.

49. *A Communion Office Taken partly from Primitive Liturgies, and partly from the First English Reformed Common-Prayer-Book: together with Offices for Confirmation and the Visitation of the Sick* (1718); reprinted in Peter Hall, *Fragmenta Liturgica* V (Bath, 1848).

50. See *Fragmenta Liturgica* V, pp. 59-74. In 1713 William Whiston, an eccentric who was able to combine an Arian Christianity with a passion for the *Apostolic Constitutions,* published *The Liturgy of the Church of England, Reduc'd nearer to the Primitive Standard:* reprinted in Hall, *Fragmenta Liturgica* III (Bath, 1848). Whiston's *Primitive Liturgy,* pp. 175-176, included the 1549 BCP form for anointing of the sick. In another work, *Memoirs of the Life and Writings of Mr. William Whiston . . . written by himself* (1733), pp. 448-453, Whiston, by this time a General Baptist, tells of several cures in his day resulting from the Jacobean unction of the sick. Although Whiston's *Primitive Liturgy* preceded the Nonjurors Liturgy of 1718, it is difficult to determine what, if any, direct influence he may have exerted on the Nonjurors. Both Whiston and the Nonjurors had this much in common: a preoccupation with the liturgy of the primitive Church. For further background on Whiston, see Grisbrooke, pp. 56-66.

51. *Fragmenta Liturgica* V, p. 5.

52. *Ibid.,* p. 68.

53. The "Usages" in question were primarily associated with the Communion Service: the mixing of water and wine, the prayer for the dead, the epiclesis and the prayer of oblation. In addition to unction of the sick, the revived ceremonies also comprised a three-fold immersion at baptism and the use of chrism at confirmation.

54. *A Compleat Collection of Devotions: taken from the Apostolical Constitutions, the Ancient Liturgies, and the Common Prayer Book of the Church of England. Part I. Comprehending the Publick Offices of the Church* (1734): reprinted in Hall, *Fragmenta Liturgica* VI (Bath, 1848), pp. 213-229.

55. Together with "the Oil for the Sick", Deacon also allows for the consecration of "the Oil for Baptism", "the Milk and Honey for the Baptized", and "the Chrism for Confirmation".

56. *A Full, True, and Comprehensive View of Christianity* (1747), p. 68:

> The Lesser Sacraments are all the ceremonies of the Church, the most considerable of which are Ten: Five belonging to Baptism, with which they shall be explained, namely Exorcism, Anointing with oil, The white garment, A taste of milk and honey, the Anointing with Chrism or Ointment: The other five are the Sign of the cross, Imposition of hands, Unction of the sick, Holy Orders, and Matrimony.

57. *Ibid.,* p. 89.

58. *Ibid.,* pp. 421-423.

59. The English Nonjurors were in close contact with the Scottish Bishops. After the Nonjurors' gradual re-absorption into the Established Church, there were still sparse traces of a probable administration of unction of the sick in the Episcopal Church in Scotland. L. Pullan, *The History of The Book of Common Prayer* (3rd ed., 1901), p. 228, tells of a case belonging to Bishop Alexander of Dunkeld which contained two vials: one for chrism and another for oil of the sick. Percy Dearmer, *Body and Soul,* p. 305, relates that a MS. form for unction of the sick was found on the fly-leaf of a Prayer Book belonging to Bishop Jolly of Moray (*d.*1832).

60. See J. Wickham Legg, *English Church Life. From the Restoration to the Tractarian Movement* for examples of the High Church or Catholic tradition re-asserting itself during this period.

61. The centennial of the beginning of the Oxford Movement occasioned studies by Sparrow Simpson, *The History of the Anglo-Catholic Revival from 1845* (1932); Yngve Brilioth, *The Anglican Revival. Studies in the Oxford Movement* (1933); E. A. Knox, *The Tractarian Movement 1833-1845* (1933); Christopher Dawson, *The Spirit of the Oxford Movement* (1933). For a study of the later Cambridge Movement, with its keen interest in ceremonial, see James F. White, *The Cambridge Movement. The Ecclesiologists and the Gothic Revival* (Cambridge, 1962). See also Horton Davies, *Worship and Theology in England. III. From Watts and Wesley to Maurice 1690-1850* (Princeton Univ. Press, 1961), pp. 243-282; and *idem, IV. From Newman to Martineau, 1850-1900* (Princeton Univ. Press, 1962), pp. 114-138. But none of these works mentions the revival of unction in the nineteenth century.

62. John H. Newman, *Tract Ninety, or Remarks on Certain Passages in the Thirty-Nine Articles,* ed. A. W. Evans (1933), pp. 54-58.

63. See Edward B. Pusey, *The Church of England A Portion of Christ's One Holy Catholic Church and a Means of Restoring Visible Unity. An Eirenicon in a Letter to the Author of "The Christian Year"* (1865), pp. 222-228.

64. As quoted by Pusey, p. 224. See Robert Bellarmine, *Controversiarum de Sacramento Extremæ Unctionis,* ed. Justinus Fèvre, *Roberti Bellarmini Opera Omnia* V (Paris, 1873), pp. 48-49.

65. Pusey, p. 225.

66. Alexander P. Forbes, *An Explanation of the Thirty-Nine Articles* (1867-68) II, pp. 463-472, esp. p. 464.

67. J. H. Pye, *Ought the Sick to be anointed? A Theological essay* (1867).

68. Charles S. Grueber, *The Anointing of the Sick, commonly known as Extreme Unction: A Catechism* (Oxford, 1881), p. 1.

69. *Ibid.,* pp. 10-11.

70. *Ibid.,* pp. 39-40.

71. Forbes II, p. 472. The justification for unction set forth by these Tractarians is all the more interesting in light of the "ritualistic controversy" raging in the Church of England during this period.

72. Pye, pp. 10-15.

73. Grueber, pp. 43-44.

74. W. K. Lowther Clarke, *Eighteenth Century Piety* (1944), p. 25, cites popular manuals used in ministering to the sick dating from the early nineteenth century: W. Assheton, *A Discourse concerning Deathbed Repentance* (16th ed., 1825); John Warton, *Death Bed Scenes and Pastoral Conversations* (4th ed., 1830) 3 vols. As might be expected, neither of these works mention the possibility of anointing the sick.

75. Pye, pp. 21-23.

76. *Ibid.,* p. 23. The exhortation is entitled: "General Form for the Introduction of the Subject of the Anointing to the Notice of the Sick Person previously to using the Office for the Visitation of the Sick".

77. Brother Cecil, SS.J., ed., *Manual for the Unction of the Sick containing instructions for the Preservation, Benediction, and Use of the Holy Oil* (1868).

78. Joseph Oldknow and Augustine D. Crake, edd., *The Priest's Book of Private Devotion* (Oxford, 1872), pp. 52-54.

79. *Ibid.* (Oxford, 1877), pp. 247-248.

80. *The Priest's Book of Private Devotion* was revised once again in 1929 by J. E. Briscoe, although most of the material on ministering to the sick from the 1884 edition was retained. The seventh and most recent revision was in 1960 by J. Stobbart, in which the content was put more in accord with newer insights into sickness and healing.

81. In this century a High Church or Catholic conception of anointing of the sick was advanced by Arthur P. Loxley, *Holy Unction: A Plea for its Restoration* (Oxford, 1904), whose booklet also concerns itself with the unctions at baptism and confirmation; Archdale A. King, *Holy Unction. A Dogmatic Treatise on the Unction of the Sick* (1921); and Francis J. Hall, *Dogmatic Theology. IX. The Sacraments* (1921), pp. 307-331, who was a professor at the General Theological Seminary in New York City. In the person of Charles Harris, the cause of the Catholic wing and of the healing movement are conjoined for the restoration of unction.

82. A number of remarkable studies have been written about this curious practice. For the most important literature of recent years see Raymond Crawfurd, *The King's Evil* (Oxford, 1911); Helen Farquhar, "Royal Charities", *The British Numismatic Journal* XII (1916), 39-135, XIII (1917), 95-163, XIV (1918), 89-120, XV (1919), 141-184; Marc Bloch, *Les Rois thaumaturges. Etude sur le caractère surnaturel attribué à la puissance royale particulièrement en France et en Angleterre*. Publications de la Faculté des Lettres de l'Université de Strasbourg, Fasc. 19 (Strasbourg, 1924).

There was also a second healing rite practised by English royalty which consisted of "cramp rings": talismans blessed by the king on Good Friday as a protection against "falling sickness" or epilepsy. This custom, whose origin is even more obscure than the Touching for the King's Evil, failed to survive the sixteenth century. A service for the blessing of cramp rings is reprinted in Maskell, III, pp. 391-397. See also Bloch, pp. 159-184; Raymond Crawfurd, "The Blessing of Cramp Rings. A Chapter in the History of the Treatment of Epilepsy", in *Studies in the History and Method of Science,* ed. Charles Singer (Oxford, 1917), pp. 165-188.

83. Thomas Lathbury, *A History of the Convocation of the Church of England from the Earliest Period to the Year 1742* (2nd ed., 1853), pp. 428-439, was highly indignant that such an unauthorized service found its way into the Prayer Book.

84. *Le Toucher des écrouelles* was practised in France as late as 1824 at the coronation of Charles X. See Crawfurd, *King's Evil,* p. 161.

85. See Ailred of Rievaulx, *Vita S. Edwardi Regis,* PL 195, 761.

86. The history of the coinage of the Angel, so-named because of the figure of the Archangel Michael on the obverse side of the coin, has been exhaustively researched in the articles of Helen Farquhar.

87. As translated by Crawfurd, *King's Evil,* p. 25, from *Epistola CL. Ad clericos aulæ regiæ.* PL 207, 440:
    Fateor quidem, quod sanctum est domino regi assistere; sanctus enim et christus Domini est: nec in vacuum accepit unctionis regiæ sacramentum, cujos efficacia, si nescitur, aut in dubium venit, fidem ejus plenissimam faciet defectus inguinariae pestis, et curatio scrophularum.

88. "The Ceremonies us'd in the time of King Henry VII for the Healing of them that be diseased with the King's Evil. Published by his Majesties command. London. Printed by Henry Hills, Printer to the King's most excellent Majesty, for his household and chappel, 1686". Reprinted in Maskell III, pp. 386-390. In view of James' ulterior motives, however, Bloch, p. 318 note, is sceptical about the authenticity of this particular text. In any case the service of Touching for the King's Evil appears to have been adapted from a medieval form of exorcism. See Crawfurd, *King's Evil,* p. 56.

89. In medieval times the reading from the Prologue of John's Gospel was considered an especially efficacious form of blessing. See Josef A. Jungmann, *Missarum Sollemnia* (Freiburg, Herder, 5th rev. ed., 1962) II, pp. 554-560.

90. See Maskell III, p. 390:
    Omnipotens sempiterne Deus, salus æterna credentium, exaudi nos pro famulis tuis, pro quibus misericordiæ tuae imploramus auxilium, ut reddita sibi sanitate, gratiarum tibi in ecclesia tua referent actiones. Per Christum Dominum nostrum. Amen.
    This prayer is number 1539 in Mohlberg's edition of the Gelasianum. See *Liber Sacramentorum Romanæ Aeclesiæ Ordinis Anni Circuli,* Rerum Ecclesiasticarum Documenta, Fontes IV (Rome, Herder, 1960), p. 222. The same oration is found in other pre-

Gregorian and Gregorian editions, in the Ambrosian and Celtic liturgies, and in the Roman Missal of 1570.

91. Queen Mary's MS. Manual is preserved in the library of Westminster Cathedral. Crawfurd, *King's Evil,* pp. 60-63, has reproduced the service.

92. See William Tooker, *Charisma sive donum sanationis seu explicatio totius quæstionis de mirabilium sanitatum gratia, in qua præcipue agitur de solenni et sacra curatione strumæ, cui Reges Angliæ rite inaugurati divinitus medicati sunt et quan serenissima Elizabetha, Angliæ, Franciæ et Hiberniæ Regina, ex cœlesti gratia sibi concessa, Applicatione manuum suarum, et contactu morbidarum partium, non sine Religiosis ceremoniis et precibus, cum admirabili et fœlici successu in dies sanat* (1597), pp. 94-97. Also published during Elizabeth's reign was the work of a famous English physician, William Clowes, *A right frutefull and approved treatise for the artificial cure of that malady called in Latin, Struma, and in English, the Evill, cured by Kynges and Queenes of England* (1602).

93. *The Booke of Common Prayer . . . imprinted at London by Robert Barker, Printer to the King's most Excellent Maiestie: And by the Assignes of John Bill, MDCXXXIII.* (Br. Mus. c. 130. i. 2).

94. See John Evelyn, *The Diary,* ed. William Bray, Everyman's Library (1936) I, p. 343.

95. *Ibid.* II, p. 199.

96. Crawfurd, *King's Evil,* pp. 163-187, has reproduced nineteen of these proclamations in an appendix.

97. Reprinted in Samuel Pegge, *Curialia Miscellanea* (1818), pp. 141-144.

98. J. Browne, *Adenochoiradelogia; or an anatomick-chirurgical treatise of gandules and strumaes, or king's evil swellings; together with the royal gift of healing, or cure thereof by contact or by imposition of hands, performed for above 640 years by our Kings of England, continued with their admirable effects and miraculous events; and concluded with many wonderful examples of cures by their sacred touch* (1684), pp. 197-199.

99. *The Book of Common-Prayer . . . London, Printed by John Bill and Christopher Barker, Printers to the King's Most Excellent Majesty. MDCLXII.* (Br. Mus. c. 83. e. 13.)

100. The English service, printed in London by Henry Hills, 1686, is reproduced in Crawfurd, *King's Evil,* pp. 132-136.

101. Robert Chambers, *History of the Rebellion in Scotland in 1745, 1746* (Edinburgh, 1828) I, pp. 183-184, relates a story he heard from an old Nonjuror of how the Young Pretender, Charles Edward, while holding court in Holyrood, healed a young girl of the King's Evil.

102. Thomas Babington Macaulay, *The History of England from the Accession of James the Second* (1855) III, p. 480.

103. See John W. Croker, ed., *Boswell's Life of Johnson* (1851), p. 7.

104. Helen Farquhar, *The British Numismatic Journal* XV, 152-155, has carefully investigated the editions of the BCP in which the service of Touching for the King's Evil is contained. The ceremony was printed in the English BCP for the last time in a quarto edition of 1732. As late as 1759, a "Forma Strumosos Attrectandi" is found in Thomas Parsell, *Liturgia seu Liber Precum Communium.*

105. *The Book of Common Prayer . . . London, Printed by Charles Bill, and the Executrix of Thomas Newcomb, deceas'd; Printers to the Queens most Excellent Majesty. 1709.* The ceremony is inserted between Queen Anne's Accession Service of March 8, 1701, and the Articles of Religion.

106. See Peter Heylyn, *Examen Historicum* (1659) I, p. 47; Jeremy Collier, *An Ecclesiastical History of Great Britain* (1708) I, p. 226; William Whiston, *Memoirs,* pp. 442-443, who regarded the custom as the remnant of the primitive practice of anointing the sick. Thomas Carte, *General History of England* (1747) I, p. 291, recounted the controversial story of a young man touched by the Stuart Pretender in 1716.

CHAPTER IV

1. Horton Davies, *Worship and Theology in England. V. The Ecumenical Century 1900-1965,* p. 38.

2. See F. W. Puller, *Anointing of the Sick in Scripture and Tradition,* pp. 298-311.

3. See Percy Dearmer, *The Parson's Handbook* (2nd rev. ed., 1907), pp. 474-476. The manual was first published in 1899; the 1902 rev. ed., pp. 408-412, was the first to treat unction, encouraging its restoration in terms similar to the edition discussed here.

4. *Ibid.*

5. Percy Dearmer, *Body and Soul,* pp. 414-420.

6. See *A Prayer Book Revised* (1913), pp. 158-164; *Lambeth Report, 1924,* pp. 40-43; Leslie Weatherhead, *Psychology, Religion and Healing,* pp. 520-521; *The Priest's Book of Private Devotion,* ed. J. Oldknow and A. D. Crake, rev. John Stobbart (1960), pp. 480-485.

7. See p. 120, note 90, of this study.

8. See pp. 102-103, note 52, of this study.

9. See pp. 86-87, note 19, of this study.

10. See Jacobus Goar, *Euchologion sive Rituale Græcorum,* p. 338.

11. Walter Howard Frere, *Some Principles of Liturgical Reform. A Contribution towards the Revision of the Book of Common Prayer* (2nd ed., 1914), pp. 204-206.

12. See *Royal Letters of Business 1920. No. 533. Proposals for the Revision of the Book of Common Prayer as approved by the Convocation of Canterbury*, p. 59. The alterations of the 1662 Visitation Office merely consisted of a slight rewording of the opening rubric; the removal from the exhortation of mention of St. Paul as the author of the Epistle to the Hebrews; and the provision for other psalms in addition to Ps. 71 (*In te, Domine, speravi*); viz., Ps. 23 (*Dominus regit me*) to be printed in full, or any other psalm such as the following: 27, 43, 77, 86, 91, 103, 121, 130, 142, 146.

13. See Ronald C. D. Jasper, ed., *Walter Howard Frere. His Correspondence on Liturgical Revision and Construction*, Alcuin Club 39 (1954), p. 94.

14. The principal amendments of the Proposed Prayer Book of 1927/28 to NA 60 and NA 84 were the following: the omission of one of the opening versicles and responses; the deletion of the projected intensification to the sick person's response to the Articles of Faith: "Lord, I believe, help thou my unbelief"; and the addition to the concluding note of the final scriptural theme: "20. Christian Hope on the Approach of Death".

15. On Nov. 27, 1924, the motion carried "almost unanimously". See Church Assembly, *Report of Proceedings* V, 3, 404-405. The response to the amendment for unction on February 25, 1927, was less than overwhelming (36-25). See *Chronicle of Convocation, 1928*, 59.

16. See *A Suggested Prayer Book: being the text of the English rite, altered and enlarged in accordance with the Prayer Book Revision proposals made by the English Church Union* ("Green Book" (Oxford, 1923), pp. 431-434, which suggested the 1549 form of unction; *A New Prayer Book. Proposals for the Revision of the Book of Common Prayer and for additional service and prayers, drawn up by a Group of Clergy* ("Grey Book") (1923), pp. 172-176, which advocated the inclusion of the Dearmer forms for the laying on of hands and anointing; *A Survey of the Proposals for the Alternative Prayer Book* ("Orange Book") II. *Occasional Offices* (1924), p. 70, which was prepared to sponsor either of the two above-mentioned rites of anointing.

17. See Charles Harris, "Visitation of the Sick", in *Liturgy and Worship*, p. 473.

18. *The Book of Common Prayer with the Additions and Deviations proposed in 1928* (Oxford), "The Order for the Visitation of the Sick". The Visitation Order of the Prayer Book proposed in 1927 and again in 1928 were identical. See also *A Survey of the Proposals . . .* II. *Occasional Offices*, pp. 62-75; F. E. Brightman, "The New Prayer Book Examined", *Church Quarterly Review* 207 (1927), 248-249 W. K. Lowther Clarke, *The Prayer Book of 1928 Reconsidered* (1943), pp. 58-59; T. W. Crafer, ed., *The Priest's Vade Mecum*, pp. 9-14.

19. The prayer for healing, "O God, who by the might of thy command etc.", is an ancient Roman oration which is also found in the Sarum and York Manuals: *Virtutum cœlestium Deus*. See *Sacramentarium Gelasianum*, ed. Mohlberg, p. 221, n. 1537; J. A. Collins,

ed., *Sarum Manual,* p. 100; W. G. Henderson, *Manuale et Processionale ad usum insignis Ecclesiæ Eboracensis,* Surtees Soc. 63 (London, 1875), p. 47: hereafter cited as *York Manual.* Two of the commendatory prayers are also from the Sarum: "Unto thee, O Lord, we commend the soul of thy servant etc." (*Sarum Manual,* p. 119: *Tibi domine commendamus*); "Go forth upon thy journey etc." (*Sarum Manual,* p. 117: *Proficere anima christiana*).

20. See the first topic suggested in the "Exhortation to Faith and Prayer": "Our Heavenly Father, in his love for all men, uses sickness as a gracious means whereby to correct his children".

21. As quoted in Bell, II, p. 1359.

22. Forms for unction of the sick and the laying on of hands have for some time been incorporated into the Prayer Books of other members of the Anglican Communion, most notably the American (1928), Scottish (1929), South African (1954) and Canadian (1962) Churches.

23. *Chronicle of Convocation,* 1931, xi. See also pp. 75-81, 91-97, 98-104. The reference to "favourable recognition . . . by the Lambeth Conference" pertains to the approval given by the 1930 Lambeth Conference to the *Lambeth Report on the Ministry of Healing, 1924,* by a committee appointed in accordance with Resolution 63 of the 1920 Lambeth Conference. See *Lambeth Conferences (1867-1930),* pp. 49, 178.

24. Harris, p. 529.

25. The Canterbury committee reports—No. 593 (Joint), No. 598 (Lower House), No. 601 (Upper House), No. 602 (Joint) and No. 602A with Annex (Joint)—are extremely difficult to locate. Only the last-mentioned and final report has been bound up with the *Chronicles of Convocation,* probably due to the fact that the earlier reports are all marked "Confidential". This writer was able to consult these reports only through the kindness of the Lambeth Palace Library.

26. The exorcism of evil spirits is also practised in the ministry of healing, although to a much lesser extent than unction and the laying on of hands. See Henry Cooper, *Deliverance & Healing. The Place of Exorcism in the Healing Ministry,* a pamphlet published jointly by the Guild of Health and the Guild of St. Raphael.

27. See *Chronicle of Convocation,* 1933, pp. 252-289, 371-399.

28. See *Chronicle of Convocation,* 1934, pp. 4-14.

29. See *Chronicle of Convocation,* 1934, pp. 68-74, 76-96.

30. See *Chronicle of Convocation,* 1934, pp. 206-215; 1935, pp. 110-111, 220-221, 225.

31. See *Chronicle of Convocation,* 1935, pp. 351-354, 400-401, 427-429.

32. See *Sarum Manual,* p. 99; *York Manual,* p. 46.

33. This prayer is one of the few forms whose source has been identified by Harris, p. 540. No modern edition of the Sarum Pontifical exists.

34. It is interesting to observe that in all the rubrical directions of the Canterbury services, the minister is referred to as "the Bishop (or Priest)", undoubtedly the influence of Charles Harris, who considered the ministry of healing especially entrusted to the bishop of the diocese. See Harris, pp. 475-479.

35. The first of the intercessions appears in part adapted from the intercessions in the Liturgy of St. James. See F. E. Brightman, *Liturgies Eastern and Western*. I. *Eastern Liturgies* (Oxford, 1896), p. 55. The third intercession is taken from "The Ministry to the Sick" of the South African Prayer Book.

36. See *York Manual*, pp. 52-53: *Dominus Jesus Christus apud te sit,* which belongs to the family of Irish Lorica prayers and is also found among the prayers for the sick in the Roman Ritual of 1614.

37. See *Journal of Convocation,* 1932, p. 6.

38. See *Journal of Convocation,* 1933, p. 12.

39. See *Journal of Convocation,* 1934, pp. 34-36. Report 406 contained "An Act of Prayer and Blessing" from the Visitation Order of the 1928 Prayer Book, and a service for unction derived from *A Prayer Book Revised,* pp. 160-164. In contrast to the Canterbury reports, no directions on the manner of religious treatment were included, as this was not in the terms of reference given to the committee. With little amendment, the forms first presented in Report 406 were those finally approved by the York Convocation in Report 428.

40. Report 413 consisted of three appendices: the Annex to the Canterbury Report, and the original services for unction and the laying on of hands from Report 406. See *Journal of Convocation,* 1934, pp. 102-103.

41. See *Journal of Convocation,* 1936, pp. 21, 34-35, 69-70.

42. *The Order for the Anointing of the Sick. Form for the Laying on of Hands* (Guild of St. Raphael). The St. Raphael's Forms are also reprinted in *The Priest's Vade Mecum,* pp. 22-28, 30-33, and appear to antedate the services of the Canterbury and York Convocations.

43. *Forms for the Laying on of Hands, Anointing with Oil, Exorcism of Evil Spirits, Confession and Absolution* (Guild of Health, rev. ed., 1961).

44. *Church of Christ the Healer. Order of Service for the Laying on of Hands of the Sick* (Burrswood, Kent, Dorothy Kerin Home of Healing).

45. *The Laying-on-of-Hands. An Explanation* (Divine Healing Mission), p. 8. The form is presumably the creation of Rev. George Bennett, the President of the Divine Healing Mission and author of numerous pamphlets and books promoting the ministry of healing.

46. See *Archbishops' Report, 1958,* pp. 65-71.

47. See A. F. Smethurst and H. R. Wilson, edd., *Acts of the Convocations of Canterbury and York,* pp. 157-158.

48. *The Lambeth Conference 1958,* 2.92. These suggestions have

already been incorporated into the Prayer Books of the South African (1954) and Canadian (1962) Churches.

49. See Norman W. Goodacre, ed., *Holy Communion. The 1967 Service* (1967), pp. 25-26. Discussing the five other sacraments, the author, p. 26, comments on the Canterbury service for unction: "In all probability this, or a similar service, will be included in all future Anglican prayer books. The Rev. Geoffrey C. Harding of the Churches' Council for Health and Healing has been a major spokesman for the inclusion of healing services of unction and the laying on of hands in the revised Prayer Book.

50. See A. J. Tait, *The Nature and Functions of the Sacraments* (1917); O. C. Quick, *The Christian Sacraments* (1927); J. W. C. Wand, *The Development of Sacramentalism* (1928).

51. See J. G. Davies, *The Spirit, the Church and the Sacraments* (1954).

52. The healing services themselves are sometimes ambiguous. The Dearmer forms, esp. for blessing and applying the oil, reflect a theology of unction which could be interpreted as a supernatural means for bodily healing. The St. Raphael forms have taken over many elements from the Dearmer services, while subscribing to the viewpoint that unction is one of the seven sacraments of the Church.

53. *The Revised Catechism*, p. 18.

54. See Marjory Wight, "Spiritual Healing: Towards an Interpretation", *Theology* 10 (1925), p. 91; J. R. Pridie, *The Church's Ministry of Healing*, pp. 36-38, 115-116.

55. *Lambeth Report, 1924*, p. 20.

56. See *Lambeth Report, 1924*, pp. 14-15; *Archbishops' Report, 1958*, pp. 12, 37. The contention of F. W. Puller and P. Dearmer that unction is merely a supernatural aid—a sacramental—for the recovery of physical and mental health is today largely antequated.

57. See Pridie, *The Church's Ministry of Healing*, pp. 72-73; A. H. Purcell Fox, *The Church's Ministry of Healing*, p. 56.

58. The Guild of St. Raphael, through the writings of Purcell Fox and Henry Cooper, has been in the forefront of the movement to restore unction as a sacrament to the Church of England.

59. Due to presence of charismatic lay healers, there seems to be a curious reluctance on the part of some clergymen to lay on hands. See *Archbishops' Report, 1958*, pp. 35-36; Crafer, *The Priest's Vade Mecum*, pp. 28-30, where the priest's authority to lay on hands is traced to the power of ordination. On this point see also Thomas Talley, "Healing: Sacrament or Charism?", *Worship* 46 (1972), pp. 518-527.

60. Harris, pp. 531, 534.

61. Jim Wilson, *Go Preach the Kingdom, Heal the Sick*, pp. 69-72.

62. Michael Wilson, *The Church is Healing*, pp. 36-37. See also Crafer, *The Priest's Vade Mecum*, p. 30; Norman Autton, *Pastoral Care in Hospitals*, Library of Pastoral Care (1968), p. 93.

63. See Weatherhead, pp. 201-209; H. C. Robins, *A Guide to Spiritual Healing,* p. 57; Fox, *The Church's Ministry of Healing,* pp. 92-93; J. Wilson, pp. 72-75; *Archbishops' Report, 1958,* pp. 52-54. The Archbishops' Commission found no evidence of mass healing demonstrations taking place in the Church of England. The average number of sick persons in attendance at public healing services was estimated to be twenty-five.

64. The importance attached to the Thirty-Nine Articles as a definitive statement of Anglican belief has declined in recent years. See *The Lambeth Conference 1968. Resolutions and Reports* pp. 40-41. The Report of the Archbishops' Commission on Christian Doctrine, *Subscription and Assent to the Thirty-Nine Articles* (1968), p. 59, proposed a revision of the Articles, in which the twenty-fifth of the Articles of 1571 would read as follows:

> *20. The Sacraments*
> The Sacraments ordained by Christ are not only badges or tokens of the profession of Christian men; they are also certain sure witnesses and effectual signs of grace, and of God's will towards us, by which he works invisibly in us, and not only brings to life, but also strengthens and confirms our faith in him.
> There are two Sacraments ordained by Christ recorded in the Gospels, that is to say, Baptism and the Holy Communion.
>
> Penance, Orders Matrimony, and Unction are in a different category. They are not recorded as instituted by Christ himself

> | and are not necessary to salvation where they may be had, but they may be received without scruple by Christians. | nor are they essential to the practice of the Christian religion, but they may be received without scruple by Christians. |
> |---|---|
> | God's grace is given to us through the Sacraments, but only to those who receive them in faith. | God's grace is given to us through the Sacraments, but only to those who receive them in good faith. |

65. The Report of the Commission on Christian Doctrine appointed by the Archbishops of Canterbury and York in 1922, *Doctrine in the Church of England* (1938; 1962), p. 200. This unofficial report was divided as to whether official provision in the Church of England should be made for the rite of unction.

66. See Marjory Wright, p. 93; Fox, *A Little Book About Holy Unction,* p. 9.

67. These reservations about the hallowing of oil were best summed up in a word of William Temple, then Archbishop of York (*Journal of Convocation* 1936, p. 35):

> I shrink from the thought of there being some special quality attached to the oil as it is carried about because a bishop bestowed his blessing upon it. It tends towards the more superstitious use of the rite, and I value the fact that there should be such a prayer within the service itself so that those assisting and observing the patient may actually participate

in the prayer for the blessing of the oil as the instrument for
the moment through which the divine grace for a healthy
body and soul is sought.

68. Pridie, *The Church's Ministry of Healing,* pp. 70-71; Fox, *The
Church's Ministry of Healing,* p. 58.

69. The committee of the Canterbury Convocation assigned to draw up
the services decided to leave the rubric open. Were only the bishop
to hallow the oil, there might be some dioceses where no oil would
be blessed at all. On the other hand, some bishops were already
hallowing the oil, a practice which should be recognized. See
Chronicle of Convocation 1934, p. 9.

70. Harris, p. 485. The author's psychological argument appears less
than conclusive.

71. See Crafer, *The Priest's Vade Mecum,* p. 21.

72. Fox, *The Church's Ministry of Healing,* p. 56.

73. Harris, p. 486.

74. Wight, p. 91.

75. See Howard Cobb, *Christ Healing,* p. 32; Fox, *The Church's
Ministry of Healing,* p. 57.

76. See Harris, pp. 485-505, esp. 485-487; J. G. Davies, *The Spirit, the
Church and the Sacraments,* pp. 203-211. But Davies regrets that
the definition of the effect of unction as a restoration of the indwelling of the Holy Spirit has been adopted by the *Canterbury Services,*
p. 6: "the renewal of the indwelling of the Holy Ghost in thy
living temple". Davies, p. 209, argues that the indwelling of the
Holy Spirit is restored by the prior reconciliation in the sacrament
of penance.

77. See Fox, *A Little Book About Holy Unction,* pp. 10-12.

78. See *Guild of Health Forms,* p. 5.

79. See Henry Cooper, *Holy Unction* (Church Union, 1959; 1961),
pp. 13-14; *idem., Holy Unction. A Practical Guide to its Administration* (Guild of St. Raphael, 1966), pp. 7-9. R. A. Lambourne,
Community, Church and Healing, p. 139, also notes a sacrificial
aspect of unction as "the occasion of a reparative sacrifice for all
men in Christ".

80. See *Archbishops' Report, 1958,* p. 20.

81. The *Lambeth Report, 1924,* p. 20, n. 1, lists the scriptural authority
for the laying on of hands: Lk. 4:40; Mt. 8:3; Mk. 5:22 (16:18);
Acts 9:17.

82. *Lambeth Conferences (1867-1930),* p. 113.

83. Harris, pp. 516-528.

84. Cooper, *Holy Unction. A Practical Guide,* pp. 3-4, 9-11.

85. See Harris, p. 522; Weatherhead, pp. 136-147; Robins, pp. 64-65;
Fox, *The Church's Ministry of Healing,* pp. 58-59; *Lambeth Report,*

1924, p. 19; *Archbishops' Report, 1958,* pp. 45-48, 65-66; *Canterbury Services,* pp. 17-18.

86. See Cooper, *Holy Unction,* pp. 9-10; idem., *Holy Unction. A Practical Guide,* pp. 4-7; Autton, p. 94. The Visitation Order of the Sarum Manual and of the BCP also stress these three virtues.

87. *Archbishops' Report, 1958,* p. 65. See also Harris, p. 487.

88. See J. R. Pridie, "Holy Unction", in *The Church and the Ministry of Healing,* ed. T. W. Crafer, p. 42. On the subject of vicarious faith, an interesting phenomenon is the occasional reception of the laying on of hands by proxy, for a sick person unable to be present at a healing service. See *The Burrswood Herald* (Easter, 1966), pp. 23-24.

89. See Harris, p. 510.

90. See *Doctrine in the Church of England,* p. 200; Harris, pp. 506-508; Davies, pp. 209-210.

91. Harris, p. 507.

92. Cooper, *Holy Unction. A Practical Guide,* p. 6.

93. *Ibid.,* pp. 13-14; Autton, pp. 95-96.

94. See Pridie, *The Church's Ministry of Healing,* p. 42; H. Pakenham-Walsh, "Spiritual Healing in the Mission Field", in *The Church and the Ministry of Healing,* p. 137.

CHAPTER V

1. *Archbishops' Report, 1958,* p. 48.

2. See Paula Schäfer, " 'Christliches Heilen' und die Heilige Ölung in der anglikanischen Kirche", *Liturgisches Leben* 1 (1934), 240-243; F. R. McManus, "The Sacrament of Anointing: ecumenical considerations", in *Miscellanea Liturgica* in onore di sua Eminenza il Cardinale Giacomo Lercaro (Rome, Desclee, 1967), II, p. 813; C. W. Gusmer, "Anointing of the Sick in the Church of England", *Worship* 45 (1971), 262-272.

3. Percy Dearmer, *Body and Soul,* p. 306; Charles Harris, "Visitation of the Sick", in *Liturgy and Worship,* p. 530.

4. T. W. Crafer, "Unction of the Sick in the Western Church", *Theology* 52 (1949), p. 328. The findings of this conference were published in a special issue of *La Maison Dieu* 15 (1948).

5. Josephus Kern, *De sacramento extremæ unctionis tractatus dogmaticus* (Regensburg, 1907). Most recently the viewpoint that unction is a sacrament for the dying (*Todesweihe*) has been expounded by E. Walter, *Die Herrlichkeit des christlichen Sterbens. Die heilige Ölung als letzte Vollendung der Taufherrlichkeit*

176

(Freiburg, 1937; 3rd ed., 1940), reprinted in 1965 under the title *Die zweifache Geburt. Beginn und Vollendung christlicher Existenz*; A. Grillmeyer, "Das Sakrament der Auferstehung. Versuch einer Sinndeutung der Letzten Ölung", *Geist und Leben* 34 (1961), pp. 326-336; M. Schmaus, *Katholische Dogmatik* IV/1 (Munich, 6th rev. ed., 1964), pp. 695-725.

6. A. Chavasse, *Etude sur l'onction des infirmes* (Lyon, 1942); Z. Alszeghy, "L'effeto corporale dell'Estrema Unzione", *Gregorianum* 38 (1957), pp. 385-405; P. Palmer, "The Purpose of Anointing the Sick: A Reappraisal", *Theological Studies* 19 (1958), pp. 309-344; A. Knauber, "Pastoraltheologie der Krankensalbung", *Handbuch der Pastoral Theologie* IV (Freiburg, Herder, 1969), pp. 145-178; Cl. Ortemann, *Le Sacrement des Malades,* Collection Parole et Tradition (Paris, Editions du Chalet, 1971); C. W. Gusmer, "Liturgical Traditions of Christian Illness: Rites of the Sick", *Worship* 46 (1972), pp. 528-543; *La Maison Dieu* 113 (1973): "Le Nouvel Rituel des malades".

7. P. Palmer, *Sacraments and Forgiveness,* Sources of Christian Theology, II (Westminster, Maryland, 1959), p. 312. See CT, VII. IV/I, p. 356:

> Declaratur etiam esse hanc unctionem infirmis adhibendam, illis vero praesertim, qui tam periculose decumbunt, ut in exitu vitae constituti videantur, unde et sacramentum exeuntium nuncupatur.

The original draft read as follows:

> Declaratur etiam, non esse hanc unctionem nisi infirmis adhibendam, nec illis quidem omnibus, ut ecclesiae traditio nos edocet, sed illis dumtaxat, qui tam periculose decumbunt, ut in exitu vitae constituti videantur. Quare merito et extrema unctio et exeuntium sacramentum nuncupatur, quod non nisi extreme laborantibus et cum morte congredientibus atque hinc ad Dominum migrantibus salubriter adhibeatur.

See also A. Duval, "Extrême-Onction au Concile de Trente. Sacrement des mourants ou sacrement des malades?", *La Maison Dieu* 101 (1970), pp. 127-172, esp. 171-172.

8. See *Codex Iuris Canonici,* Cn. 940, par. 1:

> Extrema unctio praeberi non potest nisi fideli, qui post adeptum usum rationis ob infirmitatem vel senium in periculo mortis versetur.

9. See Pius XI: Apostolic Letter *Explorata res,* February 2, 1923 (AAS 15, 105):

> Neque enim, ut sacramentum valide liciteque detur necesse est ut mors proxime secutura timeatur, sed satis est ut prudens seu probabile adsit de periculo iudicium . . .

See also Benedict XV: Apostolic Letter *Sodalitatem,* May 31, 1921 (AAS 13, 342-345).

10. Palmer, *Sacraments and Forgiveness,* pp. 311-312. See also CT, VII. IV/I, p. 356.

11. At the first session of the Vatican Council in 1962 an even more

radical text was proposed for the approval of the Central Commission:

> Sacramentum, quod communiter "Extrema unctio" nuncupatur, deinceps "Unctio Infirmorum" vocabitur; nam non est per se Sacramentum morientium, sed graviter ægrotantium, ac proinde tempus opportunum illud recipiendi est statim ac fidelis in gravem morbum inciderit. (III, n. 59.)

The original draft also spoke of the repetition of unction:
> Unctio sacra in diuturna infirmitate aliquando iterari potest. (III, n. 62.)

But in view of the practice of unction in the Western Church ever since the millennium, the Council Fathers were not prepared to agree to so radical a change. The revised rite of anointing, *Ordo Unctionis Infirmorum eorumque Pastoralis Curæ* (Typis Polyglottis Vaticanis, 1972), does, however, reflect the more progressive approach of the original schema.

12. The original order of reconciliation, anointing and viaticum has always been preserved by the Cistercian and Dominican Orders, and has in recent years been restored to the American, French and German rituals. See Balthasar Fischer, "Die Reihenfolge der Sakramente beim Versehgang", *Trierer Theologische Zeitschrift* 60 (1951), pp. 54-56.

13. See the detailed report on Lourdes by Bishop P. M. Theas in *Notitiae* 7 (1970), pp. 24-33. See also B. Newns, "Reforming the Liturgy of the Sick", *The Clergy Review* 56 (1971), pp. 279-286.

INDEX

THE ALCUIN CLUB—of which Dr. Walter Howard Frere was for many years the President—exists for the object of promoting liturgical studies in general, and in particular a knowledge of the history and use of the Book of Common Prayer. Since its foundation in 1897 it has published over one hundred and twenty books and pamphlets.

The annual subscription is £3 and members of the Club are entitled to the publications of the current year gratis. Subscriptions, applications for membership and for the list of publications, should be sent to the Assistant Secretary.

President
The Right Reverend H. E. Ashdown, D.D.

Committee
The Venerable G. B. Timms, M.A. (Chairman),
    St. Andrew's Vicarage, St. Andrew Street, London EC4A 3AB.
The Venerable R. C. D. Jasper, D.D. (Editorial Secretary),
    1 Little Cloister, Westminster Abbey, London SW1P 3PL.
The Reverend J. A. T. Gunstone, M.A. (Honorary Secretary).
The Reverend Canon G. J. Cuming, D.D.
The Reverend Canon J. D. C. Fisher, M.A., B.D.
The Very Reverend P. C. Moore, D.Phil.
The Reverend C. E. Pocknee, A.K.C., D.Th., F.S.A.
The Reverend H. B. Porter, Ph.D.

Assitant Secretary and Treasurer
c/o St. Andrew's Vicarage, St. Andrew Street, London EC4A
    3AB. (01-353 3544)